Specialty Competencies in Clinical Child and Adolescent Psychology

Series in Specialty Competencies in Professional Psychology

SERIES EDITORS

Arthur M. Nezu, PhD, ABPP, and Christine Maguth Nezu, PhD, ABPP

SERIES ADVISORY BOARD

David Barlow, PhD, ABPP

Jon Carlson, PsyD, EdD, ABPP

Kirk Heilbrun, PhD, ABPP

Nadine J. Kaslow, PhD, ABPP

Robert Klepac, PhD

William Parham, PhD, ABPP

Michael G. Perri, PhD, ABPP

C. Steven Richards, PhD

Norma P. Simon, EdD, ABPP

TITLES IN THE SERIES

Specialty Competencies in School Psychology, Rosemary Flanagan and Jeffrey A. Miller

Specialty Competencies in Organizational and Business Consulting Psychology, Jay C. Thomas

Specialty Competencies in Geropsychology, Victor Molinari (Ed.)

Specialty Competencies in Forensic Psychology, Ira K. Packer and Thomas Grisso

Specialty Competencies in Couple and Family Psychology, Mark Stanton and Robert Welsh

Specialty Competencies in Clinical Neuropsychology, Greg J. Lamberty and Nathaniel W. Nelson

Specialty Competencies in Clinical Child and Adolescent Psychology, Alfred J. Finch, Jr., John E. Lochman, W. Michael Nelson III, and Michael C. Roberts

ALFRED J. FINCH, JR.
JOHN E. LOCHMAN
W. MICHAEL NELSON III
MICHAEL C. ROBERTS

Specialty Competencies in Clinical Child and Adolescent Psychology

OXFORD
UNIVERSITY PRESS

OXFORD
UNIVERSITY PRESS

Oxford University Press, Inc., publishes works that further
Oxford University's objective of excellence
in research, scholarship, and education.

Oxford New York
Auckland Cape Town Dar es Salaam Hong Kong Karachi
Kuala Lumpur Madrid Melbourne Mexico City Nairobi
New Delhi Shanghai Taipei Toronto

With offices in
Argentina Austria Brazil Chile Czech Republic France Greece
Guatemala Hungary Italy Japan Poland Portugal Singapore
South Korea Switzerland Thailand Turkey Ukraine Vietnam

Published by Oxford University Press, Inc.
198 Madison Avenue, New York, New York 10016
www.oup.com

Library of Congress Cataloging-in-Publication Data

Specialty competencies in clinical child and adolescent psychology / Alfred J. Finch ... [et al.].
p. cm. — (Series in specialty competencies in professional psychology)
Includes bibliographical references and index.
ISBN 978-0-19-975870-8 (pbk.)
1. Clinical child psychology. I. Finch, A. J. (Alfred J.), 1944-
RJ503.3.S64 2012
618.92'8914—dc23 2011039549

Printed in the United States of America
on acid-free paper

To my mom for her dedicated care of my dad during his declining years.

AJF

I acknowledge the support of my wife, Linda, and my children (Lisa, Kara and Bryan) and their families (including my grandchildren: Garrett, Audrey, Jonathan and Lori).

JEL

To my family—Sarah, Will/Leah, Mer/Tim, and, of course, V.

WMN

Thanks to my grandsons, Caden and Carson, for providing distractions and a balanced quality of life.

MCR

ABOUT THE SERIES IN SPECIALTY COMPETENCIES IN PROFESSIONAL PSYCHOLOGY

This series is intended to describe state-of-the-art functional and foundational competencies in professional psychology across extant and emerging specialty areas. Each book in this series provides a guide to best practices across both core and specialty competencies as defined by a given professional psychology specialty.

The impetus for this series was created by various growing movements in professional psychology during the past 15 years. First, as an applied discipline, psychology is increasingly recognizing the unique and distinct nature among a variety of orientations, modalities, and approaches with regard to professional practice. These specialty areas represent distinct ways of practicing one's profession across various domains of activities that are based on distinct bodies of literature and often addressing differing populations or problems. For example, the American Psychological Association (APA) in 1995 established the Commission on the Recognition of Specialties and Proficiencies in Professional Psychology (CRSPPP) in order to define criteria by which a given specialty could be recognized. The Council of Credentialing Organizations in Professional Psychology (CCOPP), an interorganizational entity, was formed in reaction to the need to establish criteria and principles regarding the types of training programs related to the education, training, and professional development of individuals seeking such specialization. In addition, the Council on Specialties in Professional Psychology (COS) was formed in 1997, independent of APA, to foster communication among the established specialties, in order to offer a unified position to the pubic regarding specialty education and training, credentialing, and practice standards across specialty areas.

Simultaneously, efforts to actually define professional competence regarding psychological practice have also been growing significantly. For example, the APA-sponsored Task Force on Assessment of Competence in Professional Psychology put forth a series of guiding principles for the assessment of competence within professional psychology, based, in part, on a review of competency assessment models developed both within (e.g., Assessment of Competence Workgroup from Competencies Conference—Roberts et al., 2005) and outside (e.g., Accreditation Council for Graduate Medical Education and American Board of Medical Specialties, 2000) the profession of psychology (Kaslow et al., 2006).

Moreover, additional professional organizations in psychology have provided valuable input into this discussion, including various associations primarily interested in the credentialing of professional psychologists, such as the American Board of Professional Psychology (ABPP), the Association of State and Provincial Psychology Boards (ASPBB), and the National Register of Health Service Providers in Psychology. This widespread interest and importance of the issue of competency in professional psychology can be especially appreciated given the attention and collaboration afforded to this effort by international groups, including the Canadian Psychological Association and the International Congress on Licensure, Certification, and Credentialing in Professional Psychology.

Each volume in the series is devoted to a specific specialty and provides a definition, description, and development timeline of that specialty, including its essential and characteristic pattern of activities, as well as its distinctive and unique features. Each set of authors, long-term experts and veterans of a given specialty, were asked to describe that specialty along the lines of both functional and foundational competencies. *Functional competencies* are those common practice activities provided at the specialty level of practice that include, for example, the application of its science base, assessment, intervention, consultation, and where relevant, supervision, management, and teaching. *Foundational competencies* represent core knowledge areas that are integrated and cut across all functional competencies to varying degrees, and dependent upon the specialty, in various ways. These include ethical and legal issues, individual and cultural diversity considerations, interpersonal interactions, and professional identification.

Whereas we realize that each specialty is likely to undergo changes in the future, we wanted to establish a baseline of basic knowledge and principles that comprise a specialty, highlighting both its commonalities with other areas of professional psychology and its distinctiveness. We look forward to seeing the dynamics of such changes, as well as the emergence of new specialties in the future.

In this volume, Dr. Finch and his coauthors provide a comprehensive demonstration of the competencies involved in the specialty of clinical child and adolescent psychology. First recognized as a specialty by the American Psychological Association (APA) Commission for the Recognition of Specialties and Proficiencies in Psychology (CRSPPP) in

1998, and subsequently expanded in 2003, this specialty has a history that dates back to the turn of the century when the first psychological clinic for children was reportedly established. As it is currently applied, this broad and wide-ranging specialty took organizational shape from the 1960s through the 1990s, and today child and adolescent psychology shares many characteristics and plays a collaborative role other specialties within professional psychology. These include clinical psychology, cognitive and behavioral psychology, school psychology, and clinical health psychology. The specialty extends far beyond the scope of the age of its identified patient population, and requires a unique and comprehensive integration of multiple professional competencies from a range of other specialty areas, to achieve a best practices model of intervention.

Arthur M. Nezu
Christine Maguth Nezu

CLINICAL CHILD AND ADOLESCENT PSYCHOLOGY TIME-LINE

1896 Lightner Witmer founds the first psychology clinic at the University of Pennsylvania; most of his clients are children. Witmer is regarded as a founder of clinical child, pediatric, and school psychology.

1905 The Binet-Simon intelligence scale is published in France.

1907 The first clinical journal, the *Psychological Clinic*, is founded. Most of the articles involve children.

1908 The first clinical internship is offered at Vineland Training School.

1908 Connecticut Society for Mental Hygiene publishes a prospectus advocating prevention activities in the schools.

1909 Sigmund Freud publishes his case study of Little Hans.

1913 The Children's Bureau is established in the United States.

1920 John Watson and Rosalie Raynor demonstrate the development of fear in Little Albert through classical conditioning learning.

1924 Mary Cover Jones publishes her case study of Peter, demonstrating the removal of a phobia through application of learning principles.

1920s The National Committee establishes child guidance clinics across the country.

1936 C. M. Louttit publishes *Clinical Psychology: A Handbook of Children's Behavior Problems* (Harper & Brothers).

1960 Alan O. Ross authors *The Practice of Clinical Child Psychology* (Grune & Stratton).

1962 The Section on Clinical Child Psychology (Section 1) of Division 12: Clinical Psychology of American Psychological Association (Alan Ross, chair) is formed.

1967 Logan Wright authors "The Pediatric Psychologist: A Role Model" in *American Psychologist.*

1969 The Society of Pediatric Psychology establishes, in affiliation with the American Psychological Association through Division 12, Section 1 (Logan Wright, chair).

1971 The *Journal of Clinical Child Psychology* is established (Gertrude Williams, editor).

1976 The *Journal of Pediatric Psychology* is first published (Diane Willis, editor).

1979 Logan Wright, Arlene Schaefer, and Gerald Solomons publish *The Encyclopedia of Pediatric Psychology (University Park Press).*

1980 The Society of Pediatric Psychology becomes Section 5 of Division 12.

1983 C. Eugene Walker and Michael C. Roberts edit the first edition of the *Handbook of Clinical Child Psychology* (Wiley-Interscience).

1985 The Hilton Head Conference on Training Clinical Child Psychologists convenes (June Tuma, chair).

1985 Guidelines for training psychologists to work with children, youth, and families are published in the *Journal of Clinical Child Psychology* (Michael C. Roberts, Marilyn T. Erickson, and June M. Tuma).

1987 The first regional pediatric psychology conference is held in Cleveland, Ohio.

1988 The first Florida Conference on Children's Health Psychology is held at the University of Florida in Gainesville.

1988 The first edition of the *Handbook of Pediatric Psychology* is published (Donald K. Routh, editor).

1994 The first Kansas Conference in Clinical Child Psychology is held at the University of Kansas in Lawrence.

1996 The international journal *Clinical Child Psychology and Psychiatry* is established (Bryan Lask, editor).

1998 The journal *Clinical Child and Family Psychology Review* is established (Thomas Ollendick and Ronald Prinz, editors).

1998 "A Model for Training Psychologists to Provide Services for Children and Adolescents" is approved by the Section on Clinical Child Psychology and published in *Professional Psychology: Research and Practice* (Roberts et al.).

1998 Clinical child psychology is recognized as a specialty by the APA Commission on the Recognition of Specialties and Proficiencies in Professional Psychology.

2000 The American Board of Clinical Child and Adolescent Psychology is formed for board certification within the American Board of Professional Psychology (ABPP) under the leadership of Al Finch.

2000 Section 1 becomes the Society of Clinical Child Psychology, Division 53 (the name is later changed to Society of Clinical Child and Adolescent Psychology in 2001), and the Society of Pediatric Psychology becomes Division 54 of APA.

2005 The recognition of clinical child psychology as a specialty is renewed by the APA Commission on the Recognition of Specialties and Proficiencies in Professional Psychology.

CONTENTS

Appendices

PART I

Introduction to Clinical Child and Adolescent Practice in Professional Psychology

ONE

Clinical Child and Adolescent Psychology

Specialty Definitions and Historical Foundations

The specialty of clinical child and adolescent psychology includes research and practice applications to prevent or intervene with a range of mental and behavioral disorders; psychological aspects of physical conditions; and developmental challenges of children, adolescents, and their families.

- A clinical child and adolescent specialist might provide treatment for a child who is highly anxious about social interactions and school.
- The specialty clinician might work with the parents of a child who repeatedly disobeys and is hostile to his or her parents and teachers.
- A clinical child and adolescent psychologist might work in the schools to help children learn optimally, or to provide consultation to teachers about how to handle the challenges of a child presenting with serious emotional and behavioral problems such as mood swings, aggressive outbursts, and oppositional behavior.
- Working in a pediatric unit of a children's hospital, the psychologist might consult with pediatricians, nurses, and families about the psychosocial adjustment of a child newly diagnosed with a chronic illness such as diabetes or cancer. They might set up ways for the child to better follow the medical regimen for treating the disease or find support from others who are coping with the disease.
- A psychologist might directly work with children presenting to the clinic who are overweight to help them lose weight through nutritious

eating and exercise or implement a community-based program for preventing obesity.

- Through clinics and social service agencies, the clinical child and adolescent psychologist might provide psychological treatment for children who have been physically, sexually, or emotionally abused and neglected by caregivers.
- A clinical researcher in the specialty might investigate the etiology, assessment, and treatment of children with attention deficit/hyperactivity disorder, a problem of poor attention and overactivity such as excessive running around and inability to sit still when necessary.
- Investigators might research the development of children who are at risk for substance use and delinquency, and evaluate intervention programs by studying positive parental involvement and building self-regulation and social competence.
- In collaboration with developmental psychologists, other scientists in clinical child and adolescent psychology study how children form bonding attachments to their caregivers and how these relationships can go awry or be improved through treatment.
- Similarly, the clinical child and adolescent scientist-practitioner might work with families and children who have been maltreated to understand the effects of abuse, how to prevent child maltreatment, and how to ameliorate the negative outcomes.
- The child and adolescent specialist may study the etiology and developmental course of autism in order to find effective ways to treat the social and communicative problems presenting in children with this disorder.

These are only a few examples of the types of topics investigated by clinical scientists in the clinical child and adolescent specialty. This immense range of activities poses challenges for the clinical child and adolescent specialist as well as creates opportunities for scientific and service contributions (Jackson, Alberts, & Roberts, 2010; Johnson, Janicke, & Reader, 2008). As the specialty developed, it has drawn on and interacted with a variety of influences and traditions, including clinical psychology, child development and developmental psychology, school psychology, developmental and behavioral pediatrics, and child and adolescent psychiatry, among other disciplines (see Johnson et al., 2008; Walker & Roberts, 2001).

Definition Of Clinical Child Psychology

A formal definition of *clinical child psychology* provided to the American Psychological Association (APA) for official recognition as a specialty states the following:

> Clinical Child Psychology is a specialty of professional psychology which brings together the basic tenets of clinical psychology with a thorough background in child, adolescent and family development and developmental psychopathology. Clinical child and adolescent psychologists conduct scientific research and provide psychological services to infants, toddlers, children, and adolescents. The research and practices of Clinical Child Psychology are focused on understanding, preventing, diagnosing, and treating psychological, cognitive, emotional, developmental, behavioral, and family problems of children. Of particular importance to clinical child and adolescent psychologists is a scientific understanding of the basic psychological needs of children and adolescents and how the family and other social contexts influence socio-emotional adjustment, cognitive development, behavioral adaptation, and health status of children and adolescents. There is an essential emphasis on a strong empirical research base recognizing the need for the documentation and further development of evidence-based assessments and treatments in clinical child and adolescent psychology. (Council of Specialties in Professional Psychology, 2005)

This archival definition also outlined that the specialty of clinical child psychology had certain identifying characteristics. Specifically, the groups representing the specialty stated that clinical child and adolescent psychology was characterized by training backgrounds in the following:

- Knowledge of normal developmental processes as a prerequisite for distinguishing between normal and abnormal behavior and development, and for understanding developmental factors as they relate to assessment and intervention
- Relating normal family processes to the child and adolescent's development, including the impact of family dynamics, normal family functioning, and childrearing practices on normal child and adolescent development and on the development of problems
- Attention to child and adolescent psychopathology, including epidemiology and etiological models of child and adolescent

psychopathology; treatment options and treatment effectiveness for specific problems and children/adolescents of different ages; knowledge of family and other problems requiring treatment

- The integration of developmental psychology and clinical child and adolescent psychology reflected in developmental psychopathology
- Knowledge of the methods of assessment covering development, cognition, personality, emotion, and achievement
- Theories and research evidence bases for the treatment of infant, child, adolescent, and family problems
- Prevention of child, adolescent, and family disorders drawing upon knowledge of normal and deviant developmental pathways as well as developmentally informed knowledge of clinical problems
- Special ethical and legal issues in research and practice with children, adolescents, and their families
- An appropriate appreciation for and understanding of principles of diversity and cultural context as they related to professional behavior and clinical practice (Commission for the Recognition of Specialties and Proficiencies in Professional Psychology [CRSPPP], 2010a)

As can be seen in this characterization, the specialty integrates research and practice and has emphasized understanding children from a perspective of both normal development and of developmental psychopathology. The specialty is intrinsically related to clinical psychology and the core foundations of psychology and to developmental processes, with a unique combination not appreciated when separately present. Working with diverse populations is required, so specialists appreciate cultural and ethnic considerations, both in developing the scientific base and in clinical applications.

Populations Served by Clinical Child and Adolescent Psychologists

Clinical child and adolescent psychologists work with infants, children, adolescents, and their families. They may exhibit psychological, developmental, behavioral, scholastic, health, and family problems and be seen in various settings such as schools; independent psychological practices; community mental health clinics and child guidance centers; pediatric and family physicians' offices; children's hospitals; community, social service, and public health agencies; juvenile justice divisions and detention facilities; and advocacy organizations.

The range of problems that clinical child and adolescent psychologists might research, assess and diagnose, and treat might include the following:

- High-risk children compromised by biological vulnerabilities and/or psychosocial adversity (e.g., preterm, medically ill, or drug-addicted newborns) and their families
- Children and adolescents with emotional and developmental problems, including psychotic disorders (e.g., schizophrenia, pervasive developmental disorder, autism, retardation)
- Children and adolescents with significant mental disorders as reflected in behavioral, emotional, cognitive, and/or developmental problems in family, school, childcare, juvenile justice system, and/or peer group contexts
- Adolescents with problems including delinquency, substance abuse/dependency, and high-risk sexual behaviors
- Children and adolescents with signs of cognitive deficits or uneven development requiring an assessment of cognitive functioning and/or school readiness
- Children, adolescents, and their families coping with injury, trauma and loss as a result of natural disasters (e.g., earthquakes and hurricanes) and human-made disasters (e.g., bombings and attacks; wars and mobilization; terrorist alerts; kidnapping; automobile collisions)
- Children, adolescents, and their families in the pediatric system coping with a variety of health-related problems, including: chronic, serious, and/or life-threatening physical illnesses; adherence to medical regimens; pediatric patients with chronic pain; and amelioration of symptoms of various pediatric conditions
- Children and adolescents with physical illnesses whose symptoms may be exacerbated by psychosocial factors
- Children and adolescents with parents who have chronic physical or mental health conditions
- Children, adolescents, and families coping with developmental milestones or with the upset of divorce, single-parenting, and custody arrangements, or adjusting to remarriage and step-parenting (CRSPPP, 2010b)

Procedures and Techniques

Clinical child and adolescent psychologists utilize numerous procedures and techniques in their clinical work. As will be detailed in later pages in this book, the activities include assessment, intervention, prevention, and consultation.

ASSESSMENT

The specialist may conduct behavioral observations of the children and adolescents; interviews with parents and children/adolescents; measurement of academic achievement, intelligence, and other cognitive functioning; assessment of adaptive behavior or personality; and assessment of family.

INTERVENTION

Based on careful assessment, the clinical child and adolescent psychologist develops effective psychologically based treatments for the presenting problems. Evidence-based interventions often involve behavior management techniques implemented in the child's home through parent training for disruptive behaviors, or in the school through consultation on behavioral plans. Multisystemic programs may be implemented in other community and health-care settings. Additionally, cognitive-behavioral approaches have been developed to treat problems in self-regulation, mood disorders, and peer relationships. Interventions involving medication are often developed through consultation and collaboration with the child's physicians or with child psychiatrists.

PREVENTION

Specialists often develop and consult with youth programs for healthy child and adolescent development. Many programs are designed to prevent the onset of problems such as substance abuse, teen pregnancy, or delinquency. These efforts reflect an orientation to health promotion and problem prevention (including child injury, child abuse, and neglect).

CONSULTATION

As a consultant, clinical child and adolescent psychologists frequently provide psychological information assistance to a range of other professionals such as teachers and school personnel, pediatricians and family physicians, nurses, social workers, child psychiatrists, child protection and care workers, lawyers, and judges. In addition to concern about prevention and alleviation of children's and adolescents' problems, consultants may conduct program evaluation and research in applied settings providing given scientific methodology skills.

Clinical Child and Adolescent Psychologists' Work Settings

The settings in which clinical child and adolescent psychological researchers and practitioners conduct their work are varied but can include child guidance clinics and mental health centers, school and educational settings, medical settings and children's hospitals, residential and inpatient treatment centers, independent practice, and university and research settings.

CHILD GUIDANCE CLINICS AND MENTAL HEALTH CENTERS

Child, youth, and family services are provided by clinical child and adolescent specialists through community-based clinics (Smith-Boydston, 2005; Smith-Boydston & Nelson, 2008). The specialist may provide outpatient services of individual, group, or family therapy. He or she may also work with teams of other mental health professionals, including social workers, case workers, nurses, and psychiatrists. Outpatient services may involve individual, group, or family therapy. The specialists in these centers may provide direct services or consultation to school-based preventive programs and provide in-home interventions such as multisystemic treatment. Clinical child and adolescent psychologists also frequently take administrative roles in their service units and the center.

SCHOOLS AND EDUCATIONAL SETTINGS

Clinical child and adolescent psychologists may be employed by school districts to provide psychological services to children and adolescents who display psychological problems in these educational settings. The clinical child and adolescent specialist frequently consults with teachers and principals, and/or the child's parents about optimal ways to enhance the child's educational and developmental outcomes and about methods of managing behavior problems. For example, Roberts, Jacobs, Puddy, Nyre, and Vernberg (2003) described a psychological consultation program for children with serious emotional disturbances through a school-based model of therapeutic classrooms.

MEDICAL SETTINGS AND CHILDREN'S HOSPITALS

Clinical child and adolescent psychologists and pediatric psychologists often provide clinical services for children in the hospital and in outpatient clinics for children and adolescents such as pediatricians' offices (see Roberts & Steele, 2010). Often when working in these settings, the term pediatric psychologist maybe used. Some view pediatric psychology as a subcomponent of clinical child and adolescent psychology, and others view it as distinctive. Nonetheless, these areas are highly related for this specialty. Services may be provided directly to the child or family with a medical problem (or with psychological issues presenting in the medical setting) or indirectly through allied health professionals such as nurses who perform the interventions. A variety of issues may become the focus of clinical services in different departments and clinics, such as endocrinology, gastroenterology, oncology, and neonatal intensive care units, for such cross-cutting concerns as pain control, medical adherence, and adjustment to disease.

RESIDENTIAL AND INPATIENT TREATMENT CENTERS

Clinical child and adolescent psychologists may also function within teams of mental health professionals in inpatient settings such as psychiatric inpatient treatment units, residential treatment facilities, and psychiatric hospitals (Vargas & de Dios Brambila, 2005). In these settings, the specialist may provide consultation and/or conduct diagnostic evaluations, in addition to providing individual and group psychotherapy.

INDEPENDENT PRACTICE

The specialist may establish an independent or group practice of psychology (sometimes with other mental health professionals in the group) in a private practice clinic. The practices may be freestanding or related to an institutional base for providing psychological assessment and psychotherapy for children and adolescents with behavior problems, and receiving referrals from schools, courts, or medical settings. The practitioner frequently will intervene with the family and consult with other professionals about appropriate management techniques (Landolf, 2005).

UNIVERSITY AND RESEARCH SETTINGS

Increasingly, clinical child and adolescent psychologists (and pediatric psychologists) are employed at universities and colleges where they teach and conduct research on issues of developmental psychopathology, psychological concomitants of physical illness, psychological assessment, and effective treatment for children's problems.

Clinical Child and Adolescent Psychology as a Recognized Specialty in Professional Psychology

Clinical child and adolescent psychology as a psychology subfield fulfills the definition of a specialty which is "characterized by a distinctive pattern or configuration of competent services to specified problems and populations. Practice in a specialty is based upon broad and general education and training in scientific psychology and the foundations of practice. Practice in a specialty requires advanced knowledge and advanced skills acquired through an accredited doctoral program and may require an additional organized sequence of education and training in postdoctoral programs" (Council of Specialties in Professional Psychology, 2010).

Within the discipline of psychology, formal recognition or status as a specialty typically comes through two mechanisms: (1) by vote of the APA's Council of Representatives following review of a comprehensive petition presented to the Commission for the Recognition of Specialties and Proficiencies in Professional Psychology (CRSPPP) and (2) by certification through the American Board of Professional Psychology. *Clinical child psychology* was initially approved as a specialty through the CRSPPP and APA recognition in 1998, and recognition was reapproved in 2005 (for more information, see www.apa.org/ed/graduate/specialize/crsppp.aspx). *Clinical child and adolescent psychology* was approved to establish a specialty board, the American Board of Clinical Child and Adolescent Psychology (ABCCAP), and started conducting exams and awarding board certification in 2003 (for more information, see www.clinicalchildpsychology.com/). The specialty board certifies that the approved psychologists have demonstrated competence to deliver services to the public consumer through a credential review and examination process. ABCCAP functions within the American Board of Professional Psychology (ABPP), which recognizes boards in other specialties as well.

Relationship with Other Specialties

The clinical child and adolescent psychology specialty shares many characteristics with all specialties within professional psychology in terms of common history, theoretical foundations, research strategies, and assessment and therapeutic techniques. Three other specialties, in particular—clinical psychology, school psychology, and clinical health psychology—have strong commonality with the clinical child and adolescent specialty, but they also have distinctive elements.

For example, having derived both within and parallel to clinical psychology, the child specialty has intrinsic links to the broader field of clinical psychology, which has also been recognized as a specialty by the APA, has its own organizations (e.g., Division 12, Society of Clinical Psychology), and receives board certification through American Board of Clinical Psychology. As noted by Routh (1994), however, in the years after World War II, clinical psychology became more identified as adult-oriented, and training programs became much less focused on child, adolescent, and family clinical issues. This adult-oriented perspective has continued to the present, although the specialty petition of clinical psychology for CRSPPP recognition attempted to encompass child-related concerns. The specialty definition for clinical psychology states the following:

> Clinical Psychology is a general practice and health service provider specialty in professional psychology. Clinical psychologists assess, diagnose, predict, prevent, and treat psychopathology, mental disorders and other individual or group problems to improve behavior adjustment, adaptation, personal effectiveness and satisfaction. What distinguishes Clinical Psychology as a general practice specialty is the breadth of problems addressed and of populations served. Clinical Psychology, in research, education, training and practice, focuses on individual differences, abnormal behavior, and mental disorders and their prevention, and lifestyle enhancement. (CRSPPP, 2010d)

In another related specialty, school psychology (recognized by APA CRSPPP and with an ABPP specialty board; see Flanagan & Miller, 2010) shares a similar focus on child and adolescent issues and techniques, with an increasing number of school psychologists practicing outside of school institutions. Its specialty definition demonstrates the broad reach of what school psychologists consider in their practice:

> School Psychology is a general practice and health service provider specialty of professional psychology that is concerned with the science and practice of psychology with children, youth, families; learners of all ages; and the schooling process. The basic education and training of school psychologists prepares them to provide a range of psychological diagnosis, assessment, intervention, prevention, health promotion, and program development and evaluation services with a special focus on the developmental processes of children and youth within the context of schools, families, and other systems. (CRSPPP, 2010e)

Although pediatric psychology per se is not currently a specialty (or "proficiency") recognized by the APA CRSPPP, it is represented by the recognized specialty of clinical child and adolescent psychology (Johnson et al., 2008).

Clinical health psychology also relates somewhat to pediatric psychology, although many consider the former to be more adult-focused, similar to clinical psychology, in its relationship to child and adolescent-oriented professional activities. This specialty states its definition as follows:

> The specialty of Clinical Health Psychology applies scientific knowledge of the interrelationships among behavioral, emotional, cognitive, social and biological components in health and disease to the promotion and maintenance of health; the prevention, treatment and rehabilitation of illness and disability; and the improvement of the health care system. The distinct focus of Clinical Health Psychology is on physical health problems. The specialty is dedicated to the development of knowledge regarding the interface between behavior and health, and to the delivery of high quality services based on that knowledge to individuals, families, and health care systems. (CRSPPP, 2010c)

Some professionals who identify as pediatric psychologists may become board certified in clinical health psychology, for example, either because their training backgrounds were not in clinical child and adolescent psychology or because of a greater identity with generic health psychology. About half of those with board certification (ABCCAP) in clinical child and adolescent psychology have a primary identity as pediatric psychologists. Although not always considered critically linked, the ABPP specialties of family psychology and cognitive-behavioral psychology also have many conceptual and practical relationships with clinical child and adolescent psychology in terms of populations, theoretical orientations, and techniques (see www.cospp.org and www.apa.org/ed/graduate/specialize/recognized.aspx).

Historical Developments in Clinical Child and Adolescent Psychology

The specialty of psychological research and practice devoted to the problems of children and adolescents in the United States developed from early roots in psychology. Lightner Witmer is often credited with founding the first psychological clinic for children in 1896, consulting with parents, teachers, and physicians about children's difficulties, and attempting to intervene through psychological and educational strategies while studying the effectiveness of the techniques (McReynolds, 1987bbb; Routh, 1994). In a chapter relating the history of clinical child psychology, Routh (1994) suggested that one of the earliest clinical child psychologists may have been C. M. Louttit (1936), who wrote a book titled *Clinical Psychology: A Handbook of Children's Behavior Problems.*

Alan Ross also was an early contributor to the specialty and to formalizing its organizational home. Ross's 1959 book, *The Practice of Clinical Child Psychology*, outlined the professional development of the field regarding training, practice, and research. Ross posited that the specialty required establishing (a) a formal membership organization, (b) scientific journals, (c) professional meetings and conferences, and (d) accepted standards training and education of specialists. These goals have largely been accomplished at this point (although separate accreditation of training programs in the specialty has not yet occurred). Ross also became the first chair of the Section on Clinical Child Psychology when established in 1962 within the Division of Clinical Psychology of the APA (Division 12), which accomplished the first milestone he described. This organization (also known as Section I) set up the first professional journal in the field, the *Journal of Clinical Child Psychology*, which later become a strong scientific publication, accomplishing the second milestone Ross described.

The original Section on Clinical Child Psychology has grown into an APA Division (53) of its own as the Society of Clinical Child and Adolescent Psychology and changed the name of the scientific publication to the *Journal of Clinical Child and Adolescent Psychology.* The Society of Pediatric Psychology (SPP: APA Division 54), formed in 1969, is a closely related organization focusing on developmental and psychosocial considerations related to medical conditions, the psychological concomitants of disease, and developmental disorders, and the prevention of problems and promotion of healthy conditions. SPP publishes the *Journal of Pediatric Psychology.*

Other national and international organizations also serve interests related to clinical child and adolescent psychology and pediatric psychology, including the International Society of Child and Adolescent Psychopathology and the Society of Child and Family Policy and Practice (APA Division 37). Many scientific and professional journals—such as *Clinical Child and Family Psychology Review, Developmental Psychopathology, Journal of Abnormal Child Psychology*, and *Journal of Child and Family Studies*—publish research and practice applications for the field. A number of texts are available for trainees and professionals in the specialty (e.g., Ollendick & Schroeder, 2003; Steele, Elkin, & Roberts, 2008; Steele & Roberts, 2005; Walker & Roberts, 2001).

In another historical development, specialty board certification is now available in clinical child and adolescent psychology (American Board of

Clinical Child and Adolescent Psychology, 2007, which recognizes professional psychologists for their advanced level of competencies to provide quality services in clinical child and adolescent psychology, including pediatric psychology. Clinical child psychology has been awarded recognition as a specialty in professional psychology by the APA (CRSPPP, 2010b). Thus, by formal recognition and member participation, clinical child and adolescent psychologists have maintained and grown vigorous organizations and scientific journals to support the field.

The third element outlined by Ross (1959) for the specialty, the establishment of meetings and conferences serving practitioners and researchers, has also been largely accomplished. Specialists attend the Kansas Conference in Clinical Child and Adolescent Psychology (sponsored by Division 53), the Niagara Conference on Evidence-Based Treatments for Childhood and Adolescent Mental Health Problems (sponsored by Division 53), the Society of Pediatric Psychology National Conference in Pediatric Psychology (sponsored by Division 54), and the Scientific Meeting of the International Society for Research in Child and Adolescent Psychopathology. The meetings offer a range of topics within developmental psychopathology, child health and development, and evidence-based assessment and treatment.

Ross's fourth historical factor in establishing the specialty was the development of training guidelines and standards for clinical child psychology. After having no standards for training in the specialty for many years, a task force of APA's Division 37 developed guidelines for training programs including curricula and clinical experiences for psychologists working with children, youth, and families (Roberts, Erickson, & Tuma, 1985). The Hilton Head Conference on Training Clinical Child Psychologists, held in 1985, endorsed these basic training guidelines with a few additional emphases (sponsored by the Clinical Child Section of the Division of Clinical Psychology; Tuma, 1985). A later task force commissioned by the National Institute of Mental Health built on the Hilton Head guidelines by producing a model for training psychologists to provide services for children and adolescents (Roberts et al., 1998). Consistent with these documents, the Society of Pediatric Psychology developed recommendations for related training in pediatric psychology (Spirito et al., 2003). Across recommendations, specialty training recommendations have consistently included the following:

- The importance of developmentally oriented coursework and practicum experiences

- Training faculty and supervisors with specific expertise in assessment, treatment and research for issues associated with children, families, and youth
- Systematic opportunities for exposure to and experience with children, families, and youth to develop competencies
- Exposure to and experience with multisystemic models of intervention;
- Assessment of specific competencies in working with children, adolescents, and families (La Greca & Hughes, 1999; Prinstein & Roberts, 2006; Roberts, Biggs, Jackson, & Steele, 2011)

As noted by several commentators, these guidelines have had minimal effect on some training programs because the standards have not yet been adopted by the professional accrediting body, the APA Commission on Accreditation, which would make standards more enforceable (e.g., Prinstein & Roberts, 2006). Clinical child and adolescent psychology, as well as the focused area of pediatric psychology, have more clearly discussed and delineated necessary experiences than many other specialties in recognition of the need for quality training related to the quality of psychological services provided to children, adolescents, and families (see Johnson, 2003; Johnson et al., 2008; Roberts, 2006).

Evidence-Based Practice in Clinical Child and Adolescent Psychology

The unmet needs for psychological services for children, adolescents, and families are immense. As noted by Steele, Roberts, and Elkin (2008),

> In the last U.S. Surgeon General's report addressing the issue of children's mental health, David Satcher, M.D., Ph.D., estimated that approximately 20% of children and adolescents in the United States have mild to moderate symptoms of mental illness and that approximately 1 in 10 children has significant emotional health concerns that warrant professional intervention. (p. 3)

As the specialty evolved, it developed a strong scientific base for its practice and services. The terms embraced by the specialty of evidence-based practice and empirically supported treatments, although not synonymous, convey the emphasis on the integration of science informing practice and services, which inform sciences in a "reciprocating process" (Roberts & James, 2008, p. 10).

The primary journals in the field (e.g., *Journal of Clinical Child and Adolescent Psychology*, *Journal of Pediatric Psychology*) and the organizational websites for the two major divisions representing the specialty (www.clinicalchildpsychology.org and www.societyofpediatricpsychology.org) present the best research evidence for developmental psychopathology, assessment/diagnosis, and psychological treatment. For example, a special 1998 issue of the *Journal of Clinical Child Psychology* published a series of articles on empirically supported treatments for children and adolescents with such disorders as depression, phobia and anxiety disorders, conduct disorder, and attention deficit/hyperactivity disorder (Lonigan, Elbert, & Johnson, 1998). A follow-up special issue was published in *Journal of Clinical Child and Adolescent Psychology* in 2008 with updates on evidence-based psychosocial treatments for children and adolescents (Silverman & Hinshaw, 2008). A similar set of articles on empirically supported treatments in pediatric psychology was published over a period of time in *Journal of Pediatric Psychology* (Spirito, 1999), for example, on problems of pain, obesity, and psychological symptoms occurring with asthma, cancer, and diabetes. The Society of Clinical Child and Adolescent Psychology is partnering with another organization to provide information for the public and professionals on evidence-based mental health treatment for children and adolescents at www.abct.org/sccap/. Evidence-based practice has also been developing the related specialty of family psychology (Kaslow, Celano, & Stanton, 2009; Sexton & Coop Gordon, 2009). A recent report from an APA task force summarized the literature and emphasized a "meta-systems approach to evidence-based practice for children and adolescents" (Kazak et al., 2010, p. 85). This approach recognized the many systems in which children and adolescents are involved, and the need for research-based interventions to be tested and applied in these multiple complex systems. The specialty continues to build its knowledge base, and future developments will likely focus on implementing effective assessment and treatments and developing competence for providing services.

Summary

As you can see, the development of the specialty has been a work in progress over a long time. Despite these advancements in establishing clinical child and adolescent psychology as a distinct specialty, there remain challenges for maintenance and further progress. As noted by Prinstein and Roberts (2006), there are unique training needs of psychologists who serve children, adolescents, and families and there are problems in how to meet these needs in the more typical context of adult-focused clinical training programs with no enforcement for standards of minimal training. Some programs have seen success in training specialists both within identified child-focused training and in specialty tracks within general clinical psychology. (Programs that have self-identified as having clinical child and adolescent psychology and pediatric psychology training are listed at www.clinicalchildpsychology.org/graduate_directory.) However, caution must be used in evaluating the depth, breadth, and quality of the specialty training offered by some programs (perhaps in comparison to training recommendations of Roberts et al., 1998, and Spirito et al., 2003).

As you will see in the following chapters of this book, multiple elements characterize the specialty of clinical child and adolescent psychology, as captured in the following definition:

> The research and practices of Clinical Child Psychology are focused on understanding, preventing, diagnosing, and treating psychological, cognitive, emotional, developmental, behavioral, and family problems of children. Of particular importance to clinical child and adolescent psychologists is a scientific understanding of the basic psychological needs of children and adolescents and how the family and other social contexts influence socio-emotional adjustment, cognitive development, behavioral adaptation, and health status of children and adolescents. (Council of Specialties in Professional Psychology, 2005)

TWO

Conceptual and Scientific Foundations of Clinical Child and Adolescent Psychology

Clinical child and adolescent psychology can be conceptualized as a multi-systems approach to assessing and treating children, adolescents, and their families. Within each of the systems, we are dealing with a developing individual whose social, physical, and cognitive characteristics are rapidly changing. In developing a working conceptional model for this group, careful attention must be paid to the complexity of the developmental processes taking place. Most childhood and adolescent disorders are the result of the interaction of multiple variables over time, and therefore the nature of these problems is rarely straightforward. The widely used *biopsychosocial model* is designed to take into account the influences of biological, psychological, and sociocultural influences associated with specific problems. This model fits well with the diagnostic labeling and medical model approach of the diagnostic and statistical manuals that dominate the mental health fields. However, an expanded and developmentally based model is likely to be more useful for those working with children, adolescents, and their families. In 1974, Achenbach stated that psychopathology was different in children than it was in adults because of the incredible importance of development for all aspects of a child's behavior including both normal and abnormal (Achenbach, 1974). He was one of the leaders in the emerging field of developmental psychopathology. *Developmental psychopathology* views the development of psychological problems within the context of the developmental level of the child—psychological problems are development that encountered problems (Achenbach, 1990; Cicchetti & Cohen, 1995; Masten & Braswell, 1991; Werner, 1994). Many of these problems are the result of the systems in which the child is developing.

Given the varied systems and the developmental issues surrounding the individual child, Bronfenbrenner's *bioecological theory of human development* can serve as an overarching conceptual model that is useful for clinical child and adolescent psychology (Bronfenbrenner, 1986, 2004; Bronfenbrenner & Morris, 1998, 2006). In this model of development, five environmental systems (the microsystem, the mesosystem, the exosystem, the macrosystem, and the chronosystem) and the biological system interact to influence the development of the individual. The systems become increasingly removed from the child, but each may need to be considered to understand the behaviors of the child or adolescent. Although these terms may be somewhat unfamiliar, the systems to which they refer are very useful. Many practitioners and academics in the field might not articulate their conceptual framework in this manner, but most would agree that the combination of these two models reflects how they think about their clients.

At the center of these systems is the developing child who is influenced by multiple sources and systems. Before we consider each of these systems separately, we need to address the issue of working with a developing individual.

Development

Clinical child and adolescent psychologists deal with rapidly developing clients and consequently should be well founded in developmental psychology. Behaviors that are developmentally appropriate at one level may become issues of concern at another. Achenbach (1990) has pointed out that all behaviors must be attended to in terms of the relations between the maladaptive behaviors and the normal developmental emergence of behaviors. For example, sustained attention and self-control are greatly influenced by the developmental level of the child. When this perspective is taken, many of the behaviors that result in the child being referred for services are found not to be qualitatively different from those exhibited by most people at some time during their lives. The question becomes one of the appropriateness of the presenting behaviors for the developmental level of the child.

For example, crying is frequently seen in infants, toddlers, and young children. However, it generally becomes a concern if the behavior continues into middle childhood or adolescence. Similarly, bed-wetting is a normal developmental issue for younger children but becomes a source of concern later in development. As with a number of disorders that are diagnosed in childhood or adolescence, a diagnosis of enuresis (bed-wetting) should not be made before a certain age.

In addition to the disorders that are developmentally based, some disorders may appear differently according to the developmental level of the child. For example, in major depressive disorder the prominence of characteristic symptoms of depression may change with age and may appear different at various ages (*DSM-IV-TR*; American Psychological Association [APA], 2000). Young children with a major depressive disorder are more likely to exhibit somatic complaints (unexplained physical problems) and have their sadness implied from their sad facial expressions than are adults or even older children, who may verbalize sadness, hopelessness, and so on. This observation is consistent with the developmental finding that younger children see things more concretely and are less able to address, understand, and express abstract concepts and feelings. Consequently, younger children are less likely to articulate such abstract feelings as hopelessness and rather are more likely to exhibit the more concrete somatic complaints and facial expressions.

Another developmental issue has to do with the cognitive style of children. Youngsters have a more limited frame of reference than do adults and consequently have more difficulty identifying when certain problems began. They are more likely to focus on the present and not be able to contrast it with their past. As a result of this limitation, they are less likely to make distinctions such as how their current level of feelings compare to their past ones. In addition, they may not be able to state how long certain feelings have been present. Although this issue tends to decrease with age, it can make it difficult to obtain an accurate self-report on symptom duration from the child and the clinician must rely more on reports from others. This need to rely on others may present some problems when assessing subjective feelings such as anxiety, sadness, and anger. The data are clear about the discrepancies between child self-report and behavior ratings by parents and teachers regarding internalizing problems (Kamphaus & Frick, 1996).

As a result of the developmental issues associated with the child or adolescent, a developmental perspective is an essential part of the conceptual model of clinical child and adolescent psychology. There are simply too many issues that are either developmentally based or influenced.

Social Factors

Each child has a unique set of developmental and biological factors that have to be explored to gain an understanding of what that particular child brings to the session. In addition to these child factors, there are unique social factors that influence the child. Bronfenbrenner refers to these social systems as the microsystem, the mesosystem, the exosystem, the macrosystem, and the chronosystem.

THE MICROSYSTEM

According to Bronfenbrenner, the *microsystem* is the system in which the child lives; it includes family, peers, school, and neighborhood. Children and adolescents are influenced by all of these systems, and the degree of importance of any one system may vary over the course of the child's development. Certainly the family is initially the central system in which the child develops, and the nature of this system has to be examined to understand the behavior of the child or adolescent. In fact, the family system is considered central to many clinical child and adolescent psychologists, and the whole field of family therapy has developed because of this sense of importance. Several systems or schools of family therapy have evolved (see DeRoma, 2006, for a more detailed discussion). A common tenet that cuts across these approaches to family therapy is that one has to examine the entire family and intervene at the family level in order to bring about therapeutic change. The behavior of any one individual in the family is best understood when viewed as the product of family interactions. A more detailed discussion of the various approaches to family therapy is beyond the scope of this chapter. The major point to be taken is that the family is of major importance when examining the behavior of a child.

Historically the focus on the family has taken the form of blame, shared problems, maintaining stimuli, and a variety of other concepts. Early positions tended to blame the parents, particularly the mother, for the problems presented by the child. For example, the parents of autistic children were described as very intelligent individuals who were obsessive and detached (Kanner, 1943). Bettelheim (1967) went on to state that this condition was related to both the parents' wish that the child did not exist and the child's withdrawal from the "refrigerator" mother. Research soon discredited the theory of parental contributions to autism, but the trend of parent blaming has frequently been a roadblock to effective treatment. Even today, despite considerable evidence to the contrary, there remains the belief that such disorders as ADHD may be the result of poor parenting.

On the other hand, it is clear that parents do have an impact on their children. For example, parenting styles have been found to influence the child's behavior. Whereas boys whose parents use an authoritarian parenting style are likely to be more aggressive (Hart, Burock, London, & Atkins,

2003), children whose parents adopt a more authoritative parenting style are more likely to be cheerful, self-confident, and friendly in their peer relationships. Consequently it is important to determine the parenting style used in the child's home. In addition, how well do the parents agree on their parenting style, or do they disagree and undermine each other's efforts?

Siblings are part of the child's or adolescent's microsystem, and approximately 80% of American children have one or more sibling (Dunn, 2007). Siblings can play a variety of roles in the life of the developing child, and these roles may change depending on the circumstances of the moment. The same sibling may be a rival one minute and a teacher or helper the next. Young siblings fight frequently—about every 10 minutes between the age of 2 and 4 years of age—but gradually work out other means of resolving conflict (Kramer, 2006). Older children are frequently given child care responsibilities for younger children, whereas the youngest sibling may be pampered for a longer period of time. Some research suggests that birth order can be a factor in the child's development (Paulhus, 2008), even though this influence may be small. As a result of these potential influences, the clinical child and adolescent psychologist needs to explore the nature of the interactions among the siblings within the family.

What if there are no siblings? In 1896 G. Stanley Hall suggested that only children were spoiled and destined to be maladjusted. Although research has not supported his position, this stereotype may continue, even among psychologists.

Day care, preschool, after-school, and school arrangements are other microsystems that may play an important part in a child's development. The amount of time that a typical child spends outside of the home increasingly accounts for most of her or his waking hours. The quality and nature of all these potential microsystems vary greatly and are likely to be influenced by factors outside the system. Certainly, negative experiences in these environments can affect the child. For example, considerable emphasis may be placed on doing well in school, and a child who has difficulty in this area may develop behavioral or emotional issues.

It is estimated that there are more than two million children currently enrolled in licensed child care facilities and an uncounted number receiving child care from unlicensed providers and/or babysitters (Santrock, 2009). The quality of these facilities varies greatly: many provide excellent care, whereas others do not. Data indicate that some children are more likely to be harmed by child care than are others. For example, children who have a more difficult temperament and those who have lower levels of self-control tend to be at greater risk in day care (Santrock, 2009). On the other hand, most children do well in day care. Clinical child psychologists are more likely to see young children who fall into the at-risk category, and they need to be familiar with the issues associated with day care and goodness of fit with certain children.

School and issues faced by children and adolescents in school have received increased attention in recent years with reports of violence and bullying frequently appearing in the professional literature as well as the news. This increase interest in bullying is reflected by Swearer, Espelage, and Napolitano (2009) reporting a 200% increase in the number of published articles and books on the topic between 1997 and 2007.

Many children who are seen by psychologists have other school-related problems such as poor achievement. For example, children with conduct problems frequently have language and reading difficulty; children with anxiety disorders may be fearful of the social setting at school or fear being ridiculed, teased or judged; and children with ADHD are likely to experience a variety of social and academic problems at school. Children, regardless of presenting problems, frequently feel frustrated and demoralized by school failure, and the clinical child and adolescent psychologist needs to know the nature of the problems presented at school.

Certainly any psychologist working with school-aged youngsters needs to inquire about the social environment at school because so much of children's lives rotate around the interactions there. One of the many issues faced by a clinical child and adolescent psychologist is the need to obtain information from the school—a time-consuming task not likely to be reimbursed by insurance. However, without information about the child's behavior at school, considerable knowledge about the problem will be lost.

Running through all of the microsystems are parents and peers. The child's perception of his or her relationship with parents and peers is likely to contribute greatly to how that child feels about him/herself. In addition, problems in the parent-child interaction may lead to problems with the child's peers. For example, Dodge, Pettit, and Bates (1994) found that children who were maltreated at home were more disliked, withdrawn, and less popular with their peers. Consequently, the clinical child and adolescent psychologist must examine a complex set of variables and their potential interactions in the microsystems.

THE MESOSYSTEM

The *mesosystem* refers to the interaction of the microsystems such as the relationship between the parents and the school; the parents and the child's peers; the peers and the teachers; and the teachers and the neighborhood. For example, it is not unusual for parents and teachers to become involved in a blame game when the child has problems at school. The teacher blames the parents for the child not completing his/her homework, and the parents blame the teacher for having inadequate teaching skills or for lacking understanding and warmth. Similarly, parents are frequently dissatisfied with their child's choice of friends and criticize them or attempt to keep their child from interacting with them. Such parental behaviors make it less likely that the child or adolescent is going to be open and forthcoming with information about these and other interactions. This type of parent-child interaction is counterproductive, and the job of the clinical child and adolescent psychologist frequently involves attempting to change the nature of this relationship. At times the parents' concerns might be justified, whereas at other times the parents may be too involved with micromanaging the child or adolescent (Wagner & Reiss, 1995). One of the major conflicts that parents face in raising children is the conflict between exercising too much control over their child's interactions with the other systems and with exercising too little control. Furthermore, the nature of this conflict interacts with the developmental level of the child. Frequently the psychologist has to guide the parents through changes in the amount of control they want and need to exercise over the other systems in the child's life.

THE EXOSYSTEM

The *exosystem* involves the links between the various systems in which the child is involved and those systems that may influence his/her life but in which they are not directly involved. For example, the mother's job may demand increased attention and time so that the nature of the interaction between the father and the child changes. As the father becomes more dissatisfied with his wife's increased physical and emotional absence, his ability to provide the nurturing and support to his child(ren) may suffer. Similarly, parents who work under poor conditions are likely to be more irritable and less effective in their parenting (Crouter, 2006). Positive changes, such as a parent obtaining a less stressful job, can also affect the child. Another potential interaction might be the decreased funding for education, which results in the child being in larger classes with more limited resources. Consequently, even though the child is not directly involved in the exosystem, it may influence his psychological well-being through its effect on a system in which he is involved.

THE MACROSYSTEM

The *macrosystem* refers to the individual's culture, which involves the beliefs and behaviors that are passed down through the generations. Despite the considerable lip service given to attending to cultural differences, relatively little is known about the role played by culture in the development of most psychological disorders (Dumas & Nilsen, 2003) within or across countries. Epidemiological studies of many disorders are limited to North America. The exception to this statement may be ADHD, which seems to have a similar rate across various countries. In North America, certain disorders tend to be associated with certain cultural or ethnic groups. For example, eating disorders are relatively rare in African-American girls compared to European-American girls (Dumas & Nilsen, 2003). On the other hand, symptoms of PTSD are more common in African-American children, and symptoms of separation anxiety are more common in white children (Last & Perrin, 1993).

Certainly clinical child and adolescent psychologists need to be sensitive to a variety of cultural practices and customs in order to appropriately treat their clients. For example, Nelson (1982) presented an interesting case study of a young African-American boy with trichotillomania (a compulsive and irresistible urge to pull out your own hair) that demonstrated the need for this sensitivity. The mother and her son shared a hair-burning ritual that initially appeared very unusual. However, after consultation about local cultural customs, the behavior was found not to be unusual in that context. If consultation had not been sought, treatment planning might have taken a wrong turn.

As the United States becomes a more pluralistic culture, the clinical child and adolescent psychologist needs to be attuned to the influences of various cultural differences. How these differences affect the developing child and adolescent is an area in need of psychological research.

THE CHRONOSYSTEM

The *chronosystem* consists of the events that happen in one's life and the changes that take place. For example, economic conditions might change so that a family has fewer financial resources, resulting in the need to adjust to changes. There may be other events that bring about changes in the perception of one's self. For example, how did the self-perception of African-American children change with the election of the first African-American president? Certainly one needs to examine the impact of these types of changes. The most common form of chronosystem that most clinical child and adolescent psychologists are likely to have to address in some of their clients is divorce. Many children experience increased psychological problems following the divorce of their parents, but most improve with time (Hetherington, 2006). The need for the clinical child and adolescent psychologist to maintain awareness of the potential effects of such events is a task to be mastered.

Rarely do all the foregoing systems contribute to the problems presented by the child or adolescent. However, the clinical child and adolescent psychologist must be aware that there is likely to be an interaction of at least some of these systems. Behavioral problems are rarely simple occurrences and to conceptualize them as such leads to ineffective understanding and treatment.

Biological Factors

In addition to the developmental issues associated with child and adolescent disorders, there are the biological ones that are unique to each child. Attention has to be paid to the biology of the child, beginning with such basic issues as sex. The data are fairly clear on the advantages and disadvantages of one's biological sex in terms of how the child is treated in the environment. These differences will be discussed under the other systems. However, there are some differences in the development of certain disorders that are related to one's sex. For example, there are clear sex differences in the diagnosis of attention deficit/hyperactivity disorder. Although the exact ratio varies according to the nature of the sample studied, it is clear that boys are much more likely to be diagnosed with this disorder than are girls. On the other hand, adolescent girls are more likely to be diagnosed with depression than are adolescent boys despite the fact that there is not a difference in the frequency of the diagnosis earlier in development.

Another biological issue has to do with the individual's vulnerability to various disorders and/or problems. At the extreme end of the biological perspective continuum is the *disease model* upon which much of American health care is built. This position holds that psychological problems are diseases of the brain and nervous system that have distinct behavioral symptoms in the same way that physical diseases have biological symptoms. Psychological problems are seen as being disruptions in neurotransmitters or brain functioning (Dumas & Nilsen, 2003). A less extreme position recognizes that biological factors do influence behavior. In this position it is recognized that brain development, genetics, neurotransmitters, and hormones all need to be considered in the developing child.

Although the human brain is about 25% of its adult size at birth and contains billions of cells, it is not a miniature model of the adult brain. In addition to the growth that takes place in the brain during development, numerous more subtle changes occur. Dendrites and various connections are formed and modified during development. The development and connecting of these brain cells are not independent of experience. In animals, early stimulation has been found to have an influence on the formation and connection of these cells, which translates into better problem-solving skills. With humans, similar results have been implied. Hart and Risley (1995) found a direct relationship between parental verbal stimulation and the child's IQ by the age of 3.

Furthermore, not all areas of the brain develop and mature at the same rate, and some areas of the brain are not fully developed until adulthood (Santrock, 2009). Many of the changes that are observed in cognitive functioning correspond to changes that take place in the brain as it matures. Because of all these changes in the brain, the clinical child psychologist needs to have some appreciation of how the areas of the brain interact and how some typical behavioral problems may be related to brain maturity issues. For example, the difficulty frequently seen in regulating anger and other emotions in early adolescents corresponds to the differential rate of development during this period of the amygdala and the prefrontal cortex (Nelson, 2003). The amygdala, which is involved in experiencing emotions, develops more quickly than does the prefrontal cortex, which is involved in the self-control and regulation of emotions. As a result, it would be expected that there would be some possible difficulties in regulating emotions during adolescence. The question with the individual adolescent is whether or not the difficulty is greater than normal.

During development and even before birth, various factors can produce disruption in brain development. Prior to birth, various teratogens or disorders can have an impact on the behaviors that may bring the child to the attention of the clinical child and adolescent psychologist years later. For example, the effects of alcohol on the developing fetus may result in later learning and adjustment problems that were not manifested until the child entered school.

Genetics plays a role in the development of the individual child and is known to be a factor in the development of at least some psychological problems. However, exactly how genetic factors are manifested is more difficult to understand. Clearly some disorders do tend to run in families and are thought to have a genetic or biological component. For example, family, twin, and adoption studies all suggest that individuals inherit at least a genetic predisposition to develop mood disorders. Yet it is clear that there are other factors that contribute to the development of a psychological disorder.

For example, if one identical twin has bipolar disorder (one of the most clearly genetically linked disorders), there is a higher probability that the other one will have the disorder, compared with the probability among fraternal twins (Potash et al., 2007). If the disorder were totally genetic, we would expect 100% probability in the other twin because these two individuals contain the same genetic material. However, this is not the case. In addition, most children who have a family history of bipolar disorder will not develop the disorder.

Another confusing issue related to the genetic influences on psychological disorders is the fact that no single gene seems to be related to a particular disorder. Genetic influences are polygenic, and effects are likely to be related to the actions of a number of genes as well as the influence of the environment. Consequently, although the importance of genetic influences cannot be denied, they should be taken as only one source of information when working with children and adolescents. It is important to ask about family history, but it is inappropriate to make a final decision about the nature of the problem based only on this history. The amount of weight that should be placed on any one variable is a constant judgment call that the clinical child and adolescent psychologist must make.

Neurotransmitters are another biological factor affecting the child's behaviors. Neurotransmitters are the messengers of the nervous system. They help to transmit information from one neuron to the next, and a number of psychological disorders tend to be correlated with various neurotransmitters issues. For example, certain anxiety disorders have been linked to low levels of the neurotransmitter *gamma-aminobutyric acid* (GABA), whereas schizophrenia and attention deficit/hyperactivity disorder have been linked, respectively, to high and low levels of dopamine. Much of the research in this area is based on adults, but some similar findings have been found in children. As a result, the clinical child psychologist needs to have a working knowledge of the suspected role of neurotransmitters in the development or maintenance of childhood and adolescent disorders.

Scientific Foundations

The scientific foundation of clinical child and adolescent psychology has a checkered past. Lightner Witmer (1867–1956) is generally regarded as the father of both clinical and school psychology (Hergenhahn, 2009; McReynolds, 1987a; Reynolds & Gutkin, 1999), and his work primarily involved children. Given this beginning, it could be said that clinical psychology began as clinical child and adolescent psychology. Witmer felt that the science of psychology should yield applications useful to the betterment of people's lives. He opened a psychological clinic in 1896 to work with children and adolescents who were having psychological and/or school problems. The importance of this beginning is that Witmer felt that psychologists working with children needed the rigorous scientific training leading to the PhD in psychology. Using the scientific approach, he developed a number of tests that were reasonably well developed for their time. Witmer also published a number of carefully developed case studies so that others could evaluate and emulate his procedures. In addition, the work of Watson and Rayner (1920) and Jones (1924) clearly demonstrated the potential for the application of scientific psychology to the field. Thus the beginnings of clinical child and adolescent psychology were soundly founded in the science of psychology.

Despite this early scientific foundation, clinical child and adolescent psychology took a different turn for much of the 20th century. During the same period that the scientific foundations of clinical child and adolescent psychology were being laid, a highly energetic and charismatic movement burst onto the scene. Drawing from the works of Charcot, Janet, Breuer, and others, Sigmund Freud began to develop and publish his theory of psychoanalytic development. Although his work involved adults, his theory was a developmentally based one and placed heavy emphasis on childhood. At about the same time as the emergence of psychoanalytic theory and treatment, the mental hygiene and child guidance movement began. By the 1930s, there were some 500 child guidance clinics across the country (Carmichael, 2006). Most psychologists, including those working in the child guidance clinics, drew on the work of psychoanalytic theory during the first half of the century. Many psychologists were primarily involved in psychological assessment and conducting intellectual and personality testing. Although most of the intellectual tests employed reasonably sound psychometric practices for the time, the dominant approach used to understand behavioral problems focused on personality assessment. The assessment of personality was based on psychoanalytic theory and projective tests. It was argued that unique information was being sought, and that because it was unique, norms were meaningless as each individual was unique. For a more detailed discussion of this historically based position, see Finch and Politano (1994). For this discussion, the main issue to be considered is that attempts to understand children focused on internal states that were to be assessed by methods not based on sound scientific approaches.

The works of Melanie Klein and Anna Freud were widely adopted by many psychologists treating children (Carmichael, 2006). A later trend is noted with the emergence of Carl Rogers's (1942) nondirective or client-centered therapy. Interestingly, Rogers's search for an alternative to psychoanalytic-based treatment grew out of his work in a psychoanalytically oriented child guidance clinic. With the development of Rogers's new approach to treatment, other therapists began to apply his ideas to the treatment of children. Axline and Carmichael (1947) published their influential book on play therapy based on Rogers's work. This initial work in child therapy was followed by Axline's later works on play therapy (1964, 1969, 1989).

Although both Freud's and Rogers's theoretical approaches to treatment were very widely accepted and continue to have their advocates today, neither is scientific. Psychoanalytic concepts are rather nebulous and can rarely be operationally defined in order to be evaluated scientifically. On the other hand, Roger's humanistic position does not accept the principle of determinism (the assumptions that all events have a cause). Because determinism is one of the basic assumptions of science, his theory is not subject to scientific verification.

As behaviorism became the dominant paradigm in experimental psychology, there was more interest in bringing the finding from the laboratory to the practice of psychology. One of the early attempts to integrate science and practice is illustrated by the publication of Dollard and Miller's (1950) book, which attempted to restate psychoanalytic theory in terms of Hull's hypothetical deductive learning theory. Other cracks began to appear in the dominance of psychoanalytic theory. In 1954, Julian Rotter attempted to demonstrate the application of social learning theory to clinical psychology. What followed was a cascade of publications on the application of laboratory findings to clinical psychology (e.g., Eysenck, 1960; Ullmann & Krasner, 1965; Wolpe, 1958). A significant portion of this work involved children and adolescents. For example, in Ullmann and Krasner's book of case studies, 42% involved children or adolescents. Thus clinical child and adolescent psychology began the gradual return to scientifically based treatment approaches.

Evidence-based approaches to treatment represent the current movement in both clinical and clinical child and adolescent psychology. Division 53 (Society of Clinical Child and Adolescent Psychology) of the American

Psychological Association has focused on the promotion and dissemination of information about evidence-based treatment. Two separate issues of their journal, one in 1998 and one in 2008, have been devoted to the topic and the state of the field. Currently a website is available to both the public and professionals (http://effectivechildtherapy.com/) on the use of empirically based treatments. The number of disorders that have evidence-based interventions is gradually growing. A brief overview of these advances is provided by Spirito (2010a). However, there continues to be a wide gap between what we know from research and what is practiced by the typical clinical child and adolescent psychologist. Kazdin (2008) has discussed ways to make research more likely to be applied by clinicians and called for additional research efforts in areas that will enhance the relevance of research to practice. DeAngelis (2010) has provided a discussion of the issues related to closing the gap between research and practice. In addition, Beidas and Kendall (2010) presented a number of studies demonstrating how to change clinicians' knowledge, attitudes, and behaviors regarding evidence-based treatments.

Although some areas of assessment had maintained a foot in the scientific camp (intellectual, achievement, adaptive functioning), projective techniques were the dominant mode of learning about behavior and its causes until the 1960s. With the rise of behavioral approaches to treatment, there began a movement toward more objective techniques of learning about behaviors. Some of the early scales were the Devereux rating scales (Spivack & Spotts, 1966; Spivack, Spotts, & Haimes, 1967). These scales attempted to provide normative data and employ sound psychometric principles. Increasingly, attention began to focus on behavior rating scales and self-report measures (Merrell, 2003). This trend continues today: most assessments of children and adolescents include these more psychometrically sound instruments. However, projective techniques continue to have their advocates.

Summary

In conclusion, clinical child and adolescent psychology began with a strong scientific foundation. Although clinical psychology drifted away from these roots, it appears to be returning to a more scientific foundation.

PART II

Functional Competency—Assessment

THREE

Clinical Assessment of Children, Adolescents, and Their Families

This chapter presents the process involved in the social-emotional-behavioral assessment of children and adolescents and how this process can be conceptualized within a comprehensive problem-solving framework. The chapter covers the following:

- Discussion of the importance of assessment in clinicians' therapeutic work with children, adolescents, and their families
- The ways in which clinicians' theoretical orientations guide/define their practice, not only in terms of psychotherapeutic interventions, but also in terms of their assessment practices
- Discussion of the background in child and adolescent assessment
- How assessment can be comprehensively conceptualized as a problem-solving process for clinicians

Importance of Assessment in Clinical Work with Children, Adolescents, and Their Families

Beginning with the referral, the clinician must ask the question, "What do I need to know to best intervene in the particular problem presented by the individual child/adolescent and/or their family?" In other words, the clinician is faced with the challenge of identifying and defining the presenting problems that the client and his or her family are experiencing.

Although it is hoped that this chapter can be useful for clinicians of differing theoretical persuasions, it is assumed that the "gold standard" for conducting assessments of emotional, behavioral, and social problems is through the use of a multimethod, multi-informant, multisetting, and multioccasion process that is, as much as possible, evidence-based. It is also assumed that assessments have a clinical utility insofar as they provide the basis for determining which interventions the clinician will choose and how such assessments can be utilized throughout the therapeutic endeavor. As such, assessment methods and procedures discussed in this chapter tend to be more direct, objective, and compatible with the notion of evidence-based assessment. It is also assumed that clinicians strive to incorporate the latest research findings to better inform their clinical work, although this does not necessarily mean they are strong advocates of evidence-based, empirically validated models. Rather, it assumes that the most effective clinicians have an informed appreciation of the important link between clinical practice and research. It is this "informed appreciation" that a skilled clinician integrates with his/her clinical expertise in the context of the child/adolescent/family characteristics, culture, and preferences.

When a clinician sees the client and/or a family for the first time, it is important to recognize that assessment and diagnosis are the starting points of a decision-making/problem-solving process that optimally is conducted in a collaborative fashion with the child/adolescent and his or her family. As such, assessment and diagnosis are the foundations and launching pads of clinical practice and can be conceptualized as a therapeutic intervention in and of itself (Tharinger, Finn, Hersh, et al., 2008). It is also important for the clinician to recognize the differences between psychological testing and psychological assessment. *Psychological testing* is basically the measuring of psychology-related variables by means of devices, procedures, and/or tests designed to obtain relevant samples of behavior. Clinicians select tests not just for their psychometric properties, but also for their functional or clinical utility in treatment planning. As such, psychological testing is measurement-oriented and involves the technical skills associated with the broader task of psychological assessment, which inherently involves the processes of problem solving and decision making. On the other hand, psychological assessment involves the gathering of all information and the integration of psychological tests to generate decisions that will be useful in the planning, implementation, and evaluation of treatment. For clinicians who are strong advocates of evidence-based practice, they likely recognize that assessment and diagnosis are essential because evidence-based treatments were developed and evaluated for children and adolescents whose problems have been carefully selected and identified (e.g., conduct disorders, anxiety disorders, attention deficit/hyperactivity disorder, depressive disorders).

For most others, however, assessment is considered essential even when it does not include formal psychological testing or the collection of data of some sort (e.g., baseline) beyond a thorough clinical interview. In either case, it is essential that clinicians have a clear understanding as to "what is the problem" before they can select (guided by their theoretical orientation) the most effective way to proceed with a given problem (disorder) or set of problems (comorbid disorders). Thus, it is assumed that (1) defining the presenting problems and (2) determining how to proceed are best accomplished through an appreciation of how the problem-solving model can be applied to the psychotherapeutic enterprise and be seen within a collaborative framework that the clinician builds with the child/adolescent and his/her family.

The *collaborative problem-solving model*, when applied to the therapy process, is useful because problem solving is the most generalizable characteristic of any clinical endeavor, ranging from assessment to intervention to termination. Although the problem-solving paradigm is highly relevant to the process of assessment, it is actually the therapist's own theoretical orientation that is the foundation upon which their clinical decision making over the course of therapy rests. As such, it is the clinician's own theoretical orientation that structures how he/she will proceed/problem solve in the assessment, intervention, and termination phases of therapy. In a real sense, the therapist's theoretical orientation is similar to the principle of assimilation, which is the process by which an individual (therapist) understands and experiences (the assessment of and intervention in clinical problems) in terms of her or his current way of thinking (theoretical orientation). Assimilation is the dynamic process whereby therapists use as a "backdrop" their current ways of thinking and conceptualizing clinical issues to understand the client and develop an intervention plan that leads to change. Although many therapists claim to be "eclectic" in terms of their theoretical orientation, it is hoped that this is not used as a substitute for the careful development of a serious professional framework for conceptualizing child and adolescent emotional and behavioral difficulties. It is important to appreciate that pragmatic eclecticism (which may be appropriate in some cases) does not replace a solid theoretical foundation for understanding and guiding interventions throughout the course of therapy. Without a solid theoretical framework, therapists function more as technicians and less as skilled clinicians.

Assessment is essential in that it forms the basis for the clinician's treatment plan, the interventions selected, and the benchmarks by which therapy is considered successful or not. Assessment is also the bedrock that guides decisions about which criteria, when met, determine the termination of the case. Over the past 30 years, efforts to understand the important link between assessment and therapy, as well as to evaluate the purpose and adequacy of assessment, have been numerous and have grown (e.g., Hayes, 1998; Nelson, 1983; Reitman, 2006). For example, the *Journal of Clinical Child and Adolescent Psychology* recently sponsored a special section on "Developing Guidelines for the Evidence-Based Assessment of Child and Adolescent Disorders" (Mash & Hunsley, 2005). Textbooks written on assessment are beginning to routinely discuss the role of assessment within the context of evidence-based practice (e.g., Hunsley & Mash, 2010). Before further discussion of modern-day assessment of children, adolescents, and their families, however, the importance of the clinician's theoretical orientation needs to be more thoroughly considered.

Theoretical Orientation: The Basis/Linchpin for a Clinician's Assessment

The therapeutic contract defines the roles of the client and therapist. At the broadest level, it is the therapist's treatment model or philosophical orientation that generally determines how the clinician will carry out the six basic assessment operations as defined by Mash and Hunsley (2005):

1. What type of assessment strategies will be utilized
2. How the case will be understood (case formulation)
3. The establishment of the treatment goals
4. The intervention method/strategies that will be utilized
5. How progress in therapy is defined over the course of treatment

In working with children and adolescents, it is the parents who typically initiate therapy by bringing their child/adolescent (sometimes viewed as the "identified client" by family therapists) to therapy. Parents are the ones typically seeking professional services to deal with their child's and/or family's presenting complaints. From the outset, the therapist will "understand" their difficulties in terms of his/her theoretical orientation, which will guide the clinical treatment of any particular client. It is also important to recognize whether the therapist views assessment as simply information gathering (as in the case in the traditional assessment model) or as an opportunity to collaboratively engage the child/adolescent and his/her family in a way that can be therapeutic in and of itself by facilitating positive change (e.g., Tharinger, Finn, Hersh, et al., 2008).

A clinician's theoretical orientation offers two important elements—a way of understanding human behavior and an approach to assessment and treatment. As we all know, there are a number of different theories about the development of human emotional, behavioral, and social problems that help us conceptualize and assess the emotional/behavioral difficulties presented by the child/adolescent and his/her family. Although the debate among clinicians with different theoretical orientations is about as long-standing as the field of psychology itself, it is the behavioral, cognitive-behavioral, and social learning theories that tend to be more anchored in appreciating the importance of research that serves as a base for the knowledge we have about the assessment strategies and therapeutic intervention techniques. In essence, the assumption in this chapter is that the more our assessment intervention techniques can rely on knowledge gained through empirical research, the better. Having said that, it is important to remember that despite the criteria offered by Chambless and Hollon (1998) to define empirically supported *therapies,* there is no current framework by which to evaluate whether *assessment strategies* meet an agreed-upon criteria as being an evidence-based technique.

Mash and Hunsley (2005) attempt to offer several considerations and guidelines to promote evidence-based assessments for children and adolescents. However, the current Standards for Education and Psychological Testing (1999) offer only general guidelines to be used as the national standard for development and use of psychological tests. In addition, Mash and Hunsley argue that guidelines need to consider evidence-based methods (e.g., types of assessment techniques), as well as the assessment process (e.g., how assessment data are utilized and how divergent information is integrated in the psychotherapeutic endeavor). Despite such general guidelines, in everyday practice, it is the clinician's theoretical orientation that provides the link between data gathered during the assessment and the developed intervention plan. It is hoped that one's theoretical orientation is rooted in a thorough knowledge of assessment strategies and intervention techniques that appreciate the importance of empirical support.

Despite the fact that evidence-based practice in psychology has made significant strides to the point where the field has moved toward the issues of dissemination, implementation, and sustainability of such methods (e.g., Chu, 2008), many clinicians still do not use such methods in their actual practice (e.g., Addis & Krasnow, 2000; Chorpita & Nakamura, 2004; McHugh & Barlow, 2010; Weisz, Sandler, Durlak, & Anton, 2005). Even if there were agreed-upon guidelines for empirically based assessment (which currently there are not), it is likely that the actual use of such procedures/

guidelines by practitioners would be limited. Thus, the fact remains that the clinician's actual practice has and will continue to be a direct function of her or his theoretical orientation (Orvaschel, Faust, & Hersen, 2001a). It is a clinician's theoretical orientation, hopefully grounded in a solid theoretical background, that elevates assessment and intervention processes to something other than what might be expected from a paraprofessional who functions simply as a tester or technician.

Regardless of a clinician's theoretical orientation, all therapists typically (in the beginning of or even before initiating psychotherapeutic interventions) must select and define the problems (or target behaviors) crucial in a therapeutic endeavor. Although this chapter adopts more of the behavioral/cognitive-behavioral/social learning perspective in discussing these issues, other professionals who espouse different therapeutic orientations will likely find the discussion of assessment with children and adolescents helpful. Thus, it is hoped that this chapter will enable therapists to be effective when engaging in the assessment phase of working with a child or adolescent and his or her family. This can be accomplished by taking a broader view of assessment in which the therapist presents to children/adolescents and their families their "insights and understandings" of the case not just as something to be simply accepted by them, but rather as an opportunity to develop a collaborative approach with the client(s) that can be seen as a therapeutic intervention in and of itself (Ackerman, Hilsenroth, Baity, & Blagys, 2000; Tharinger, Finn, Austin, et al., 2008).

Background in Child and Adolescent Behavioral Assessment

The past 25 years of child and adolescent behavioral assessment primarily emphasized the diagnostic epidemiological and prognostic purposes of behavioral assessment (e.g., Mash & Hunsley, 2005). In one of the earliest efforts to articulate the importance of assessment in child and adolescent work, Ollendick and Hersen (1984) defined *child behavior assessment* as "an exploratory hypotheses testing process in which the range of specific procedures is used in order to understand a given child, group or social ecology and to formulate and evaluate specific intervention strategies" (p. 6). More recently, the definition of child behavioral assessment is seen as being comprised of several assessment operations: (a) diagnosis and case conceptualization, (b) screening and early identification, (c) prognosis, (d) treatment design and planning, (e) treatment monitoring, and (f) treatment evaluation (Mash & Hunsley, 2005). Clinicians need to remember that it was only 25 years ago that the *Diagnostic and Statistical*

Manual (*DSM*) began to include information that would be useful to behavioral work with children and adolescents. Many clinicians are developing an appreciation of the fact that assessment is not just determining a *DSM* diagnosis for billing/insurance purposes but is an ongoing process that involves the six elements articulated by Mash and Hunsley (2005). Thus, the traditional role of assessment in assigning individuals to categories (e.g., establishing differential diagnosis and/or comorbidity) or "taxonomic diagnosis" (Mash & Wolfe, 2010) has been expanded. It should also be noted that it is really only in the last 10 years that psychology has begun to embrace the concept of evidence-based practice (see Chambless et al., 1998; Norcross, 2002.) Unfortunately, explorations regarding evidence-based assessment have begun only recently.

The initial stages of therapy are important as crucial decisions are made. For example, consider the following:

- What problem behaviors are to be specifically addressed in therapy?
- How will they be defined?
- What, if any, intervention approaches are to be implemented?
- Is it best to treat the problem with an individual approach or with a family-oriented approach?
- What is the best way to facilitate, if at all, the extent to which family members will be involved?

It is important to note that diagnostic assessment traditionally involves, at a general level, two major activities. The first involves collecting information (e.g., conducting clinical interviews with the child and/or significant others such as parents, teachers, peers; the use of child self-ratings, parent/teacher ratings, and peer sociometric ratings) to evaluate any deviance from normative samples. The second involves direct observations and other behavioral assessment procedures that are idiographic in nature (e.g., self-recording, monitoring, simulated observations, role-playing). Considering the differences in these assessment activities, the clinician needs to reflect upon whether diagnosis primarily involves classifying child/adolescent problems into discreet categories of disorders (as is the case with the *Diagnostic and Statistical Manual*) or whether assessment is to be individualized, gathering detailed information about a child/adolescent's problems and their maintaining conditions. These differing viewpoints about the purpose of assessment and diagnoses still remain an ongoing issue in the field of psychology and are beyond the scope of this chapter.

Despite these differences, the role of assessment throughout the therapeutic process has recently attained even more importance. It should also be noted that assessment processes with children, adolescents, and their families evolved within the behavioral tradition, which emerged in the 1980s when the purpose of diagnosis had been expanded to include determining cause and/or function of behavior. This was referred to as *functional assessment/analysis* (e.g., Iwata, Dorsey, Slifer, Bauman, & Richman, 1982). Functional assessment, often based on interviews of the child/adolescent and significant others, as well as formal testing and other assessment procedures, is designed to elicit information about the circumstances under which the problem/target behaviors first arose, as well as the determining factors that maintain the frequency, duration, and/or intensity of such problems. In essence, a *functional analysis* is an analysis of the contingencies responsible for behavior problems. In other words, at the broadest level, the clinician asks, "What maintains an inappropriate behavior before trying to eliminate it?" or "What prevents an appropriate behavior before trying to reinforce it?" In other words, "What function does problem behavior serve for the child/adolescent/family?" The systematic, empirical search for an answer to such questions, before implementing therapeutic interventions, is called a *functional analysis* (a term inspired by Durand, 1987), the process of which can be seen in Figure 3.1.

This functional analysis of behavior is the clinician's assessment-derived integration of the functional relationship among the important variables that are the focus of therapy—judgments about the child/adolescent/family's problems and goals, their effects, related causal and mediating variables, and the functional relationships among them (Haynes & O'Brien, 2000). This tradition in behavior therapy has evolved into the case formulation model. Basically such a functional analysis involves five basic steps:

1. The clinician identifies the problem/target **b**ehavior (**B**) and the frequency, duration, and/or intensity with which it occurs.
2. The **c**onsequences or outcomes (**C**) are clarified. Is the consequence a reinforcer or an aversive condition?

FIGURE 3.1 **Functional analysis of behavior**

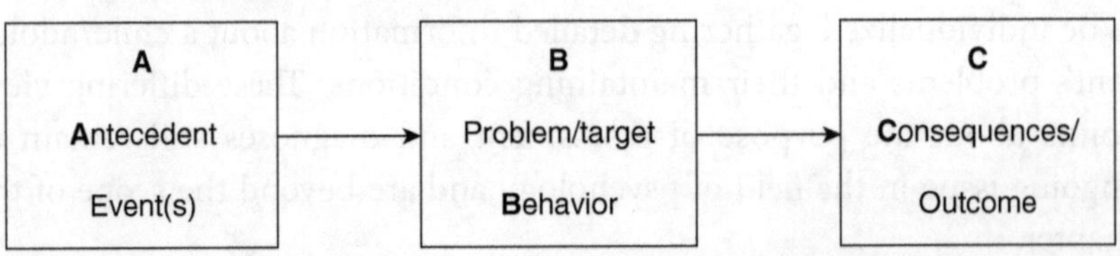

3. The **a**ntecedent events (**A**) or motivating conditions that lead to the problematic/target behavior are identified.
4. The problematic A → B → C relationship or cycle is described.
5. The **c**onsequences/outcomes (C) are defined as contingencies—as reinforcement, punishment, penalty, escape, or avoidance. Does the problem/target behavior increase or decrease as the result of the consequence? Note that if more than one contingency controls the behavior, the foregoing process needs to be used in assessing each problem.

Such an analysis facilitates a more thoughtful selection of an intervention strategy:

- Reinforcement (presentation of a reinforcer or avoidance of the removal of an aversive condition)
- Punishment (presentation of an aversive condition or prevention of the presentation of a reinforcer)
- Penalty (removal of a reinforcer)
- Escape (removal of an aversive condition)
- Avoidance (prevention of the presentation of an aversive condition)

From a behavioral perspective, it is in such a way that assessments are conducted to facilitate the selection of the most effective intervention strategy. This form of behavioral or cognitive-behavioral assessment has been likened to a "problem-solving analysis" (Mash & Wolfe, 2010) and has evolved over the past decade to the point where the problem-solving orientation in case formulation is viewed as the important "mind-set" of clinicians to guide their attempts to understand, explain, predict, and change problematic behavior (Nezu, Nezu, & Cos, 2007).

Another important trend in the psychological assessment of children/adolescents and their families is related to how the feedback that psychologists routinely provide to parents (and sometimes their children) is conducted after the psychological assessment of the situation has been performed. In traditional assessment, after such feedback, the client or clients are then expected to accept this and move on to the therapeutic intervention stage where the problems are attempted to be altered in some fashion. In a collaborative model of assessment, the process of assessment can be viewed as an equally essential part of the therapeutic intervention and goes beyond the guidance that others have offered regarding the parent/child feedback session that occurs at the conclusion of a psychological assessment of the child.

It has been suggested that the feedback session occur in three stages:

1. First, the purpose of assessment is reviewed, the therapist's impressions are shared, and the therapist evaluates the parents' level of understanding and openness to feedback (Oster, Caro, Eagen, & Lillo, 1988).
2. Then, the therapist discusses the specific assessment findings (Groth-Marnat, 2003).
3. Finally, the therapist summarizes the major findings and recommendations with the parents, being sensitive to their reactions and then answering any remaining questions.

It should be noted that the collaborative model for providing assessment feedback to parents and children is only beginning to be better articulated (see Tharinger, Finn, Hersh, et al., 2008, for more information in this regard). Such an approach is designed to help clients and their families conceptualize their problems more systematically and to see themselves as being part of the system that contributes to or maintains their child's behavior problem. It is through such a paradigm shift that the importance of contextual influences on a child's behavior (in addressing the larger interpersonal/family as well as social systems in planning for effective treatments) can be facilitated by the therapist. It should be noted, however, that there has not yet been a great deal of actual research conducted to evaluate the efficacy of clinicians making such a paradigm shift (Finn, 2007). Such therapeutic assessment can be seen as a hybrid of traditional psychological assessment and short-term intervention, as it uses the ongoing process and results of the traditional psychological assessment to enhance parents' understanding of their child and what can be done to facilitate change (Tharinger, Finn, Gentry, et. al., 2009).

Assessment with Children, Adolescents, and Their Families: The Collaborative Problem-Solving Model

When a clinician contracts with the parents or legal guardians to provide therapeutic services for a child/adolescent, the clinician begins an interpersonal relationship that involves trying to solve the family's problems, which is the discrepancy between their current state/situation and some desired state or goal they would like to obtain. In doing this, the clinician evaluates both the extent to which the child/adolescent's behavior deviates from the normal "developmental curve or trajectory," and the child/adolescent's vulnerability and strengths within the context of their family and culture.

Spearheaded by the initial work of D'Zurilla, behaviorally oriented therapists have been refining problem-solving procedures and adapting them to treat and prevent psychological problems (e.g., D'Zurilla & Goldfried, 1971; D'Zurilla & Nezu, 1982; D'Zurilla & Nezu, 1999, 2001, 2007). Initially, problem-solving therapy (also referred to as social problem-solving therapy) was developed as a psychotherapeutic intervention in which clients were taught to apply problem solving to the difficulties for which they specifically sought treatment. Problem solving was viewed as a broadly applicable coping skill serving a dual purpose—first to treat immediate problems for which clients and families seek treatment, and second to prepare clients and/or their families to deal with future problems on their own, which might help prevent further psychological problems from developing. Problem-solving therapy was applied to diverse problems and populations (e.g., Chang, D'Zurilla, & Sanna, 2004). This problem-solving model has more recently been adapted to the assessment procedures in clinical work.

Historically, there have been several attempts to articulate how clinicians basically function as systems-level "problem solvers" (Barker, 1965; Fein, 1974; Kaufman, 1971; Reilly, 1973, 1974; Sarason, 1971; Schmuck, Martell, & Derr, 1972). Sloves, Docherty, and Schneider (1979) proposed a rather comprehensive scientific problem-solving model of psychological assessment consisting of three primary elements: (1) levels of organizational action, (2) methods, and (3) a six-stage problem-solving process. The *levels of organizational action* in psychological assessment refers to the gathering of information across various levels such as the individual (the traditional level of assessment), small groups (families, classrooms, and/or school that is part of a larger system), systems (outpatient clinics, hospitals, and/or school districts), and supra systems (state and federal agencies, corporations, policy organizations). Although psychological assessment has traditionally been at the individual and small-group levels, it is essential for the clinician to consider the broader connections across interrelated systems, especially when dealing with children, adolescents, and their families. Bronfrenbrenner's (1977, 1989) contextual model is discussed later in this chapter as providing a useful way for clinicians to consider such multiple systems.

Methods, another basic component of this problem-solving model, consist of the hierarchical arrangement of skills, tactics, and strategies when using instruments that make up psychological assessment. It should be noted, however, that it is the six-stage problem-solving process that primarily fueled the momentum to the paradigm shift in the clinical assessment that has occurred: (1) problem clarification, (2) hypothesizing as to the nature/cause of the problems, (3) development of the plan needed for assessment, (4) implementation of data collection, (5) outcome determination as to whether sufficient information was collected, and (6) the collaborative process of disseminating or communicating useful information to significant others.

Others have further contributed to our understanding of how the problem-solving model can be applied to the assessment work of clinicians. For example, Nezu (1993) viewed the clinician as a problem solver and the problem to be solved as the discrepancy between the client's presenting problems and the desired state/outcome. Extending this work, the clinician can now view assessment throughout the therapeutic process as a collaborative problem-solving endeavor involving eight basic stages: (1) adopting a problem-solving orientation, (2) defining the problem, (3) collecting data, (4) setting treatment goals, (5) generating interventions, (6) choosing the most efficacious intervention, (7) implementing the intervention, and (8) evaluating the effects of intervention. See Figure 3.2.

In applying the collaborative problem-solving model to assessment, it is assumed that the essential questions at each stage can integrate assessment practices with the most appropriate therapeutic interventions so that assessment and intervention become complementary throughout the treatment of the child/adolescent and family. The child/adolescent and the family are viewed as essential "partners" in assessment and are actually

FIGURE 3.2 Schematic representation of eight stages of collaborative problem-solving assessment with children, adolescents, and their families. Dotted lines indicate the possibility that difficulties at one stage may necessitate returning to prior stages (Adapted from Spiegler and Guevremont, 2010)

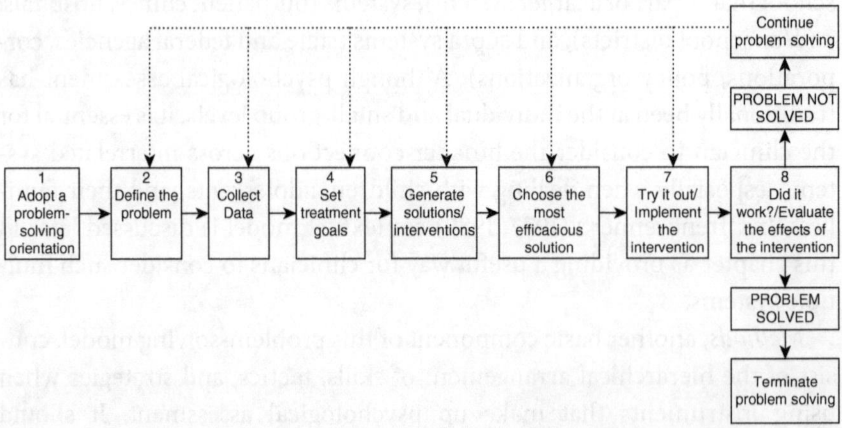

involved in every stage (with the exception of Stage 1, which involves the "attitude" or approach adopted by the therapist as he/she engages in the assessment process) (see Table 3.1).

TABLE 3.1 A Stage Model for Assessment of Children and Adolescents: Questions to Be Considered

Stage 1: Adopting a Problem-Solving/Collaborative Orientation
What are the problems presented by the child/adolescent and the family?
How have the child/adolescent and family members previously tried to solve the problem?
How can the assessment process be conducted in a collaborative fashion to foster new understandings of the problems into being rather than simply view presenting them to children and/or their families as simply "truths" to be accepted?

Stage 2: Defining the Problem
Who is the client (or who are the clients)? Again, this depends on the therapist's own theoretical orientation.
From the parent, child/adolescent, or family's perspective, what is the problem?
What is the intended purpose of the assessment?

Stage 3: Collecting Data
Does the clinician view the assessment process in a broad-based fashion when considering the domains of behavioral, emotional, and social assessment of children and adolescents?
What are the factors that appear to contribute to the problem?
What information is needed and from whom?
What assessment methods, procedures, and tests will best provide this information?
Which of the potential means of gathering information are most appropriate for this specific client, problem, and situation?
Does the assessment information confirm the problem?
What other information regarding the problem do the assessment data provide?
Is there any missing assessment information that is needed to help analyze this problem? If so, how can it be obtained and from whom?
How can the assessment information be used to answer specific referral questions?
[It is at this stage that relevant information on the case formulation forms is most likely to be entered—see Chapter 4.]

Stage 4: Setting Treatment Goals
Based on all the available information, what should be the *target* of intervention?
Have the child/adolescent/family's problems been clarified sufficiently and behaviorally framed for specific goals to be formulated within a collaborative therapist-client framework?
Have the problems been developed within the context of familial and sociocultural factors?
Once the goals have been established, are they stated in a specific, unambiguous, and measurable fashion (treatment plan)?
Is this done in a collaborative fashion with the child/adolescent and his/her family so that they understand and have hope in the treatment process?

Stage 5: Generating Solutions (Intervention Strategies)
What appear to be the most appropriate types of intervention?
Does the child/adolescent's family "buy into" the collaboratively developed treatment plan?
What is the child/adolescent/family's level of "readiness to change"?
What resources are available to implement the intervention?
What assessment information is needed and from whom over the course of therapy to assist in evaluating the effectiveness of treatment?

(Continued)

TABLE 3.1 **A Stage Model for Assessment of Children and Adolescents: Questions to Be Considered (Continued)**

Stage 6: Choosing the Best One

On the basis of the information obtained in the previous stages, the therapist (likely in conjunction with the child/adolescent and especially the parents or other adults) chooses the best solution from among the alternatives generated in Stage 5. The "Collaborative Problem-Solving Work Sheet" should be helpful in this regard (see Appendix A). After examining the potential consequences of each course of action and considering what is likely to happen in the short- and long-run for the child/adolescent in the context of the family, the choice of intervention is made.

Stage 7: Initiating the Intervention (Trying It Out)

At this stage, the planning that took place in the first five stages is "put to the test," as the chosen intervention is implemented. In working with children and adolescents, it is particularly important to ensure not only that such interventions are coordinated with other important individuals from within both the family and the community (e.g., siblings, teachers), but also that the child/adolescent and his/her family have the requisite skills to implement the chosen solution and are motivated to do so.

Stage 8: Evaluating the Effects of the Intervention (Did It Work?)

Once an attempt is made to implement the intervention, its effectiveness is carefully evaluated employing the outcome criteria that have been considered in the previous stages. If the problem is resolved, the therapist moves toward termination. If it still exists, the therapist gets "back to the basics" of the problem-solving process with the child/adolescent and his/her family by either collaboratively tinkering with the implemented solution or attempting a new approach. This entails going through one or more previous stages. Again, if no acceptable alternative solutions remain, further solutions are generated (Stage 5). If the difficulty lies in the goals that were selected (Stage 4) or how the problem was defined (Stage 2), it is necessary to repeat those processes. In doing this, it provides another opportunity for the therapist to teach the child/adolescent and his/her family how to address their difficulties within the problem-solving orientation. It is this approach to solving life's problems that is an important (although oftentimes not directly stated) therapeutic goal because it teaches individuals not just how to solve presenting problems but how to deal with further problems as they go through life. In this way, it is hoped that the child/adolescent/family can generalize treatment gains to solve other problems that will arise. If assessment has been viewed as a collaborative process with the child/adolescent and their family from the outset, it becomes a therapeutic intervention in and of itself.

STAGE 1: ADOPTING A COLLABORATIVE PROBLEM-SOLVING ORIENTATION

Viewing the psychotherapeutic process from beginning to end within a problem-solving framework can be very useful in working with children, adolescents, and their families. This may be somewhat of a paradigm shift for some clinicians but fairly easy for others such as those who are behaviorally oriented or cognitive-behavioral in approach. One of the essential features in therapy, which therapists from all theoretical orientations recognize, is the importance of "joining" with or establishing a good working relationship with the child/adolescent and the family. In the process of doing this, it is important for the therapist, especially from a collaborative problem-solving perspective, to also help clients view their dilemmas as problems that are amenable to change. It should be noted that such a problem-solving perspective is, in fact, atheoretical and broad enough in scope to accommodate therapists with varying theoretical orientations (e.g., Eells, 1997).

STAGE 2: DEFINING THE PROBLEM

Although identifying the problem seems rather straightforward in the sense of asking "Who is the client and what is his/her problem?", the answer to this question is defined by the clinician's theoretical orientation. The following are some examples:

- From a family perspective, the "identified patient" is viewed as a symptom-bearer or official patient viewed by the family as being the "sick one" or "the one who has the problem." Some "identified patients," particularly from a structural or strategic viewpoint, were initially viewed as being basically "innocent" or scapegoats whose deviance maintained family stability (homeostasis) and, as such, help keep the families together at their own emotional cost (e.g., Nichols, 2010).
- From a more psychodynamic perspective, this child/adolescent was chosen because of some trait that makes him/her a suitable target for parental projected emotions and may even be viewed as a symbolic symptom of denied parental emotion (e.g., Nichols, 2010). The child/adolescent's problems are viewed as the result of unconscious motives and thoughts and their dynamic interrelationships, and these interactions determine both normal and abnormal behavior.
- From the more traditional behavioral viewpoint, the focus is on how the problematic behaviors are maintained by environmental events/consequences proceeding and following these behaviors. The central understanding of a client's behavior, both normal and abnormal, is understood in terms of the learning processes over the course of the development (operant and instrumental conditioning, modeling). Thus, from a behavioral perspective, family interactions (adaptive and maladaptive) are viewed as being maintained by the environmental events proceeding and following each member's behavior.
- From a cognitive-behavioral perspective, it is these events or contingencies, together with mediating schemas/attitudes/beliefs, that determine the form, as well as the frequency, of each family member's behavior (e.g., Epstein, Schlesinger, & Dryden, 1988). More specifically, a child/adolescent's normal/abnormal behavior is a function of how his

> or her thoughts, beliefs, and information processing can become distorted and lead to maladaptive emotions and behavior. Schema are highly personalized, core cognitive structures for processing the wide range of stimuli/experiences that impinge on the individual. They represent an individual's cognitive themes about oneself, family, others, and the world that develop as a result of temperament, abilities, and experiences.

As previously discussed, it is the therapist's theoretical orientation that shapes his/her understanding of what the problem is, what types of assessment to conduct, what needs to be done to resolve the problem, and just how important others in the family are in solving the problem.

All therapies, whether specifically recognized or not, provide the parents and, depending on the developmental level and age of the child, the child/adolescent with a conceptual framework (ideally in their lay terms) for understanding the nature of their problem and responses to various difficulties. Again, it is the therapist's theoretical orientation and her or his acceptance of a collaborative approach to assessment that shapes the logic of the "education" of the family and the identified child/adolescent about his/her problem. By adopting such a collaborative approach, the therapist (from any theoretical orientation) will likely increase the acceptance and willingness of the child/adolescent and family to try out the specific intervention strategies or techniques (Stage 7). The purpose of providing such a framework in therapy is not necessarily to convince the family and the child/adolescent (perhaps against their will) that a particular understanding of the presenting problem is valid, but rather to urge them to view the problem from a particular perspective (namely, that which is determined by the clinician's theoretical orientation) and thus accept and collaborate in the therapeutic plan that follows.

Issues of face validity and even an "air of plausibility" for the parents and their child/adolescent are at least as equally important as the scientific validity of a particular conceptualization. Without this plausibility on the family's part, it is not likely that they will buy into or become actively engaged in the further steps of the therapeutic process.

Those ardent supporters advocating empirically supported assessment and treatment for children and adolescents based on evidence-based practice (e.g., Barrett & Ollendick, 2004) often expect that such techniques will be wholeheartedly embraced by clinicians. This view has proven to be naïve, particularly in light of the fact that many clinicians do not treat their clients using such manualized empirically based interventions (e.g., Addis & Krasnow, 2000; Chorpita & Nakamura, 2004). A firestorm of debate within the field of psychology has arisen about such issues despite arguments that evidence-based practice is not wedded to any one theoretical orientation and that treatments of whatever theoretical position need to be based on objective and scientifically credible evidence (i.e., obtained from randomized clinical trials whenever possible). This disagreement can clearly be seen in terms of how controversial the arguments for empirically "validated" treatments have been (e.g., Chambless, 1996; Chambless & Ollendick, 2001; McHugh & Barlow, 2010) since the original report issued by the Society of Clinical Psychology (Psychology Division 12) of the American Psychological Association in 1995. Such reports have fueled this sometimes bitter debate within the profession of clinical psychology and other related mental health disciplines (e.g., Ollendick & King, 2000).

At this stage within the problem-solving model, the clinician also needs to further clarify the problem by asking, "What is the purpose of my assessment?" Is it simply diagnosing the problem, helping screen for the problems during the initial phases of psychotherapy, determining eligibility for specific services (e.g., as might be the case in the school system), generating predictions about the course of problems if left untreated, or gathering data for forensic purposes (e.g., competency to stand trial, custody/visitation matters)? Thus, the purpose of assessment is also important to consider in defining the problem and developing a "problem list."

STAGE 3: COLLECTING DATA

The third phase of this problem-solving model is to structure the assessment, based upon its purpose, and to gather data in a multitrait, multimethod, multi-informant, multisetting, and multioccasion fashion. Such assessment results in a more comprehensive evaluation than does employing any single method, as it provides collaborative evidence from different assessment procedures, across different individuals, across different settings, and at multiple times—thus providing unique information that will aid not only in assessment but also increasing the reliability and validity of the assessment. It is the clinician, however, who determines which means of gathering information is the most appropriate. Appreciating multiple types and sources of assessment information is important because psychological disorders of children and adolescents often involve a range of issues, as reflected in rather high rates of comorbidity for various disorders and the low levels of agreement among multiple sources and types of information concerning children and adolescents (e.g., Johnson & Murray, 2003). Any significant discrepancies among the assessment findings should lead to further investigation before a diagnosis is made and treatment goals are set. Although some clinicians and/or agencies employ a standard battery of assessment procedures that is the same for everyone, a master problem solver/skilled clinician will be guided by the problem-solving method that considers the purpose of the assessment as well as the particular characteristics of the child/adolescent and family within the context of their culture and preferences. Thus, the clinician must determine what assessment methods, procedures, and tests (both objective and projective) will best provide the information to answer the referral question and interventions over the course of therapy.

Again, the clinician needs to develop a keen appreciation for the importance of multiple assessments on different occasions employing multimethods, multi-informants, and multisettings, particularly when considering the behavioral, emotional, and social domains of children and adolescents. Figure 3.3 is a graphic representation of the components of data collection for children and adolescents in actual practice. It needs to be considered within the varied contexts of child/adolescent/family functioning and ideally occurs over the course of treatment. These components are integrated

FIGURE 3.3 **Components of collaborative data collection with children, adolescents, and their families across treatment: multimethod, multi-informant, and multisetting**

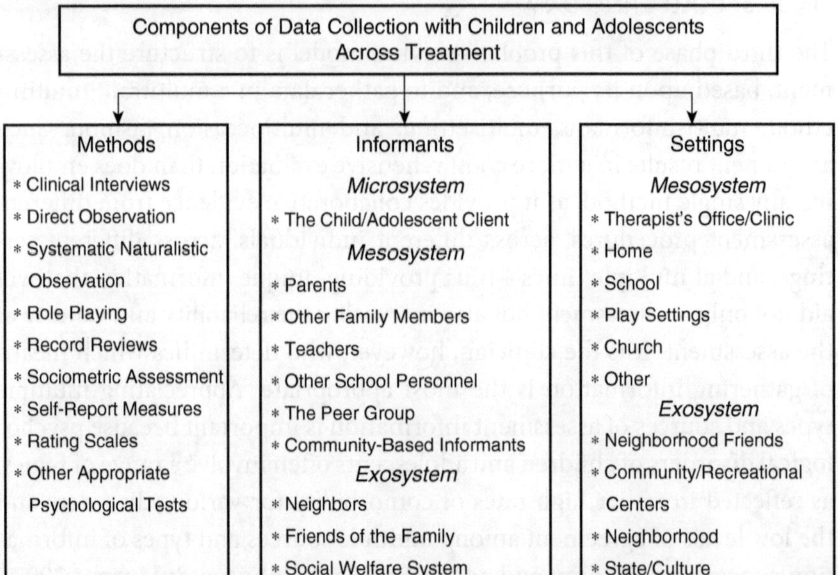

within Bronfenbrenner's (1977, 1979, 1989) bioecological approach more thoroughly discussed in the previous chapter and later in this chapter, since it is essential that the child/adolescent be understood in light of the various contexts and environments that so profoundly influence a child/adolescent's behavior and development.

The methods of data collection may vary from one clinician to another but almost always include clinical interviews, either individually and/or jointly with the children and their parents. Rating scales, self-report measures, and possibly behavior observations may also be part of the assessment. There are a variety of tests/instruments or specific techniques that can possibly be used within each method. A listing of such a wide variety of tests and assessment techniques is beyond the scope of this chapter. Nevertheless, it may be difficult for the clinician to include more than several methods of data collection with any one client and his/her family.

In terms of informants, it is necessary, at a minimum, to collect data from the child/adolescent and his/her parents. If possible, it is desirable to include other relevant sources, specifically teachers, other family members, or (less likely) community-based individuals such as recreation center group leaders or clergy. In reality, however, it is not possible to include all relevant informants and settings. Sometimes it is difficult to include more than just several (i.e., child, parents, and possibly teachers) in data collection. It is important for the clinician to remember, however, that as assessment becomes more broad-based, an aggregate or more extensive picture of a child's behavioral, emotional, and social functioning is obtained, thus providing unique information important in one's clinical work with the child/adolescent/family.

At this stage, the clinician is now faced with the challenge of analyzing/interpreting all of the assessment information to develop the goals and treatment plan that will be utilized. How the clinician uses this information is also a function of his/her theoretical orientation and how various problems are viewed. Case formulation strategies can be most helpful at this point (this is discussed in greater detail in Chapter 4).

STAGE 4: SETTING TREATMENT GOALS

In setting goals, therapists must work with the family to answer the question "What must happen so that the problem is resolved?" In considering this, it is important to remember that how the problem is defined is extremely important, as it determines the type of goals that will ultimately be selected. It is also important to recognize that the goals of therapy are clearly influenced by the therapist's theoretical orientation and often take one of two forms in the behavioral/cognitive-behavioral tradition: solution-focused (the goal is to alter the problematic behavioral cycle itself) or reaction-focused (the goal is to alter one's cognitive, emotional, and/or overt behavioral reactions to the problem situation). In setting treatment goals, the therapist considers the old adage "God grant me the serenity to accept the things I cannot change [reaction-focused interventions], the courage to change the things I can [solution-focused interventions], and the wisdom to know the difference." In a very real sense, the youth/family's goals guide and determine what solutions are likely to be generated in the next stage.

STAGE 5: GENERATING SOLUTIONS (INTERVENTION STRATEGIES)

In this stage, therapists work collaboratively with the client and family to generate solutions or courses of action that will hopefully solve the particular problems that have been identified. At this point, the principle of *brainstorming* is paramount, since developing solutions can best be accomplished by keeping in mind three different principles: quantity, judgment deferment, and variety. The quantity principle dictates that any possible solution, no matter how impractical or outlandish it appears, might be the most viable and practical solution. The more solutions, the greater likelihood the most effective solution will be generated. It is important to defer judgment during this stage, because discussions about the viability of any specific solution can derail/sidetrack the problem-solving process that occurs among the therapists, youth, and/or family. Brainstorming hopefully frees the problem-solving process from the more constricted, rigid thinking that young people and their families often bring with them into the therapeutic situation. Brainstorming also encourages individuals to think "outside the box," which might lead to other solutions that they otherwise might miss. In other words, brainstorming facilitates creativity in considering new ways of looking at and working on the problems that brought the child/adolescent/family to therapy.

STAGE 6: CHOOSING THE BEST ONE

In this problem-solving phase of treatment, the therapist's task is to offer a solution to the clinical problem/dilemma that is presented to him/her—namely, the discrepancy between the client's present state and a desired state. The therapist needs to consider the consequences of each potential intervention and collaboratively work with the child/adolescent and family to choose the most effective one. Again, the proposed solution, in large part, is dependent upon the therapist's theoretical orientation. For example, in children and adolescents who experience significant externalized (typified by severe acting out) conflict, all theoretical approaches recognize that such acting out is basically determined by multiple factors. The behavioral and cognitive-behavioral approaches characteristically view such acting out as being strongly influenced by the environment in which the child lives—at home, school, and in the neighborhood. Such approaches also view problematic acting-out behavior as the result of reciprocal influences from those environmental events, because behaviors are influenced by the contingencies following such behavior. The cognitive-behavioral approaches also hold that such acting-out behavior needs to be viewed in light of the person's understanding of his/her environment (i.e., schema, attitudes/beliefs, self-talk), because these are important factors influencing an individual's overt behavior. As such, cognitive events are seen as being potential sources for behavioral change.

Some individuals, particularly evidence-based proponents from a behavioral perspective, suggest that a structured evaluation of available research evidence would best determine the most effective intervention approach. For example, the following continuum has been proposed for clinicians to evaluate existing research from best to worst (Silverman & Saavedra, 2004):

Best 1. Systematic reviews of randomized controlled trials RCTs
2. Single RCT, all-or-none series
3. Systematic review of cohort studies
4. Single cohort studies or RCT with less than 80% follow-up
5. Outcomes research in ecological studies
6. Systematic review of case-control studies
7. Single case-control study
8. Case series

Worst 9. Expert opinion

Family therapists, from their systems perspective, view the problem directly as a result of maladaptive family relationships that arise out of disturbance in the family's subsystems/structure. In contrast to these approaches, analytic/self-psychology and pharmacological approaches view such acting out as related to variables (intrapsychic or biological) within the person. Although there are differences within the psychodynamic perspective (e.g., psychoanalytic, ego psychology, object-relations theory, interpersonal perspective, attachment theory), the focus for such therapists is basically to help restart the development of the self that has become blocked in the client for various reasons. Thus, the goal is to develop an internal sense of cohesion and resilience so that the individual does not "come apart" or "fragment" in the course of development.

When dealing with children and adolescents, it should again be remembered that it is the therapist's theoretical orientation that plays a major role in determining the type of interventions approach that will be selected. In dealing with children and adolescents, decisions of whether to treat the identified patient using individual and/or family therapy become essential. In individual therapy, the basic assumption is that the important variables for change are internal/intrapsychic dynamics or trait deficits. Either way, treatment is directed at the child's personal makeup. On the other hand, family and behavior therapists believe that the dominant forces in children's/adolescents' lives are located externally, in the family and immediate environment. As such, therapy is directed at changing the way in which the family functions or its organization. Cognitive-behavioral therapists may focus primarily on the schemas, attitudes/beliefs, and/or dysfunctional self-talk that mediate external influences. Thus, determining just who the client is will be influenced by the therapist's theoretical orientation. It is also crucial to consider "What is the problem from the child/adolescent's perspective as well as from the significant others in his/her lives (e.g., parents, teachers)?" It is likely that there will be disagreements among these individuals as to just what the problem is and what should be done about it. Using different sources in the assessment process helps the clinician to consider these different views of the child/adolescent at this stage when deciding what interventions would be most effective.

STAGE 7: IMPLEMENTING THE INTERVENTION (TRYING IT OUT)

The therapist works with the child/adolescent and/or family in implementing the agreed-upon intervention from among the alternatives considered in Stage 6. This is one of the most important stages in the therapeutic process, because it directly involves efforts to change the specific problems that were framed by the therapist in defining the problem (Stage 2). At this stage, it is also important for the therapist to also assess consequences for the child/adolescent/family's "readiness to change" (e.g., Prochaska & DiClemente, 2005):

- In the precontemplation phase, individuals are basically unaware of their problems and have no real intention of changing their behavior.

- In the contemplation stage, they are aware of their problems and are seriously thinking about grappling with them within the next 6 months but have not yet made a real commitment to take action.
- In the preparation phase, clients have made some attempt to actually change the problematic situation but these attempts have proven only sporadic or partially effective.
- In the action stage, clients are ready to take concrete steps to change the problem/target behavior in a way that has been developed through their joint efforts with the therapist.

Thus, it is important not to assume that all clients are ready to take concrete steps to change the problem/target behavior in a way that has been developed through their joint efforts with the therapist. In other words, all clients would not be at the action stage, or even want to be, at this point in therapy.

STAGE 8: EVALUATING THE EFFECTS OF THE INTERVENTION (DID IT WORK?)

When a specific intervention plan has been chosen, it is also incumbent upon the clinician to consider how to continuously collect data during the intervention to assist in determining whether the specific intervention strategies are achieving the desired effect. In other words, assessment needs to guide our treatment practices on an ongoing basis for each individual case. If the problems have been resolved, the therapist moves toward termination. If the problem still exists, the clinician reevaluates the intervention strategies that have been attempted to clarify if that intervention strategy was properly implemented by the child/adolescent and/or family. If it was not, the therapist needs to consider the factors that led to the less-than-successful resolution of the problem.

It may be because the child/adolescent and/or the family did not entirely understand how to actually implement the intervention strategy, whether they actually had the requisite skills to do so, and/or were not fully motivated to carry through with the specific intervention strategies selected in Stage 6. It is important for the clinician to utilize a problem-solving approach with such less-than-successful attempts to resolve problems and not simply just view the problem as being one of "resistance" by the child/adolescent and/or family. From the problem-solving perspective, the clinician needs to determine the reason for lack of success in redefining the problem and/or treatment goals (Stage 2 and 4) and/or generating other solutions to this therapeutic problem (Stage 5). The therapist then needs to decide how to proceed (Stage 6) by either recommending trying to fine-tune the previously selected intervention strategy (if it was not implemented in an effective fashion) or selecting another intervention strategy that is more likely to succeed given the knowledge obtained from the less-than-successful intervention attempt.

Considering the "Big Picture": Contextual Considerations in the Assessment of Children, Adolescents, and Their Families

It is helpful to have an overarching system beyond the individual theoretical orientations that predominate current psychological thought (e.g., behavioral, cognitive-behavioral, psychoanalytic, humanistic/existential, systems theory). Particularly in work with children and adolescents, it is generally recognized by most practitioners that the social context or environment is important, even critical, in understanding children's development and the difficulties they encounter along the way. Thus, it is important for the clinician to also thoroughly assess the different environments that influence a child/adolescent's behavior. This evaluation needs to be part of a comprehensive evaluation (e.g., Carlson, 2003; Liaupsin, Jolivette, & Scott, 2004), even when working from models that generally view disorders as primarily residing within the child/adolescent rather than in the ongoing reciprocal interactions between the child/adolescent and his/her family or even larger social system. Bronfenbrenner's (1977, 1979, 1989) bioecological approach, as discussed in the previous chapter, offers just such a contextual perspective, because it aides clinicians in appreciating the interrelationships among youth in their physical, cognitive, and personality, family, and social worlds. This contextual perspective is not a specific theoretical perspective in the same way that behavioral, cognitive-behavioral, psychodynamic, humanistic/existential, and family therapies are, but rather offers a specific framework for understanding the importance of the varied social systems and contexts in which children and adolescents, as well as their families, develop and function. Figure 3.4 illustrates the four major components of this contextual model as offered by Bronfenbrenner. At the center of the model is the *microsystem*, which includes the everyday, immediate environment in which children/adolescents lead their daily lives. Homes, caregivers, and teachers are all immediate influences that are part of the microsystem.

The microsystem (including individual/family/school/peer contexts) is the level at which traditional clinical work with children occurs. It should be noted, however, that even Bronfenbrenner recognized that his theory was

FIGURE 3.4 **Bronfenbrenner's four levels of the environment that simultaneously influence children and adolescents (Based on Bronfenbrenner, 1979)**

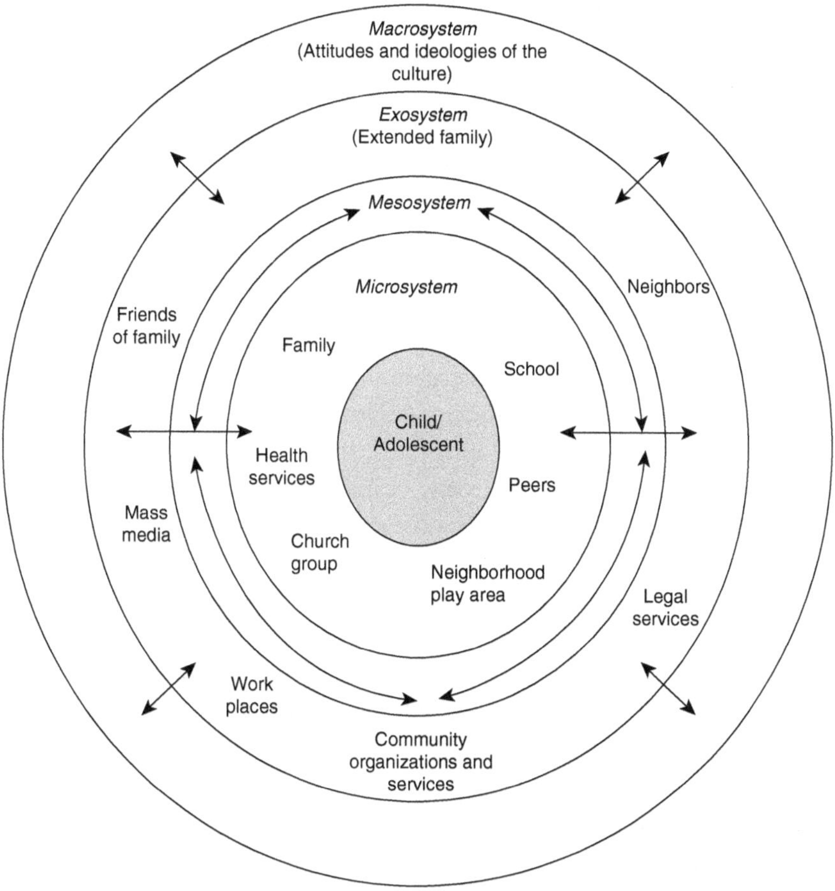

incomplete in that he needed to include the levels of the individual functioning (biology, psychology, and behavior) that fuse so dynamically with the microsystem and the other more general systems he described. Thus, Bronfenbrenner recognized that better articulation of the individual in terms of his/her individual repertoire of biological, emotional, and behavioral characteristics was needed to broaden his model. It is just at this level that the analytic and cognitive theorists primarily conceptualize clinical problems—namely, the individual him/herself and any intrapsychic or cognitive/physiological processes that are related to a person's actual behavior in any given situation. Behavioral and family therapists have traditionally had a keener appreciation of the other contextual factors in which a child's behavior is viewed within the context of their everyday microsystem.

The *mesosystem* encompasses the reciprocal connections between the various aspects of the microsystem. Similar to links in a chain, the mesosystem binds children to parents, students to teachers, employees to bosses, and friends to friends. It acknowledges the direct and indirect influences that bind us to one another, such as those in which the child desires contact/approval with the father who has had a bad day at the office and becomes short-tempered with his son at home who then finds support within his peer group. It is within the mesosystem that clinicians are alerted to the fact that it is often essential to assess not just the emotional/behavioral problems and strengths/competencies of individual children themselves but also parental well-being/psychopathology (e.g., Connell & Goodman, 2002; Kane & Garber, 2004; Marmorstein & Iacono, 2004) and the parental relationship or interparental conflict (e.g., Fincham, 1998; McMahon, Grant, Compas, Thurm, & Ey, 2003). These parental elements have been linked to the developmental psychopathology in children and adolescents and relate either directly or indirectly to a child's well-being.

The *exosystem* represents broader influences encompassing societal institutions such as the local government, the community, schools, parents' workplaces, the extended family, places of worship, and the local media. For example, a child raised in a high-crime area of the city where violence and gang activity are more normal will be impacted at the exosystem level more than the youngster who is reared in a safe community. Another example is how the quality of the school will affect the child's development and potentially have long-term consequences.

The *macrosystem* represents the broader cultural consequences on the individual and has a more indirect influence on the individual child. Social institutions, such as types of governments, religious and political value systems, and other broad encompassing factors, are parts of the macrosystem. For example, children living within the United States are exposed to a culture that more likely emphasizes normative values of individualization and, depending upon broader factors, the importance of education for the family. It should be noted, however, that practicing psychologists are typically most concerned about the individual and, depending upon the clinician's theoretical orientation, might directly involve other family members, possibly the schools, and occasionally even peers or other health service providers in the community. This contextual perspective is important because it helps practicing clinicians understand the level at which their interventions are primarily directed. Thus, it offers an atheoretical, practical approach to assessments that can guide practitioners' clinical work.

Summary

Besides the typical ways of determining the "goodness or badness" of tests (namely, psychometric data regarding reliability and validity), the concept of clinical utility has been articulated not only in terms of assessment tools, (e.g., Hunsley & Bailey, 1999; Yates & Taub, 2003) but also diagnostic systems (e.g., Kendell & Jablensky, 2003). Unfortunately, not much attention has been paid to the clinical utility of different assessment instruments (McGrath, 2001), even though there is a multitude of studies on the reliability and validity of a wide range of psychological instruments. As such, clinicians basically determine on their own whether any specific instrument will be used in their assessment of a particular case. Despite advances in evidence-based practice in therapeutic interventions, evidence-based practice in assessment lags far behind, even though it is now standard practice for clinicians who work with children/adolescents and their families to employ a multimethod, multi-informant, multisetting, multioccasion evaluation that is so necessary in dealing with the wide range of emotional/behavioral difficulties of youth.

There are several exceptions to this as reflected in the special issue of the *Journal of Clinical Child and Adolescent Psychology* (September 2005), which provided seven reviews of evidence-based assessment with different child/adolescent disorders. It is by employing such assessment processes that clinicians can best intervene in the lives of children, adolescents, and their families. Despite such advances, the fact still remains that everyday clinicians seldom employ evidence-based assessment and therapeutic approaches. Their selection of assessment instruments and intervention techniques still remain firmly tied to their particular theoretical orientation/understanding of social and emotional behavior.

Bronfenbrenner's ecological systems theory was suggested as an atheoretical way to better integrate clinicians' thinking about human environments when conducting assessments with children and adolescents. Conceptualizing the assessment of youth and their families as a problem-solving process is emphasized. Nevertheless, practitioners have not enthusiastically endorsed this paradigm shift either. Practitioners still tend to view the assessment of children/adolescents and their families as a distinct endeavor from treatment, rather than as one part of an overall process. The collaborative problem-solving model of assessment has been offered as a way of integrating these two important tasks faced by any clinician working with a child, adolescent, or their family. Within this framework, practical questions can be viewed by a clinician who adopts a problem-solving orientation—defining the problem, collecting data, setting treatment goals, generating solutions, initiating interventions, and evaluating the effects of such interventions.

The case formulation model (see Chapter 4) fits neatly into the collaborative problem-solving model and can not only aid the clinician in better integrating assessment throughout the therapeutic process, but also enhance the clinician's compliance and commitment to his/her therapeutic work with children, adolescents, and their families. The case formulation approach can cut across different theoretical orientations of therapists by including four basic components: (1) symptoms and problems, (2) predisposing life events or stressors (i.e., preexisting vulnerabilities), and (3) hypothesized causal mechanisms that link all of these components together, resulting in (4) an explanation for the development and maintenance of the symptoms/problems (Eells, 1997; Eells, Kendjelic, & Lucas, 1997).

Overall, evidence-based psychotherapeutic interventions are slowly transforming how we can treat children, adolescents, and their families. Evidence-based assessment has the potential to streamline how we gather and synthesize data about the youth and their families we treat, in an effort to facilitate decision making, improve clinical outcomes, and even optimize the cost-benefit of how we serve our clients. At this point, such a knowledge base is likely to be further developed by researchers. It remains to be seen whether clinicians will actually integrate such knowledge into their practices. Such questions are raised with the recognition of the significant challenges associated with the task of narrowing the formidable gap between research and practice in working with children, adolescents, and their families. Advancement of quality assessment and its importance to optimal treatment/care will require a collaborative partnership between not only researchers and practitioners, but also families and policy makers.

FOUR

Case Formulation Models with Children, Adolescents, and Their Families

Introduction

Particularly over the past decade, the practice of psychotherapy has taken a decidedly scientific turn. The notion that therapists just have to be "good listeners" to help clients "feel better" (an ambiguous, nondefined state) has shifted to viewing therapists as active participants in the therapy process whose focus is to help clients "get better" (determined by specific goals directly related to their life's problems).

Although many in psychology bemoan managed care, it has certainly shaped the delivery of health care in our country. Although some managed care companies may be concerned more with maximized profits for owners and shareholders than quality of care, they often require therapists to clearly delineate client problems, use the most effective treatments, and work quickly. Depending somewhat on the therapist's own theoretical orientation, these last two requirements (clear problem definition and use of the most effective treatment interventions) may or may not be seen as positive movements in the delivery of mental health care. The downside of managed care is that with overemphasis on financial concerns, profit-making considerations will simply encourage ineffective treatment by therapists who have the least training and charge the lowest fees. In addition, the growing popularity of brief, goal-oriented therapy may not be driven as much by concerns with outcome as it is by the sometimes questionable needs of managed care systems. The upside, however, is that therapists are now more focused on the psychological problems their clients want to resolve and on their clients' desire to do so as quickly as possible so they can move on with their lives. Thus, regardless of one's therapeutic orientation, therapists have been "pushed" toward short-term treatments based on clearly established treatment goals and objectives.

Over the past 4 decades, cognitive-behavioral therapists, family therapists, and some psychodynamic therapists (e.g., interpersonal therapy) have also contributed to this paradigm shift in the delivery of health care in this country. Those who work with children, adolescents, and their families have also grown to realize the importance of taking into account the social context of their clients' difficulties. There must now be a structure to therapy, as opposed to viewing the therapeutic endeavor as a free-flowing, unfocused enterprise, in which change is hoped for without specifying what this is particularly and what specifically will bring it about. Thus, both managed care and advances in psychotherapy have been significant forces in shifting therapies to become more active, directive, and symptom-focused. In short, the financing and practice of psychotherapy with children and adolescents has been transformed and restructured.

The case formulation approach has been one area of practice that has more recently been developed to facilitate the clearly defined, specifically targeted, and symptom-focused advances in the psychotherapeutic endeavor. It is designed to guide the clinician's decision-making process that occurs over the course of treatment. The primary focus of this chapter is to outline the case formulation approach specifically as it applies to therapeutic work with children, adolescents, and their families. Such assessment formulation was also integrated into the problem-solving framework of assessment presented in Chapter 3.

The therapeutic endeavor for child/adolescent therapists usually begins with the parents, guardians, or courts seeking mental health services for a child/adolescent who presents with sometimes complex and comorbid difficulties for which no single approach clearly fits. The pros and cons of empirically based treatments have been vehemently, sometimes bitterly, argued in our profession over the past 15 years, although no universally accepted model for empirically based assessment has been delineated. Despite this, Mash and Hunsely (2005a) have proposed several key considerations that are needed for the development of clinical guidelines for evidence-based assessment in light of the following:

- High comorbidity
- Broad scope assessments to achieve an adequate understanding of the child within his/her life's context
- Consideration of the amount and timing of assessment activities
- Consideration of possible common factors in targeted population (e.g., relationship variables for the child, other family members)

- Qualities of the measures
- How clinicians integrate assessment data

Still, the therapist must conceptualize problems and define them in a way that makes interventions as effective as possible. In the process of doing this, the therapist also assesses the client's skills and motivation and has to choose among the various strategies and techniques (guided by their theoretical orientation) to select what they decide is the best way to proceed with a particular child/adolescent and family.

In regard to treatment interventions, certainly we cannot assume that "one size fits all" given the relatively few number of empirically validated interventions. Nevertheless, such therapeutic interventions need to be continued to be developed and carefully evaluated. In the meantime, the content and direction of therapy need to be established early in the therapeutic process to maximize success. This involves carefully developing a problem list and then structuring sessions in a way to maximize outcome and solve the particular problems presented by the child/adolescent and his/her family.

It is a premise of this chapter that case formulation helps therapists take just such an active and directive role in the collaborative endeavor of psychotherapy. How problems are defined, the types of changes that can be expected, and how to reach these goals all derive from the therapist's conceptualization of the case. More specifically, case conceptualization is the framework for providing interventions that flexibly meet the specific needs of the client and guide the therapist's decision making, which hopefully is based on a knowledgeable appreciation of relevant evidence-based interventions. Case formulation is not a new form of assessment or therapy but, rather, a collaborative process in which the therapist and child/adolescent/family come to a focused understanding of the presenting problems that brought them to therapy and then the therapist guides effective and efficient treatment interventions (e.g., Kuyken, Padesky, & Dudley, 2009; Sacco & Beck, 1995).

In short, all therapists are faced with the same question at the beginning of therapy—"How can I best use my clinical skills to help my client and his/her family deal with particular problems that they present?" Although theoretical assumptions about the relevance of certain kinds of information vary from theory to theory, it is just such assumptions or beliefs that affect the clinician's perception of what the problem is, how to assess the problem, how to select the intervention strategies that will be used, and eventually how and when to terminate treatment. The case formulation approach helps clinicians place psychological problems in their context because, in doing so, it is more likely that appropriate interventions will be selected (e.g., Beck, Emery, & Greenberg, 1985). In essence, case formulation can be viewed as a refinement of therapist's theoretical orientation, because it is this orientation that has traditionally been the backdrop against which therapists understand their clients' problems and guide their therapeutic interventions over the course of therapy. In short, the case formulation approach is a clinician's "road map" for understanding the dynamics of the case and helps guide the therapy process until termination.

The importance given to formal psychological testing and the care in which a thorough assessment is made not only differs among practitioners but is heavily influenced by their theoretical orientation. For example, on one end of the family therapy continuum are experiential family therapists who pay less attention to assessment than almost any other school of family therapy and deliberately eschew categorizing people. They make an effort to better understand the barriers that keep their patients from experiencing the full range of their feelings, thus resulting in greater freedom of choice and expanded emotional experiences. Strategic and structural family therapists also do little in the way of formal assessment, although they carefully observe particular aspects of the family's behavior around the presenting problem and consider difficulties with individuals within the context that can extend beyond the nuclear family to include the influence of extended family members as well as social agencies.

On the other end of the family therapy continuum are the behavioral and cognitive-behavioral therapists who view problematic behavior as essentially a result of (1) a failure to learn the necessary adaptive behaviors or competencies to deal with the various kinds of problems, and/or (2) the learning of ineffective or maladaptive behaviors. Careful assessment is the hallmark of these approaches, and greater emphasis is placed on clearly and behaviorally defining, observing, and recording the frequency of behaviors to be modified, as well as the events that proceed and follow those behaviors. From a behavioral/learning perspective, behavior is viewed as being maintained by its consequences and careful attention is paid to evaluate the A (antecedents), B (behaviors), and C (consequences) of problematic behavioral sequences and how the contingencies of reinforcement maintain the problem/target behaviors.

Cognitive-behavioral therapists also carefully evaluate the way in which a child/adolescent and family interpret an environmental event and how their dysfunctional schema, irrational beliefs, and self-talk effect the emotional/behavioral consequences in specific problematic situations. Thus, a formal assessment is conducted in order to (1) provide a clear description of the presenting problem(s), (2) set clearly defined goals for treatment, and (3) use these goals in the process of establishing a baseline to measure progress throughout therapy. As such, assessment is viewed as an essential ongoing part of the treatment.

There are a number of commonly agreed-upon elements that are incorporated into the case formulation model (Persons, 2008):

1. All of the child/adolescent *symptoms*, disorders, and problems are assessed and described.
2. Hypotheses about the *mechanisms* causing these disorders are proposed, although this is in large part determined by the therapist's theoretical orientation.
3. The current precipitant/activating events of the current problems are articulated
4. The *origins* of the proposed mechanisms causing the problems are ascertained.

To maximize the usefulness of a case formulation, an appreciation of the *principle of parsimony* (the simplest explanation should be selected if it is as effective as a more complex one) is important. In other words, therapists should attempt to identify the fewest number of causal mechanisms related to the problems that can comprehensively explain the child/adolescent's behavioral problems (Persons, 2008). Thus, in the process of using a case formulation approach, therapists and clients are better able to "see the big picture" in terms of identifying specifically what the problem is, what has caused it, what is maintaining the problem, and what needs to be done about it.

In a very real sense, a case conceptualization not only helps the therapist understand the child/adolescent and family and what needs to be done in therapy, but also provides the client and family with a conceptual model, articulated in their own language, to understand the nature of their difficulties and what will be done in therapy to accomplish the jointly established treatment goals. Because case formulation is for both the therapist and client (child/adolescent/family), it is important that this conceptual framework be plausible to client and its acceptance should lead naturally to the understanding of and increased motivation to actively work with the therapist in terms of the specific intervention strategies that will be employed. Although it is important to evaluate the scientific validity of the case formulation approach (as only limited research to date has attempted to do), the face validity or plausibility for the client and his/her family in helping them understand their difficulties is essential.

Thus, another purpose of case formulation is to provide a framework, not necessarily to convince the child/adolescent and family that any particular explanation of the identified client's problem is valid, but to encourage them to view the problem from a particular perspective and thus accept and collaborate in the therapeutic interventions that will follow. At one level or another, all therapists with different theoretical orientations engage with the client and the family in such an "educational phase."

A good case formulation is internally consistent and presents a compelling analysis that pulls together many aspects of the client's history and current functioning based on a multifaceted assessment (see Chapter 3 for a more thorough discussion). Again, it is important to recognize that the therapist's theoretical orientation will guide the hypotheses he/she forms about the origins of the mechanisms causing the disorders and problems, as well as determine which therapeutic strategies will be employed.

Case formulation can be perceived as being atheoretical, as many clinicians regard it as akin to a "working hypothesis" that includes a variety of factors such as information about early biological influences, early childhood experiences, developmental history, maladaptive schemes/irrational beliefs, and/or reinforcers (Eells, 1997). Because case formulation is generic, the specific dynamics and hypotheses that arise from this process are a direct function of the theory of psychotherapy espoused by the clinician (Orvaschel, Faust, & Hersen, 2001a). Thus, it is important that an effective case formulation be clearly rooted in an identified theory.

Assumptions about the importance of certain kinds of assessment information vary from theory to theory, directly alter the clinician's perception of the problematic behavior, and directly influence the selection of assessment strategies used to evaluate the child/adolescent/family's problems. For example, the Greek physician Hippocrates (460–377 BC), father of modern medicine, viewed mental disorders as arising from a person's temperament, which was determined by establishing which of the four essential fluids of the body or humors were dominant—blood (sanguine), phlegm (phlegmatic), bile (choleric), and black bile (melancholic). Although our understandings of causal factors of problematic behavior certainly have evolved over the centuries, they are still rooted in the clinician's perceptions about "what makes us tick."

Case formulation methods have evolved from the three current traditions in psychotherapy—psychoanalysis, behavioral/cognitive-behavioral, and phenomenological/humanistic. Eells (1997) compared case formulations from these three current traditions in psychotherapy and has noted that they share several features:

1. After obtaining clinical information, there are separate components to case formulations that are combined into narrative formulations or graphically depicted.
2. Clinical judgment is most important in case formulation, rather than just relying on traditional psychological testing.
3. Case formulation emphasizes the notion of parsimony by making low-level clinical inferences, which renders them amenable to a wide range of cases.

This chapter presents case formulation summary forms (see Appendices B and C) for therapists who work with children, adolescents, and their families and who espouse a behavioral or cognitive-behavioral orientation. There are several case formulation sheets/models developed for adults within the behavioral/cognitive-behavioral traditions, including the following:

- Persons's (2008) case formulation sheet consists of the following: identifying information, chief complaint, problem list, hypothesized mechanism that underlies the client's various problems, relationship of the mechanism to the problems, precipitants of current problems, origins of the central problem, treatment plan, and predicted obstacles to treatment.
- Beck's (1995) cognitive conceptualization diagram provides the following salient information: relevant childhood core data, beliefs, conditional assumptions/beliefs/rules, and compensatory strategies, along with a way to integrate automatic thoughts and the meaning of automatic thoughts, emotions, and behavior into the case conceptualization plan.
- Needleman's (1999) case conceptualization summary form provides a listing of the problems and therapy-relevant behaviors, a list of relevant beliefs, origins of the core beliefs, as well as a working model outlining the cognitive/behavioral cycles, maintaining factors, treatment goals, possible obstacles to treatment, and the working plan.

As is typical with most assessment and treatment procedures for children and adolescents, existing case formulation models were originally designed more for adult clients. The case formulation summary forms presented in this chapter are proposed as an integration of the selected elements from these previous approaches with adults and offer a downward extension of such ideas for use with child/adolescent clients within the context of their families. Two summary forms are provided—the behavioral version (Appendix B), based on an analysis of clinical problems from a learning theory/behavioral viewpoint, and the cognitive-behavioral version (Appendix C), based on cognitive-behavioral theories.

A description of the fundamental principles of major learning theories (classical conditioning, operant conditioning, and observational learning), as well as cognitive-behavioral learning theories, is beyond the scope of this chapter, although more detailed information can be seen in reviews of the extensive empirical support that underlies them (e.g., Kazdin, 2001; Lieberman, 2000; Martin & Pear, 2003; Masters, Burish, Hollon, & Rimm, 1987; Persons, 2008). Based on learning theory, the clinician conducts a careful assessment or a *functional analysis* in order to clarify the antecedents (A) and consequences (C) that are considered essential in understanding/controlling the problematic overt behavior (B) that is the focus of clinical treatment. With some variations, learning theories basically propose that all behaviors (B) need to be viewed in the context within which they occur—namely, in terms of their antecedents (A) and/or their consequences (C). Overt behaviors can be involuntary and autonomic (e.g., heart rate, respiration) or voluntary (e.g., hitting someone, fleeing situation), and are accompanied by internal thoughts and emotional reactions (even though the importance of such thoughts and emotional reactions are not viewed by all as essential in formulating clinical assessments). In general, antecedents (A) are those events that occur *before* the problematic behavior (B), and cue or elicit this behavior. Consequences (C) are events that *follow* the problematic behavior and are the mechanisms that facilitate behavioral change. The "Case Formulation Summary Form for Children and Adolescents: Behavioral Version" (Appendix B) can be used to assist the clinician in conceptualizing the case.

Although there are also some variations in the cognitive-behavioral theories, they all propose that psychological problems—negative emotions and maladaptive behaviors—are maintained by the interpretations that children/adolescents and their families make of events in their lives. Thus, it is an individual's beliefs about events, not the events themselves, that make us frightened, angry, frustrated, annoyed, upset, and so forth. The sequence is typically the same, however—some event activates (A) an irrational/dysfunctional belief (B) that results in problematic consequences (C; negative emotions/maladaptive behaviors). In both cases, the learning and cognitive-behavioral models are presented in A-B-C terminology to make it user-friendly for the child/adolescent and the family. It should be noted, however, that the A-B-C sequence represents different elements depending whether the problematic sequence is viewed more from learning theories (**A**ntecedent → **B**ehavior → **C**onsequence) or cognitive-behavioral theories (**A**ntecedent → **B**elief → emotional/behavior **C**onsequence).

The Case Formulation Process and Summary Forms for Children and Adolescents

The first step in the case formulation process is to conduct a thorough assessment to understand the relevant developmental history and also to identify the current focus of treatment. As can be seen in the two versions of the summary form, the assessment analysis is anchored in the child/adolescent's *relevant developmental history* (risk and protective factors that involve the child, family, social and/or school contexts). The clinician identifies the target behavior or problematic behavioral cycles that will be the focus over the course of treatment and the *problem list and other issues to be addressed* is then determined. The *problem list* categorizes all the difficulties that are related to the child/adolescent, his/her family, school, and social and/or other situations. More specifically, the problem behaviors that the child/adolescent and/or family want to decrease (e.g., aggressive outbursts, avoidance of frightening situations) or increase (e.g., staying in his/her seat, engaging in problem-solving activities to help control anger and subsequent acting out). The behaviors that are selected to be specifically addressed in treatment need to be high-priority ones that are described in a very concrete, specific, behavioral fashion so that they can be identified and measured over the course of treatment (e.g., school phobia vs. not going to school; conduct disorder vs. yelling or spitting when told "no").

Although the importance of selecting the appropriate problem/target behaviors is beyond the scope of this chapter, useful reviews are available (e.g., Hawkins, 1986; Haynes & O'Brien, 2000, Kazdin, 2001; Watson & Tharp, 2002). In the behavioral version, after identifying the *problem/target behavior* (B), the clinician assesses the *antecedents* (A) and *maintaining consequences* (C) that are triggering and maintaining the problematic/target behavior. The information reported in the case formulation plan is then used to develop an intervention plan based upon a functional analysis that are the A's, B's, and C's of the problems to be addressed throughout therapy. In the cognitive-behavioral version, *antecedents* (A) trigger the *developing schema/core beliefs* that are being formed and the *antecedents*

(A) trigger the *thoughts* and *feelings* that mediate the *problem/target behaviors* (B). This problematic cognitive-affective behavior chosen is subsequently maintained by the consequences.

At this point, the clinician records the antecedents (A), problem/target behavior or beliefs (B), and maintaining consequences (C) of each problem on the specific summary form. The specific origins/hypotheses about how the problem/target behavior(s) was (were) learned and is (are) now being maintained are then entered on the form. In completing the forms, it is likely that the clinician will develop a more thorough, comprehensive understanding of the functional relationship among the problem/target behavior (B) and the antecedents (A), and at a later point the maintaining consequences (C). It should be noted that other issues to be addressed in the problem list and especially the relevant developmental history are not likely to be immediately understood by the therapist, but rather will be more thoroughly ascertained over the course of working with a child/adolescent and family.

In short, the case formulation process guides the therapist's decision making over the course of therapy and, in the process, increases the therapist's confidence in his/her clinical decisions during the course of working with the child/adolescent and family. It is important to note that these summary forms are not designed to be filled out by the clinician in a lock-step fashion, but rather are dynamic in the sense that they are to be utilized and altered over the course of therapy as more information is obtained during the work with the child/adolescent and family.

An important question to consider when treating children/adolescents is "How is case formulation different when the client is a child?" To better understand this, one needs to consider how assessment of the child differs from that of an adult, as assessment is an integral part of the case formulation process. When the first book about behavioral assessment, *Behavioral Assessment: A Practical Handbook* (Hersen & Bellack, 1976), was written, there were only two chapters devoted to children. Since that time, we have come to understand some of the essential components in the assessment of child and adolescent disorders, which, although varying across theoretical perspectives, primarily refer to (1) assessment processes (e.g., generating hypotheses, case formulation, decision making, integration of information), and (2) assessment methods and specific measures (i.e., the use of specific tests, questionnaires, observations, and other means of gathering data in order to evaluate a child and develop appropriate interventions) (Fernandez-Ballesteros et al., 2001; Mash & Hunsley, 2005a).

In this regard, it is important to note that behavioral assessment has expanded over the years from the traditional operant perspective (see the behavioral version in Appendix B) in which assessment relied on a description of current behavior and specification of organismic and environmental conditions that elicited and maintained the problem behaviors to include cognitive and affective components of child behavior (Mash & Terdal, 1997) (see the cognitive-behavioral version in Appendix C). It is now widely accepted that efficient child behavioral assessment involves multiple assessment strategies used with multiple sources of information in formulating an effective understanding of and treatments for children and adolescents.

More recently, assessment with children has focused on developing guidelines for evidence-based strategies paralleling the call for evidence-based treatments with both children and adults (Mash & Hunsley, 2005b). In fact, Mash and Hunsley (2005b) called for the development of the "assessment equivalent" of the evidence-based treatments movement that is currently so dominant in clinical and clinical child and adolescent psychology. This is a daunting task because the assessments of children necessarily involve not only understanding the developmental changes in the domains being assessed (e.g., Lahey et al., 2004) but also a keen appreciation of` viewing children in the context of their family, school, and peer groups (see Bronfenbrenner's model in Chapter 3 for the three levels of the environment that simultaneously influence a child/adolescent).

As such, a much larger number and variety of assessment methods have typically been utilized with children than is typically the case with adults. Thus, compared to adult assessments, youth assessments commonly involve seeking information from multiple methods (e.g., interviews, ratings, direct and indirect observations), informants (e.g., child, parents, teachers, peers), and settings (e.g., home, classroom) and not just the use of a collection of psychometric methods that have defined adult assessments (e.g., Evans & Meyer, 1985; Mash & Terdal, 1997). In a real sense, assessment of children has become multifaceted. It has moved from a generic battery to the use of more disorder/specific assessment techniques that can be readily integrated into treatment interventions (e.g., Hunsley & Mash, 2008).

Another important consideration in the assessment and treatment of children and adolescents is to view their difficulties from a developmental perspective, which involves an analysis of risk and protective factors. Factors that create developmental risk include, among others, vulnerabilities in the child (e.g., mental impairment, chronic illness), external factors (e.g., impaired parenting), and socioeconomic and institutional factors (e.g., lack of access to medical care, poverty, social disadvantages). Likewise, resilience/protective factors (e.g., easygoing temperament, high self-esteem, high intelligence, superior school achievement) can be viewed as a transactional processes in that resilience can exist *in* the child or within supportive factors in the environment (e.g., responsive/protective parents over time, parental employment, excellent school system, safe/stable neighborhood) (Davies, 2001; Masten, 2007; Masten & Coatsworth, 1998). In general, infants and young children depend more on external protective mechanisms (e.g., secure attachment, protective parents, a stable family, a predictable environment) than older children and adolescents who are developing their own internal resources or skills that enhance their capability in responding to stress. Thus, in assessing children, adolescents, and their families, it is important to understand a particular child's development in the context of the transactions between the individual child and the layers of ecological context that surround him/her.

The task of the clinician in assessing a child or adolescent is to identify the cluster of present risk factors, as well as the protective factors. Generally, unless some risk factors are eliminated, or protective factors are added, there may be a negative outcome for the child or adolescent (Werner, 2000). In essence, it is the balance of risk and protective factors across development and the timing of the new stressors or opportunities in the course of a child's life that will determine the course of development. Assessment must examine the balance of risk and protective factors because protective factors tend to offset or minimize risk. It is for these reasons that the "relevant developmental history" in both the behavioral and cognitive-behavioral versions within case formulation are presented as "weaknesses/risk factors" and "strengths/protective factors." These issues are directly relevant to developing a "problem list and other issues to be addressed" in these summary forms.

Case Examples Employing the Case Formulation Summary Forms for Children and Adolescents

CASE STUDY 1 (INTERNALIZED PROBLEM): THE CASE OF MEREDITH

- Those who get lost on the way to school never find their way through life.—German Proverb

The following case using the "Case Formulation Summary Form for Children and Adolescents: Behavioral Version" (Appendix B) is offered in the work with Meredith, a 9-year-old girl, brought to therapy by her parents after she began steadfastly refusing to attend classes 2 months into the school year.

Meredith is in the second grade and was brought to therapy by her 30-year-old mother, Sarah, and her 31-year-old father, Paul. Meredith's mother would describe herself as a "busy housewife" and her father was a white-collar insurance salesman who was the sole provider for this upper-income family. Meredith's teachers were concerned because of her school absences prior to this and having to give her special assignments "just to keep up." Although Meredith had been somewhat reluctant to attend school previously, she would usually do so with the encouragement of her parents.

Her excessive and unreasonable fears of school intensified, however, and she complained of having more severe headaches, an upset stomach, and a sore throat just before the time to leave for school (rather conveniently after her father had left for work). She began to "feel better" when her mother relented and allowed her to stay at home, only to become "sick again" the next morning. When Meredith's mother would inform her husband about Meredith's absence from school that day and about her own helplessness in being able to do anything about it, he would become angry and would give Meredith a stern lecture, which occasionally included rather boisterous yelling at his daughter. Meredith would become teary-eyed, and feebly reiterate that she "really was sick" as her mother would assuage Meredith's hurt feelings, comfort her, and promise that "everything will be all right." Meredith was an only child whom her mother, a full-time homemaker, doted upon. The only other stressor that appeared to be impinging upon the family was a "breast cancer scare" that her Meredith's mother had dealt with near the end of the previous summer, although follow-up testing was negative. Nevertheless, this still was a notable concern for Meredith's parents. Meredith's school refusal seemed to be related to a fear of leaving her parents, particularly her mother.

Separation anxiety disorder is one of the two most common disorders occurring in childhood, the other being specific phobia, which occurs in about 4–10% of all children (Mash & Wolfe, 2010). School refusal is a fairly common problem, affecting up to 28% of American school-age children (Kearney & Albano, 2000) As Kearney and Albano (2000) also note, children generally refuse to go to school for one or more of the following reasons: to avoid school-related situations that cause general distress (e.g., anxiety, embarrassment, dread, physiological symptoms), to escape aversive social and/or evaluative situations, to receive attention from others considered important outside of school, and/or to pursue what they consider important things/activities outside of school. The first two reasons typically involve negative reinforcement or the child attempting to "get away from" something unpleasant at school (e.g., buses, playgrounds, social interactions, bullies, or situations in which they are evaluated, such as tests, recitals, and speaking in front of others). The latter two reasons are typically reinforced, as children (usually older adolescents) want to pursue something or someone outside of school that they view as being rewarding (e.g., watching television at home, sleeping, shopping, engaging in social activities with friends, using alcohol or other drugs). Younger children who refuse school, however, may engage in such activities to force parents to attend to them, are possibly worried about their parents for some reason (probably her mother's cancer scare, in Meredith's case) or simply to demand more physical closeness or additional comfort. Thus, some children may refuse to attend school for multiple reasons and may require more involved treatment interventions than children who refuse school for one reason.

Within the problem-solving framework, the following steps are suggested to guide the therapeutic process (see Chapter 3).

Stage 1: Adopting a Problem-Solving Orientation In the initial sessions, I listened carefully to Meredith and her parents speak about the specific issues that motivated them to seek therapy. The therapeutic alliance was begun by listening to their "story," and "joining" with them around the theme that Meredith's difficulties are "problems to be solved" by a joint collaborative effort among the therapist, Meredith's parents, and Meredith herself. Thus, the problem-solving framework is introduced in the very beginning stages of the therapeutic process. The therapist offers a sense of hope that the presenting "problems can be solved." In addition, framing the therapeutic work as a problem-solving endeavor demystifies the psychotherapeutic process, which many children/adolescents and their families do not thoroughly understand. Therefore, the process of adopting a problem-solving orientation can facilitate the development of a solid therapeutic relationship, which is essential in effective treatment.

Stage 2: Defining the Problem (Developing the Problem List and Other Issues to Be Addressed Using the "Summary Form: Behavioral Version") In dealing with any problem that is likely multifaceted, the case formulation approach can clarify not only for the therapist but also for the child and his/her parents the nature of the problem and what will be done about it over the course of treatment. Although it seems self-evident that practitioners should tailor their assessments and interventions toward the specific characteristics and circumstances of the child/adolescent and family, in reality many therapists may typically provide the same or at least similar assessments and interventions for the majority of their clients. All assessments and interventions with children, adolescents, and their families are ultimately grounded in the specific theoretical orientation with which the therapist is most familiar.

The child's age is important in understanding school refusal separation anxiety, because most children ages 5 to 11 years tend to refuse school to avoid general negative affectivity and/or to receive attention. Adolescents ages 12–17 years who refuse school often do so to escape aversive social and/or evaluative situations, and/or to pursue more enjoyable activities/reinforcers outside of school (Kearney & Albano, 2000). Just as knowing the age and family factors are important, in this case, assessment in pinpointing what is causing and maintaining such behavior is crucial. Basically, a child's school refusal should be analyzed to see which components (behavioral avoidance, cognitive distortions, and/or physiological reactions) are most prominent. Thus, the clinician needs to determine what is maintaining the school refusal behavior and, based upon this analysis, decide just what the best treatment is. The case formulation summary form can help the clinician most effectively organize his/her understanding of the case (see Figure 4.1). Although it is clear that Meredith's parents view her as "the problem," the therapist sees Meredith's behavior as being a part of an interactional cycle that has existed among Meredith, her mother, and her father.

Stage 3: Collecting Data A functional analysis of behavior is important in such cases in which identifying antecedent and consequences behavior, at least from a behavioral viewpoint, is most beneficial. Most therapists conduct a clinical interview that may be augmented by self-report instruments—for example, the Negative Affect Self-Statement Questionnaire (NASSQ; Ronan, Kendall, & Rowe, 1994), the Fear Survey Schedule for Children-Revised (FSSC-R; Ollendick, 1983), the Social Anxiety Scale for Children-Revised (SASC-R; La Greca & Stone, 1993), and the School Refusal Assessment Scale (SRAS; Kearney & Silverman, 1993). In addition, parent and teacher measures—Child Behavior Checklist (CBCL; Achenbach, 1991a), Conner's Parent Rating Scale (CPRS; Conners, 1990), Teacher Report Form (TRF; Achenbach, 1991b)—may be helpful.

FIGURE 4.1 **Case formulation summary form**

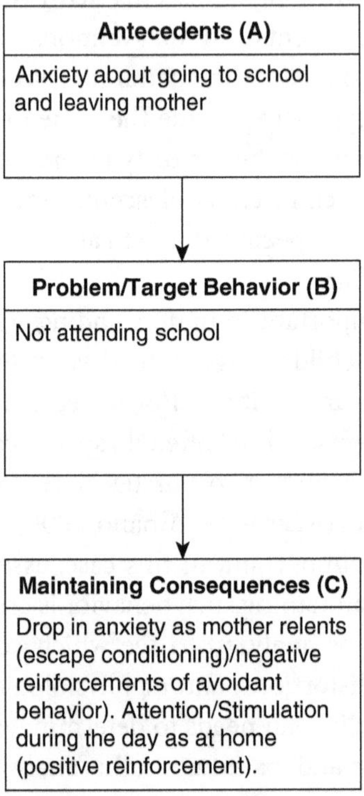

Stage 4: Setting Treatment Goals Meredith's parents and I worked together on understanding her problem and developed the following *problem list*:

1. Poor school attendance and associated emotional distress (defined by frequent negative complaints about school, crying, pleading with her mother not to go to school) and, when at school, telling her teacher that she was sick and had to go home, demanding to call her mother.
2. Separation anxiety defined by excessive emotional distress (frequent complaints about leaving her mother, complaints about harm befalling her mother) and frequent attempts to sleep in her parent's bed at night.

Meredith's difficulties were viewed within the problematic interactional relationship pattern with her mother and father—Meredith refusing to go to school and being worried (at least to a moderate extent) in a number of situations in which she was away from her mother, and her mother's concern/fears about Meredith and Meredith's ability to cope with or handle various situations, particularly those in which Meredith exhibited anxiety; Meredith being "soothed" by her mother following her father's efforts to "fix the problem" by sternly yelling at Meredith after his wife had informed him about Meredith's absence from school again upon his return from work. He becomes baffled and frustrated by his wife's coddling of Meredith and occasional reprimand of him for his "yelling at her too loudly." According to the *DSM-IV-TR*, it should be noted that Meredith met the criteria for separation anxiety disorder in that she exhibited excessive anxiety concerning separation from her home and mother beyond that which is expected for her individual developmental level. However, giving her such a diagnosis and framing Meredith's behavior as symptom of anxiety might simply reinforce this view for Meredith and her parents, inadvertently facilitating the helplessness of Meredith's parents (especially her mother) in solving this problem. By stating the problem as a *DSM-IV-TR* diagnosis, the therapist may also inadvertently define him/herself as the primary change agent and minimize the role of the parents in solving this problem that they face with their daughter.

As a result, I chose to define the problem (determined by my own behavioral/family systems theoretical orientation) as one of *parental leadership* in which both parents have been unable to reassure Meredith that they have confidence in her ability to successfully go to school and remain there each day. Thus, the problem is defined in a way that hopefully will mobilize the parents to take appropriate action to ensure that Meredith not only starts attending school but then does so regularly.

Stages 5 and 6: Generating Solutions (Intervention Strategies) and Choosing the Best One(s) School refusal has been addressed by mental health professionals and educators in a variety of ways. Behavioral treatments for children with specific phobias such as school-related issues have included systematic desensitization (e.g., Lazarus, Davison, & Polefka, 1965); forced school attendance (Kennedy, 1965); and/or family-treatment interventions such as education in communication skills, training, and/or written contracts between the child/adolescent and parents (e.g., Stuart, 1971). In this case, Meredith's school refusal was conceptualized by the family's therapist as an operant behavior that allowed her to escape from a variety of situations at school that caused her general distress/negative affectivity. Contingent upon exhibiting such behavior, her mother backed off and permitted her to stay home, which simply reinforced such behavior. As Meredith began to "feel better" during the course of the day, she was permitted to stay in her room and watch TV, as well as make lunch with her mother, to the point at which it was "too late" to go to school that day. Such behavior was negatively reinforced (escaping from school) and positively reinforced (attention from her mother, in addition to engaging in activities she viewed as more interesting than school) at home. Thus, this part of the case formulation process leads to a clearer understanding of what needed to be done in therapy.

The functional analysis of Meredith's school refusal can be effectively developed in the "Origins/hypotheses" section of the "Case Formulation Summary Form: Behavioral Version." At this stage, it would also be helpful for the therapist to consider using the problem-solving grid previously discussed (see Chapter 3) to optimally develop and ultimately choose the best therapy strategy/intervention by brainstorming possible therapy strategies/interventions and rating the likely outcomes of implementing each strategy.

At this time, it is also important for the therapist to assess consequences for the child/adolescent/family's "readiness to change" (e.g., Prochaska & Norcross, 2006) (see Chapter 3). Meredith's mother was clearly at the action stage as she was ready to do "whatever it takes" to get Meredith to school, considering that her daughter was falling behind because of her school refusal. At this point in treatment, the therapist should consider sharing the summary form with the child/adolescent and family in a jargon-free fashion. If the therapist judges this form to be too complicated or confusing for the parents, a simplified version of it can be shared with the clients during this "educational phase."

Stage 7: Trying It Out (Initiating the Intervention) At this stage, the therapist has the child/adolescent and family implement the chosen intervention decided upon in the previous stage. It is important to recognize that assessment does not stop at Stage 6; it is important throughout the therapeutic endeavor as the therapist attempts to ascertain the effects of the intervention (Stage 8).

Stage 8: Evaluating the Effects of the Intervention (Did It Work?) In evaluating the effects of the intervention, the therapist determines whether or not the problem has been resolved. If it has been resolved, movement toward termination is initiated. If the problem still exists, the therapist teaches the child/adolescent/family to consider one or more of the previous stages within the problem-solving framework. Thus, another solution might be attempted (Stage 6), or, if there are no acceptable alternatives, other solutions must be generated (Stage 5). Perhaps the difficulty lies in the goals that were originally established or how the problem was originally defined (Stage 4). Thus, the problem-solving process continues to guide the work with the family. In this way, the clients are further taught about problem solving and how this can be an effective paradigm to deal with not only the current but also future problems.

CASE STUDY 2 (EXTERNALIZED PROBLEM): THE CASE OF WILL

- Parents are the bones on which the children sharpen their teeth.—Peter Ustinov, *Dear Me*
- Children today are tyrants. They contradict their parents, gobble their food, and tyrannize their teachers.—Socrates (470–399 BC)

The following case, using the "Case Formulation Summary Form for Children and Adolescents: Cognitive-Behavioral Version" (see Appendix C), is presented in the work with Will, a 14-year-old eighth-grader who was brought to therapy by his mother who was upset about his acting-out behavior.

Will's 41-year-old mother, Mary, divorced her husband (Will's father) 1 year ago, after finding out that he had a 6-month affair with a married woman. Will's relationship with his father was described as not particularly close or particularly difficult. They were more like acquaintances who occasionally did things together. After the multimethod/multisource/multisetting assessment was completed, the following *problem list* was developed: verbal aggression/"below-the-belt" insults of his mother, a decline in academic grades over the past year, frequent defiance of curfew, and disobedience especially at home with his mother. Will met the *DSM-IV-TR* criteria for adjustment disorder with disturbance of conduct because over the past year he had exhibited a recurrent pattern of negativistic, defiant, disobedient behavior toward authority figures (especially his mother and occasionally toward his teacher in school).

His mother was not much concerned about peers with whom Will had been associating, because there were no major changes in his friendship patterns over the past year. She also had always approved of Will's friends and described them as "basically good boys." She was particularly concerned, however, about Will's "short fuse and hot temper," stating that Will sporadically became so angry and even threatened to hurt his sister on several occasions (2 years younger than he, and a "perfect daughter"). Although Will exhibited verbal aggression and some threatening behavior toward his mother and sister, he had never behaved in a physically aggressive fashion at school, nor had he ever actually physically aggressed against his sister or mother. He had done some minimal damage to nonvaluable things, such as accidentally breaking a vase in the family room when he threw a ball after becoming angry 2 weeks prior to the initiation of therapy. His mother complained that "Will had a hot temper just like his father's"; she reported that her ex-husband was never physically abusive with her but was frighteningly verbally confrontational at times.

Within the problem-solving framework (see Chapter 3), the "Case Formulation Summary Form: Behavioral Version" can be helpful in guiding the therapeutic process.

Stage 1: Adopting a Problem-Solving Orientation In the initial sessions, I listened carefully to both Will and his mother about various issues that brought them into therapy, and in the process of empathetically listening to their "story," the beginnings of "joining" with them (the therapeutic alliance) were initiated. Issues brought up by both Will and his mother were labeled as "problems" that could be dealt with and essentially solved in therapy. In the process of framing the precipitating events and dynamics that brought them to therapy within a problem-solving framework, I tried to convey a sense of hope from the onset of therapy that these presenting problems can be solved by Will and his mother. It was fairly clear from the beginning, however, that Will's father, a blue-collar worker whose factory work provided a modest income for the family, was not interested in becoming an active participant in the therapeutic process. He did not think his son's difficulties were that severe and certainly not so severe as to warrant "going to the shrink."

Stage 2: Defining the Problem (Developing the Problem List and Other Issues to Be Addressed Using the "Summary Form: Cognitive-Behavioral Version") The clinician determines, along with the parent(s) and child/adolescent (depending upon his/her age), the child's/adolescent's most problematic behaviors. The clinician "understands" the problem in light of his/her own theoretical perspective and reemphasizes the therapeutic process as being a "problem-solving" process. The case formulation approach can "sharpen" this process and facilitate the therapeutic process. The cognitive-behavioral model has been previously articulated as being rooted historically in social learning theory (e.g., Bandura, 1977; Rotter, Chance, & Pharres, 1972) and in the development of children's self-regulation capabilities (e.g., Giancola, Zeichner, Yarnell, & Dickson, 1996; Meichenbaum & Goodman, 1971). It should be noted that cognitive-behavioral interventions have been made more user-friendly by practitioners and researchers for a wide range of child/adolescent problems, including the following:

- Aggression (e.g., Lochman, Wells, & Lenhart's [2008] *Coping Power: Child Group Program*)

- Anger and aggression (e.g., Nelson & Finch's [2008b] *Keeping Your Cool: The Anger Management Workbook*)
- Anxiety (e.g., Kendall and Hedtke's [1992] *The Coping Cat Workbook* [2nd ed.])
- Depression (e.g., Stark, Simpson, Schnoebelen, Hargrave, & Molnar's [2007] *ACTION Workbook: Cognitive-Behavioral Therapy for Treating Depressed Girls*)

It should also be noted that the therapist recognizes that acting out/aggressive behaviors are multidetermined, often involving different causal pathways, and that these pathways can vary across children who show severe acting-out behaviors (Dodge & Pettit, 2003; Frick, 2006). For anger and aggression, the following cognitive-behavioral model depicts the way in which the therapist can understand the problems presented in therapy, in a user-friendly way that can be readily understood by Will and his mother. This model (see Figure 4.2) was selected because of its application to Will's subjective state of anger and his subsequent aggressive acting out, as well as fitting my primary cognitive-behavioral theoretical orientation. Such a theory has been elaborated, as previously indicated, in a number of places in the literature, and cognitive-behavioral interventions have a good evidence base.

It is at Stage 2 in the problem-solving model that the therapist begins to develop the case formulation plan (more structured than a traditional

FIGURE 4.2 **Cognitive-behavioral model of aggression**

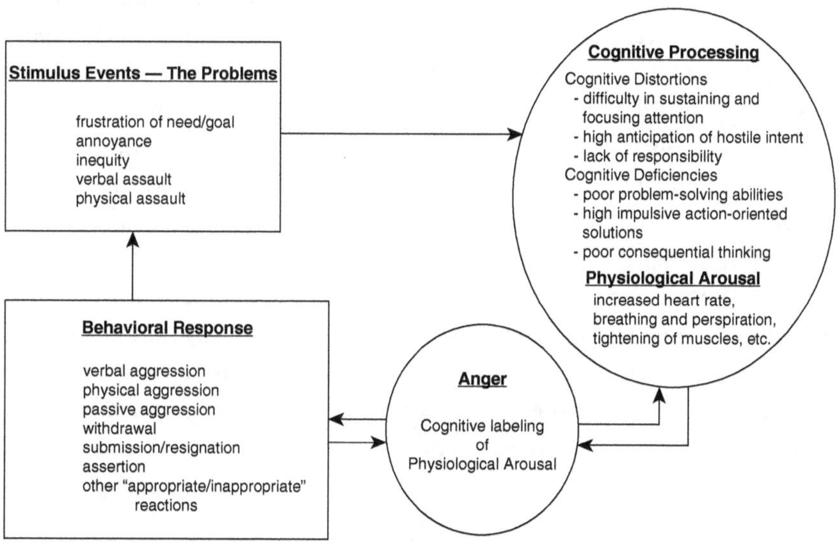

treatment plan that will best help the family achieve its goals). In essence, the case formulation is an extension of the therapist's own theoretical orientation. Ideally, it is one that provides the most parsimonious account of the child/adolescent's problems and the one that is most acceptable and understandable to the identified client and his/her family.

Stage 3: Collecting Data The *problem list* was derived from a through multimethod/multisource/multisetting assessment, including clinical interviews with Will and both parents, completion of the Child Behavior Checklist (Achenbach, 1991a, 1991b) by both Will's mother and teacher, the CBCL Youth Report Inventory (Achenbach, 1991a), the Children's Inventory of Anger (Nelson & Finch, 2000), the Children's Depression Inventory (Kovacs, 1999), and direct observational reports/monitoring of Will's verbally aggressive behavior by his mother. In addition, a number of risk factors relevant to Will's relevant *developmental history* were noted. Will's difficulties were seen as being an adjustment reaction to an identifiable psychosocial stressor: namely, the divorce of his parents 1 year prior. There were no other clear distal or proximal factors that appeared to be related to his more severe acting out.

When it comes to such oppositional, aggressive behavior, there are no simple or single causes. There were no behaviors that seemed to run in either the maternal or paternal families across generations (genetic influences). Likewise, there did not appear to be any prenatal or birth complications that are sometimes correlated with aggressive problems (Mash & Wolfe, 2010). Will had always been a sociable youngster whose friends were judged by his mother as basically "good kids" (social factors). His parents' difficulties were long-standing, however, which eventually culminated in their divorce 1 year prior (family factors). The parents exhibited at least moderate deficits in their parental management skills with Will, who was always considered to be rather "high-strung" and resentful of his sister. She received much of the parents' attention because she was considered to be a "star" student who was popular and involved in many after-school activities. Although Will was never subjected to any physical abuse by either parent, his father was more cold, distant, and authoritarian.

Overall, Will met the *DSM-IV-TR* criteria for adjustment disorder with mixed emotional features. Although exhibiting some oppositional defiant behavior and mood disturbances, he did not meet criteria for a disruptive behavior disorder or depressive disorder. His problems began subsequent to his parents' marital difficulties and divorce 1 year prior.

Stage 4: Setting Treatment Goals Will, his mother, and I worked together brainstorming the following *problem list,* which included his most problematic behaviors, along with the accompanying/mediating automatic thoughts and emotions for each problem:

1. Verbal aggression: "Below-the-belt" verbal attacks were judged to be the most problematic for Will's mother, who characteristically became alternately withdrawn/dejected and angry/upset. Will became particularly angry when his mother would verbally criticize his father for not providing what she felt was appropriate parental assistance in helping rear their son, as well as for nonpayment of child support. Related to this was Will's irrational belief that it was "terrible and horrible" that his parents not only divorced in the first place but also continued to argue and criticize each other; he wished they would reconcile and even wondered what he could do to facilitate this. He would became overwhelmed by his anger (which is a subjective state, as opposed to the overt behavior of verbal/"below-the-belt" aggression) and reportedly felt indifferent and rather hopeless in being able to "control [his] temper." Will would also become angry when his mother would try to set limits on his behavior or not agree to what he wanted to do.
2. Depression: Although not meeting the criteria necessary for a formal diagnosis of a mood disorder, Will experienced such feelings surrounding the separation/divorce of his parents about 1 year prior. About 50% of youngsters with externalized problems also are diagnosed with depression or anxiety (Wolfe & Ollendick, 2006). Automatic *thoughts* included sporadic upsetting ruminations such as "My parents hate each other and I can't stand this," "I'll never have the same relationship with my mother and father," "They wouldn't have divorced if they really loved me," and occasionally "I was the cause of their breaking up and should have been able to do something to stop them from divorcing." In addition, he thought that he was responsible for his mother's happiness and could not tolerate her becoming depressed at times.
3. Deterioration of grades at school during previous year: This occurred shortly before his parents' divorce, indicating that it also was an adjustment reaction to this marked stressor. Other *developmental* stressors included going through the physiological changes associated with puberty and concerns about where he should apply to high

> school, particularly because of his parents' disagreement (his mother thought that he should go to a Catholic high school while his father wanted him to attend a less expensive public school).

Will's description of his problems suggested several developing schemas or core beliefs that were problematic about himself and about his family. As a young adolescent, he was learning to construct reality through his early experiences with the environment, especially with his parents. He was struggling with core needs for safety, stability/predictability, love, and nurturance.

In trying to understand and deal with his parents' divorce, Will's behavior was mediated by his existing cognitive structures (schema) or core beliefs about his self, others, and the world. There were two *schemas* that were activated and directly influenced the screening, coding, and evaluating the troubling events that impinged upon him—(1) helpless schema: "I'm vulnerable" and "I'm helpless in getting my parents back together"; and (2) unlovable schema: "I'm unlovable and I'm bound to be abandoned."

In dealing with the divorce of his parents, Will was further developing schema regarding abandonment/instability related to the unreliability of his father and his availability for support. He was struggling with and questioning whether his parents would be there to continue to provide emotional support, connection, and protection because they were not present in a way that characterizes a typical two-parent family. Thus, his anger and subsequent aggressive acting-out were globally mediated by his *developing schemas/core beliefs,* which in turn were mediated by his thoughts/self-talk in specific problem situations. The relationship among these cognitive processes is shown in Figure 4.3.

These developing, early maladaptive cognitive schemas that seemed to underlie Will's problems are important in understanding Will's current anger problems. In specific anger-arousing situations, Will's automatic *thoughts* that are triggered included "I can't stand it that my parents are divorced and they argue" (about self); "I must have an intact family to be happy" and "It's terrible and horrible if my mother criticizes my father" (about family); and "I must have things the way I want them to be" (about self).

External precipitants seemed to be triggers for Will's aggressive acting out (e.g., mother criticizing the father; mother setting limits on Will's behavior); these external stressors articulate Will's *developing schema* about himself and his family and trigger the irrational beliefs that influence his

Figure 4.3 **The A-B-C mediational model**

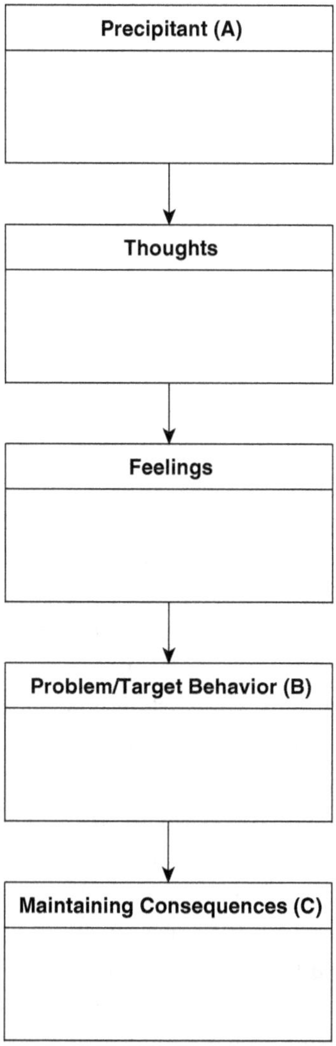

feelings (internal/physiological sensations) (e.g., burning mad feeling, hot face, clenched fists, tight muscles) and his overt *problem/target behavior.*

"The Case Formulation Summary Form for Children and Adolescents—Cognitive-Behavioral Version" was used to understand and integrate the treatment plan addressing the problems that Will experienced. It helped me to more carefully consider factors in Will's upbringing that were important in further understanding the schema that mediated his current problems (e.g., being the oldest child and having a younger sister who was "a star" in terms of her academic, athletic, and social interactions). It also helped to identify some of Will's automatic thoughts, emotional/physiological reactions, and behaviors, which enabled me to further educate him about the components of anger (thoughts, feelings/physiological events, and behaviors), decrease his subjective experience of anger, and sensitize him to "high-risk" situations in which he is most likely "to lose it."

At this juncture in the therapeutic process, the case formulation summary form is completed to the point at which it begins to offer a structured guide for the therapist, client, and family over the course of treatment. The therapist begins to fill out the summary form as soon as information is gathered about the child/adolescent in Stage 3. As previously indicated, the summary form is dynamic in the sense that it should be altered as more information is obtained and the effectiveness of the specific interventions is evaluated.

Stages 5 and 6: Generating Solutions (Intervention Strategies) and Choosing the Best One(s) Because I decided that an individualized approach would be taken, I selected Nelson and Finch's (2008b) *Keeping Your Cool: The Anger Management Workbook* to guide therapy, as this workbook was designed for youngsters at Will's age level. Our meetings primarily involved individual sessions with Will. The workbook would also be adapted to integrate direct involvement of his mother in treatment (as his father did not seem to be much interested in becoming directly involved in therapy).

At this point, the therapist is ready to "try it out" by specifically implementing the chosen interventions and evaluating the effectiveness of such interventions. As mentioned in the case of Meredith, the therapist needs to consider the stages, or the child/adolescent/family's "readiness to change" because psychological interventions are differentially effective depending on the client's relative readiness to change (in Will's case, this meant initiating treatment employing Nelson and Finch's [2008b] *Keeping Your Cool Workbook*).

Stage 7: Trying It Out (Implementing the Intervention) The most effective way of intervening, as determined by the therapist in conjunction with Will and his mother, is now implemented.

Stage 8: Evaluating the Effects of the Intervention (Did It Work?) Continued assessment over the course of therapy is also essential to evaluate whether and when the treatment goals have been met (Nelson & Politano, 1993). When the treatment goals are met, termination is initiated. If treatment goals are not met, the problem-solving framework is reemphasized and the therapist revisits previous stages to determine how best to proceed at this point. Again, this becomes another "teachable moment" in therapy to assist clients in coping with resolution attempts that do not always turn out as hoped or planned.

Summary

By offering case formulation forms to be used within the problem-solving model for use in assessment with children, adolescents, and their families, it is hoped that these will be further used by clinicians to guide and shape their decision-making processes that characterize the psychotherapeutic endeavor. At this point, it is clear that case formulation will increasingly become researched and its acceptance into clinical practice will hopefully grow in a similar fashion as some have embraced empirically supported clinical interventions. The closing of this gap between research and practice in clinical assessment with children and adolescents will also likely present a fundamental change for both researchers and clinicians. It is hoped that these groups, both so important in our field, work together to best serve the ever-growing mental health needs of children, adolescents, and their families.

PART III

Functional Competency—Intervention

FIVE

Clinical Child and Adolescent Intervention Strategies

This chapter will provide an overview of a clinician's functional competencies with regard to psychological interventions with children and adolescents. As with other aspects of this text, the focus is on levels of intervention competency that permit a psychologist to provide good quality care to the child clients and their families. This is a level of competency that is expected to be attained by well-trained psychologists in the years shortly after they have received their terminal degrees.

This chapter will first briefly overview basic procedural issues in establishing the therapy contract, and then will overview types of therapeutic procedures that psychologists may competently use with their clients. When a candidate pursues certification through the American Board of Clinical Child and Adolescent Psychology, it is important to stress that the successful candidate may perform interventions that take the form of any modality of psychological treatment or environmental modification. Thus, there is no presumption that there is only one correct way to intervene with a given child or family. However, it is incumbent on the candidate to provide a detailed rationale for the treatment plan used with the child or family. This treatment rationale typically involves attention to the theoretical and empirical basis for the procedures to be used with a particular child.

Establishing the Therapeutic Contract and Treatment Plan

After an intake evaluation or full psychological assessment of a child is completed, the psychologist establishes a therapeutic contract with the child/adolescent and his or her family. The psychologist typically summarizes the initial assessment information and begins to identify intervention goals based on the identified problems and concerns. In some cases, assessment and intervention are integral parts of the same process, but in other forms of psychological practice, assessment and intervention represent more differentiated clinical steps. As part of the process of establishing therapeutic goals for a case, it is important that the psychologist ask about the intervention goals that the child and family might have. Because some clients are more expressive at this stage of therapy about their wishes and perceived needs than others, the therapist should proceed slowly through this phase, with frequent opportunities for client input. The establishment of the treatment goals and of the related treatment plan should be a collaborative effort among the clinician and client and client's family. Frequent efforts by the clinician to check on the client's perceptions of intervention goals, and later of the intervention process, can be useful in adapting intervention to the specific needs of a given client. This will help to avoid early intervention termination due to clients' frustration that their preferences are not being elicited or addressed.

Identification of intervention goals is a key step in creating a treatment plan, which should also be developed in collaboration with the client and family. The treatment plan should lay out the nature and length of the planned treatment. The following section in this chapter on intervention strategies provides examples of different types of interventions that have been used with children and adolescents, and which could be included in the treatment plan. The treatment plan should be based on a clear and specific rationale about the particular intervention approach that is selected for the client. The rationale typically includes an understanding of the evidence base and/or of the theoretical basis for the particular approach. This rationale permits the clinician to tell the client and family *why* this approach will be pursued, and the likelihood of its success, based on prior reports and research.

The treatment selected should be appropriate for the particular type of problems and psychopathology that the child or adolescent displays. Thus, the ability to use an intervention effectively requires that the clinician understand the risk and protective factors associated with the development and maintenance of the client's problem behaviors, the active psychological mechanisms associated with the problem, and how the chosen intervention can target those active mechanisms associated with that disorder. The use of psychological interventions with children requires that we integrate knowledge about developmental psychopathology into our assessments and treatment planning. The procedures in the treatment plan should also be appropriate for the developmental level of the child and for the resources and culture of the family. Because a specific child client with a given disorder typically has only a subset of the risk factors and active mechanisms that have been identified in the literature to be associated with the disorder, the clinician can potentially tailor and adapt the chosen intervention to meet the specific risk factors present.

The initial therapeutic contract with the client and family should also include not only a discussion of why this particular intervention was chosen, but also whether there are any effective alternative therapies that were *not* chosen (and why). Concrete contractual issues should also be addressed, including a discussion of the payment arrangements, confidentiality, the boundaries of the services offered, and the clinician's/clinic's availability in crises. The clinician should ensure that records are kept in a way that is consistent with existing standards of care.

Throughout this phase of intervention contracting, the clinician should begin to establish a strong therapeutic relationship with the client and the family. The maintenance of the therapeutic bond is an important nonspecific aspect of intervention with children and families, and can be a key focus even when the treatment plan involves the use of a manualized and highly structured intervention.

Intervention Approaches

In this section, we will discuss three prominent approaches to working with child/adolescent psychopathology:

1. Behavioral therapy, including behavioral parent training
2. Cognitive-behavioral therapy with children and adolescents
3. Family therapy (apart from behavioral parent training)

In actual practice, it is not unusual to use several different methods with a given case, such as cognitive-behavioral intervention with the child and behavioral parent training with the parent. In a similar manner, some manualized, structured interventions have multiple components integrated together (e.g., Lochman & Wells, 2002a).

The emphasis in these sections is on interventions and programs that have accumulated an evidence base in efficacy and effectiveness studies. There have been a number of advances over the past 10 to 15 years in the development and implementation of evidence-based practices for children's and adolescents' emotional and behavioral difficulties (Kazdin & Weisz, 2003; Lonigan, Elbert, & Johnson, 1998; Mayer, Van Acker, Lochman, &

Gresham, 2008; Stoiber & Kratochwill, 2000; Walker et al., 2004). There has been debate concerning the level of evidence necessary for determining whether particular interventions are effective with specific problems (Gresham & Lochman, 2008), but in general evidence-based interventions have empirical support that is based on appropriate experimental design features using either group or single-case experimental designs. Studies using group experimental designs should have randomly assigned participants to experimental and control conditions.

BEHAVIORAL THERAPY

Behavioral therapy is based in some of the earliest efforts in psychology to systematically change children's behavior. In the early 1900s, behaviorism became a major approach in psychology, following the research of John B. Watson first on rats and then on humans (Scott & Yule, 2008). Watson's work demonstrated that an organism's behavior (such as avoidant reactions when fearful) could be altered by changing the immediately preceding events. These early demonstrations of antecedent control were followed by systematic research by B. F. Skinner in the mid-1930s, which found that changes in the events subsequent to given behaviors could substantially change the behavior. These roots in basic behavioral principles led to the development of behavioral therapy as a treatment approach, which was first labeled by Hans Eysenck in the early 1950s.

Behavioral therapies developed rapidly for children and adolescents in the 1970s, initially in single-case studies and small group comparisons, and in more recent years in large-scale randomized trials. In recent decades, behavioral therapy approaches have often been combined with cognitive therapies (as will be seen in the section on cognitive-behavioral therapies) and have become integral parts of some family system interventions (as will be seen in the section on family therapy). In the last decade, a "third generation" of behaviorally based cognitive therapies has emerged (Scott & Yule, 2008) that emphasizes that sometimes unpleasant thoughts and feelings cannot be changed but can be accepted as less concerning. These third-generation approaches include *acceptance and commitment therapy* (Hayes, Luoma, Bond, Masuda, & Lillis, 2006), *mindful-based cognitive therapy* (Segal, Williams, & Teasdale, 2001), and *dialectical behavior therapy* (Linehan, 1993), and child and adolescent versions of these approaches are just beginning to be examined.

Behavioral Principles Behavioral approaches are rooted in classical conditioning and in operant conditioning. In *classical conditioning*, an unconditioned stimulus (such as food) presented at the same time as a conditioned stimulus (such as bell), can lead the conditioned stimulus to lead to conditioned responses (such as salivation) that are similar to those that followed the unconditioned stimulus. Systematic desensitization (Wolpe, 1958) used a derivation of this theory to help patients replace their unconditioned fearful responses to a stimulus with acquired and competing conditioned responses of relaxation in response to the stimulus. *Operant conditioning*, which was the central feature of Skinner's work, suggested that behaviors increased or decreased depending on the rewards and punishments that followed the behaviors. The central focus of behavioral approaches are thus on environmental events that occur prior to and following behavioral responses, and do not address internal motivation or beliefs of the individual.

In behavioral therapy, positive and negative reinforcements are used to increase the rates of children's positive behaviors. In positive reinforcement, a consequence that is positively valued by the child will increase the rates of the child's behaviors that occur just prior to the positive reinforcement. The behavioral therapist may wish to reinforce a behavior that is a prosocial opposite (e.g., compromising during a conflict) of one of the problematic behaviors (e.g., scathing insults during a conflict) that led to the child's referral; this has the advantage of increasing the rate of the positive behavior while indirectly reducing the rate of the negative behavior. The rewards used can be either tangible (food, time on the computer, staying up late) or social (praise). When children and adolescents are initially resistant to identifying what they perceive to be rewarding, the Premack (1965) principle can be useful. It suggests that whatever adolescents like to do at a high frequency on their own (e.g., playing a video game) can likely be used as a reinforcer for a targeted low-frequency behavior (e.g., completing homework sheets).

Negative reinforcement is a sometimes misunderstood concept in behavioral therapy. Negative reinforcement occurs when a child's behavior leads to the removal of something aversive, thus causing the frequency of the behavior to increase; negative reinforcement is not punishment. If a child eventually complies with a parent's instruction to clean up his room, but only after the parent has been threatening to remove his privileges unless he complies, then the child has been negatively reinforced (cleaning up behavior has increased because the aversive stimulus has been removed). Shaping and prompting are often used to increase children's response to operant conditioning, and more elaborate reinforcement schedules in token economies can be useful in increasing positive behaviors among children who would be resistant to positive change following simple rewards (Scott & Yule, 2008).

Behavioral techniques used to decrease problem behaviors fall into one of three primary approaches: extinction, stimulus control, or punishment:

- Extinction can be used with mildly problematic behaviors, such as a child's whining, and involves the removal of parents' or teachers' attention to that behavior. When planned ignoring is used in this way, the child's problem behavior typical increases at first (an extinction burst) before eventually declining in frequency.
- When stimulus control is used, a stimulus that tends to elicit a problem behavior is removed and replaced with another stimulus (e.g., a peer who sits beside a child who gets into trouble for talking in class is moved to a different part of the classroom).
- Punishment can be the removal of something that is reinforcing following a child's behavior (planned ignoring, or time-out from positive reinforcement) or the provision of something that is aversive following the child's behavior. Many parents of children with problem behaviors use punishments such as physical hitting of the child, but although physical punishment typically does lead to short-term reductions of the problem behavior, it often does not lead to long-term behavior change because the child has not learned a competent alternative behavior and the child may model the parent's aggressive control behaviors. To be effective, punishment should be applied quickly and consistently, and does not need to be intense (Kazdin & Benjet, 2003). Punishments used in behavioral therapy can include removal of a child's privileges, or assignment of work chores, contingent on the occurrence of the problem behavior.

Use with Internalizing Disorders Anxiety disorders, obsessive-compulsive disorder (OCD), and posttraumatic stress disorder (PTSD) all respond well to behavioral therapy. The basic aim is to expose the child to the feared stimulus (in imagination, and then live) and to teach an alternative conditioned response that is characterized by calm and relaxation (Scott & Yule, 2008). During graded exposure, response prevention is used to prevent the child from carrying out the typical obsessive or avoidant behavior. Most contemporary behavioral approaches, tested in randomized control trials to treat anxiety disorders (Silverman, Kurtines, Ginsburg, Weems, Rabian, & Serafini, 1999), OCD (Barrett, Healey-Farrell, & March, 2004), and PTSD (Chemtob, Nakashima, & Hamada, 2002; Stein, Jaycox, Kataoka, Wong, Tu, Elliott et al., 2003) now include cognitive elements as well (focusing on children monitoring and challenging their erroneous cognitions), and would be classified as cognitive-behavioral.

Use with Disruptive Disorders Behavioral methods had a major influence on the treatment of children's aggression and conduct problems starting in the 1960s, largely through the use of behavioral parent training. A series of manualized parenting programs exist, including Triple P (Markie-Dadds & Sanders, 2006), Helping the Noncompliant Child (McMahon & Forehand, 2003), Parent-Child Interaction Therapy (Brinkmeyer & Eyberg, 2003), Defiant Children (Mash & Barkeley, 2006), and the Incredible Years (Webster-Stratton & Reid, 2003). More than a hundred clinical trials have been conducted, and mean effect sizes from meta-analyses indicate that the programs are effective in reducing children's antisocial behavior, especially with children in the 3- to 10-year age range (McCart, Priester, Davies, & Azen, 2006), and that the effect sizes are in the moderate to large range of 0.4 to 1.0 standard deviations (Barlow, 1999; Scott, 2008). These structured programs typically last 8 to 12 sessions and cover a relatively common set of skills, starting with helping parents to provide reflective attention to children's play; to increase their use of social reinforcement and rewards; to provide more specific instructions, expectations, and "house rules" for children so that the antecedents for children's behavior are clearer; to use effective methods for reducing children's problem behaviors (ignoring, time-out, withdrawal of privileges); and to use family problem-solving techniques.

Use with ADHD Behavioral therapy for ADHD children is similar in content to the behavioral approaches used with conduct problem children, and typically involves training for parents and teachers in contingency management. Because of the characteristics of ADHD children, behavioral programs for ADHD children typically include giving more frequent and rapid rewards, changing the reinforcement menu more often to reduce boredom, and giving directions more concretely and clearly (Scott & Yule, 2008). Common behavioral procedures, such as time-out, have led to more significant reductions in aggressive and noncompliant behavior in ADHD children than have been evident in no-treatment control groups (Fabiano, Pelham, Manos, Gnagy, Chronis, Onyango, et al., 2004). Behavioral programs for ADHD children have less effect on the core symptoms of ADHD than on the associated conduct symptoms (MTA Cooperative Group, 1999). Although behavioral therapy added to medication has not led to better outcomes overall than medication alone (MTA Cooperative Group,

1999), inclusion of behavioral therapy has improved children's aggression at home and led to lower doses of medication required.

Use with Developmental Disorders A clear effective use of behavioral therapy has been with nocturnal enuresis. In the systematic development of procedures designed to generate an aversive conditioning response based on classical conditioning, Mowrer (1980) found that when a loud bell sounded as soon as pads in children's underwear became wet, nocturnal enuresis was decreased. In their review of alarm interventions for nocturnal enuresis, Glazener, Evans, and Petro (2005) found that two-thirds of children across 55 studies were dry at night after treatment. When overlearning is added, by increasing fluid intake at night, the long-term relapse rate is decreased to 20% (Houts, 2003). Other research has disputed whether these effects are due only to classical conditioning. Bollard (1982) has had similar rates of success using only an operant conditioning approach, with parents providing reinforcement for dry beds and without using an alarm. Thus, the active treatment mechanism is likely to be due to both classical and operant conditioning (Scott & Yule, 2008).

Behavioral procedures have been widely used with children with autism spectrum disorders (ASD) to develop these children's language and social skills and to reduce their stereotyped behaviors. For this group of participants, behavioral therapy should be introduced in a predictable, gradual, and structured way within the children's daily routines, and instructions need to be delivered concretely and calmly (Scott & Yule, 2008). The intensive and comprehensive behavioral approach developed by Lovaas (Lovaas & Smith, 2003) can take up to 3 years and has produced increases in IQ scores of 15 points or greater in initial randomized trials (McEachin, Smith, & Lovaas, 1993) and in less intensive replication studies (Smith, Groen, & Wynn, 2000). Less intensive programs using only parent training have produced encouraging increases in educational behaviors in some small-scale research (Panerai, Ferrante, & Zingale, 2002) but has not produced intelligence or language gains in other studies (Kabot, Masi, & Segal, 2003).

Behavioral procedures that have been used effectively with temper tantrums and self-injurious behavior of children with intellectual disabilities include a focus on teaching alternative responses to attain valued rewards (e.g., getting adult attention, escaping from disliked school activities; Carr, Levin, McConnachie, Carlson, Kemp, & Smith, 1994) and on stimulus control by changing activities that occur before problematic behaviors. An emphasis is placed on developing a thorough functional analysis of the problem behavior, and then changing triggers (e.g., transitions in daily routines, closeness of interpersonal contact) that appear to immediately precede the behavior (Scott & Yule, 2008).

COGNITIVE-BEHAVIORAL THERAPY

A large portion of empirically supported treatments for child and adolescent psychiatric disorders are cognitive-behavioral (Kazdin & Weisz, 1998). *Cognitive-behavioral therapy* integrates behavioral therapy approaches with the assumption that cognitions or thoughts can influence emotions and behaviors across a variety of situations. By altering maladaptive, distorted, or deficient thoughts, cognitive-behavioral therapy (CBT) can be effective in treating various forms of psychopathology.

Although the widespread application of cognitive-behavioral treatments to emotional and behavioral problems in youth began in the mid-1980s (Graham, 2005), the theoretical and empirical underpinnings of these treatments began as early as the 1950s. Rotter (1954) developed one of the first social learning models, and stressed that behavior was influenced by cognitive processes, such as the subjective value individuals placed on reinforcers and their expectations that specific behaviors would result in rewards. As a result, this model expanded upon existing behavioral theories by introducing cognitive representations of social information and reinforcement contingencies as mediating processes (Lochman & Pardini, 2008). It is not just the behaviors that are important but also the individual's perceptions and thoughts about events. Early observation learning theories also stressed the important of cognitions by recognizing that a child's observations of real life and symbolic models could influence subjective reward contingencies and decision-making processes. Studies in this area found that children tended to imitate aggressive behavior when they observed a model being reinforced for aggression, and were less likely to imitate aggressive behavior when they observed a model being punished for aggression (Bandura, Ross, & Ross, 1963).

Mischel (1973) proposed a cognitive social learning model of human behavior that combined developments in social learning theory (Bandura, 1969) with research on cognitive processing and symbolic mental representations (Neisser, 1967). He posited that the relation between environmental stimuli and behavior was mediated by individual difference characteristics such as construction competencies, encoding strategies, outcome expectancies and values, behavioral regulation systems, and planning abilities. Mischel (1973) theorized that children's overt behavior could also modify the nature of the situations they experienced. As a result, children were viewed as active participants in their social environment, with the ability to influence social exchanges and reinforcement contingencies, as well as be influenced by them.

In conjunction with the development of cognitive social learning models, researchers also began stressing the importance of deficient cognitive problem-solving in the development of emotional and behavioral problems in children. These early models suggested that ineffective interpersonal problem solving in daily life could produce a wide variety of social and emotional adjustment difficulties (Jahoda, 1958). Findings from an early problem-solving study suggested that children who received the interpersonal cognitive problem solving (ICPS) intervention showed improvements in alternative, consequential, and causal thinking, as well as behavioral improvements, in comparison to a no-treatment control group (Shure & Spivack, 1980). Consistent with the theoretical underpinnings of the program, children who showed improvements in problem-solving skills were more likely to exhibit sustained behavioral improvements 1 year later. Over the years, Shure (1992) has further developed the program (now called "I Can Problem Solve") for use as either a primary prevention or preventive-intervention program during the preschool and elementary school years.

Inspired by the use of cognitive therapies to treat adult depression (Beck, 1963) and guided by Lev Vygotsky's and Alexander Luria's studies of children's development of internalized self-talk to guide their behavior (Akhutina, 1997), Donald Meichenbaum developed the first cognitive self-guidance treatment program for impulsive children (Meichenbaum & Goodman, 1971). The program taught children to control their own behavior by modeling self-control verbalizations and instructing children on how to engage in private self-speech while performing sustained attention tasks. Findings suggested that impulsive children who underwent this treatment improved their ability to use private self-speech to orient attention and think carefully when making important decisions.

Cognitive-Behavioral Principles A core feature underlying all cognitive-behavioral therapies is the idea that altering dysfunctional or deficient thoughts that accompany or precede problematic emotions or behaviors can be effective in treating various disorders (Graham, 2005). In addition, cognitive-behavioral interventions for children with conduct problems often teach parents how to use the behavioral principles of reinforcement, extinction, and shaping to change their child's behavior (Brestan & Eyberg, 1998). Cognitive-behavioral interventions seek to integrate these behavioral strategies into an overarching treatment approach that emphasizes the influence of both cognitive factors and behavioral contingencies in the development of problematic emotions and behaviors.

Perhaps the most influential and comprehensive social information processing (SIP) model relevant for cognitive-behavioral interventions with children and adolescents was developed by Dodge (1993; Crick & Dodge, 1994). The model explicitly describes the "online" cognitive processes steps that occur when children are engaged in social interactions and social problem solving. In the most recent version of this model, a series of six sequential steps are outlined: (1) encoding of external and internal cues, (2) interpretation of these cues, (3) determining goals or desired outcomes for the situation, (4) generating possible responses, (5) evaluating and selecting a response, and (6) enacting and evaluating the chosen response. Social adjustment problems in youth are believed to arise due to difficulties at one or more of these information processing steps. CBT programs thus include elements to help children more accurately perceive their social world and other elements that assist the generation of competent solutions to their social problems and their consideration of consequences of behaviors as they make decision to act. Children who have different types of problems (e.g., conduct problems versus depression) and different variations of the phenotype behavioral problem (e.g., reactive aggression versus proactive aggression) have been found to have deficiencies and distortions at certain processing steps but not at others. As a result, CBT interventions can be targeted at the specific areas of a child's cognitive dysfunctions.

CBT also addresses how children's acquired social schemas filter and guide their information processing. Preexisting schemas, such as a belief that others are typically controlling and dangerous, can narrow children's attention to specific facets of their social environment and reduce their attention to other interpersonal cues. As a result, children can be hypervigilant to signs of threat and can make erroneous interpretations of others' behavior and intentions (thus influencing their processing at steps 1 and 2 in the SIP model). Strongly held schemas usually operate outside of children's conscious awareness and lead to automatic, emotion-laden responses. Thus, CBT interventions often distinguish between children's automatic versus deliberate cognitive processing, and assist children to make the more competent strategies hidden deeply in their memory bins to become more salient and more likely to be accessed when responding automatically to threats in the future. In addition, a central feature of many CBT interventions are emotion awareness and emotion regulation components that help the child to better manage the surges of emotion (e.g., anger, anxiety) that they experience.

Cognitive-behavioral therapies with youth often make distinctions between cognitive distortions and cognitive skills deficits when treating social information processing problems. Cognitive distortions are self-defeating interpretations of people or events that do not accurately represent reality (Daleiden & Vasey, 1997). These thinking errors are believed to help maintain negative emotions and often result in dysfunctional social interactions and poor social problem solving. A common cognitive distortion is an overgeneralization, in which an individual assumes that a specific negative event is part of a continual or pervasive pattern. For example, a depressed child may think "All people I care about will leave me" when a friend moves out of town, or an aggressive child my think "Everyone is out to get me" after being ridiculed by a single peer. Within the context of cognitive-behavioral therapies, children and adolescents are often taught to recognize and refute these distortions, which is a process commonly referred to as *cognitive restructuring*. Replacing these distorted cognitions with more realistic and adaptive thinking patterns is designed to reduce negative emotional reactions to aversive social events and promote more competent social problem solving. In other instances, the child may have a deficiency in cognitive skills, as evident when they have an impoverished menu of possible solutions to the social problems they face, or when they do not understand the consequences for their behavior. Cognitive-behavioral therapy with a child or adolescent exhibiting social cognitive deficits focuses primarily on social problem-solving training.

Use with Conduct Problems One of the largest applications of cognitive-behavioral therapy to child and adolescent psychopathology has focused on the treatment of conduct problems (e.g., aggression, defiance, oppositional behaviors, rule breaking). Although cognitive-behavioral therapies for conduct problems differ based on the developmental level of the target population (e.g., preschool children vs. adolescents) and the severity of the behavior problems being targeted (e.g., treatment for conduct disorder vs. preventive-intervention for minor aggressive behavior), common elements pervade most empirically supported cognitive-behavioral approaches (Lochman & Pardini, 2008).

Anger management sessions involve assisting children in recognizing the level of arousal and anger they experience in difficult interpersonal situations and identifying the triggers that lead to these high-arousal reactions. Perspective-taking sessions are commonly used to help participants understand how others can have a range of intentions in a given situation that are often unclear. This is done in an attempt to prevent children from assuming that other people are always trying to be cruel or mean in conflict situations, which often triggers increased anger. Children often practice using coping self-instructions and distraction techniques within the group, sometimes while being teased directly by other group members or by using puppets.

Cognitive-behavioral interventions for conduct problems also focus on teaching youth appropriate social problem solving strategies and social skills. These skills are often taught through a combination of verbal instructions, modeling, and in-session role-plays. The in-session role-plays frequently focus on dealing with interpersonal conflicts experienced by youth (e.g., being teased by a peer), as well as other social situations that are difficult for youth with conduct problems, such as making new friends. As therapy progresses, children are often given homework assignments in which they are asked to apply their newly learned problem-solving and social skills to real-life interpersonal situations of increasing complexity.

Research on cognitive-behavioral programs for conduct problem youth typically involves a behavioral parent training component in addition to CBT for the youth. Reviews indicate that a vast majority of the empirically supported treatments for conduct problems in youth are based upon a cognitive-behavioral theoretical framework (Brestan & Eyberg, 1998; Eyberg, Nelson, & Boggs, 2008; Farmer, Compton, Burns, & Robertson, 2002; Nock, 2003). Meta-analytic studies suggest that the effect size (ES) for cognitive-behavioral interventions targeting conduct problems ranges from medium to large, from 0.47 to 0.90 (for review, see Nock, 2003). Research suggests that cognitive-behavioral interventions that include a child component focusing on social problem-solving and social skills development together with a parent management training component produce broader positive effects and better maintenance of behavioral improvements over time than interventions with either component in isolation (Kazdin, Siegel, & Bass, 1992; Nock, 2003; Webster-Stratton & Hammond, 1997). However, the parenting component of these interventions has been shown to produce particularly robust reductions in conduct problems and delinquent behaviors (Beauchaine, Webster-Stratton, & Reid, 2005; Lochman & Wells, 2004).

An example of a CBT program for preschool children is the Incredible Years program, which consists of a parent and child intervention designed for children ages 4 to 7 who have conduct problems significant enough to warrant a diagnosis of either oppositional defiant disorder or conduct disorder (Webster-Stratton, Reid, & Hammond, 2004). Research findings regarding the effectiveness of the child and parent training interventions alone and in combination are impressive. The Incredible Years child intervention has been shown to produce significant reductions in the amount of conduct problems children exhibit at home and at school, as well as increases in social problem-solving skills in comparison to waitlist control conditions (Webster-Stratton & Hammond, 1997; Webster-Stratton, Reid, & Hammond, 2004). There is also evidence indicating that at 1-year follow-up, approximately two-thirds of children who participated in the intervention have parent ratings of behavioral problems in the normal, rather than clinically significant, range (Webster-Stratton & Hammond, 1997).

The Coping Power program is an example of a CBT program for preadolescent aggressive children, and its effectiveness in comparison to no treatment has also been demonstrated in several studies. For example, aggressive boys randomly assigned to an early version of the program (i.e., Anger Coping) displayed less parent-reported aggressive behaviors, fewer observed behavior problems in the classroom, and higher levels of self-esteem at posttreatment, in comparison to aggressive boys who did not receive treatment (Lochman, Burch, Curry, & Lampron, 1984). At a 3-year follow-up, the intervention boys exhibited lower substance use involvement and increased self-esteem and social problem-solving skills in comparison to controls (Lochman, 1992).

Aggressive children who have participated in the expanded Coping Power Program, which includes a parent component as well as a child component, have been shown to exhibit posttreatment reductions in self-reported substance use and proactive aggression, as well as improved social competence and teacher-rated behavioral improvements, in comparison to nontreated controls (Lochman & Wells, 2002b). One-year follow-up studies in two separate samples have found that Coping Power led to lower levels of delinquency, lower levels of substance use, and lower rates of behavioral problems at school, in comparison to nontreated controls (Lochman & Wells, 2003, 2004). The longer term intervention follow-up effects were found to be mediated by intervention-related improvements in hostile attributions, expectations that aggression will result in positive outcomes, and an external locus of control regarding positive outcomes (Lochman & Wells, 2002a).

Longer term effects on substance use have been evident in a 4-year follow-up of a randomized control study of oppositional defiant disorder and conduct disorder children treated with a Dutch version of Coping Power (Zonnevylle-Bender, Matthys, van de Wiel, & Lochman, 2007). Dissemination research has found that the Coping Power program can be successfully implemented by real-world counselors in school settings, and that when the counselors receive intensive training, they can produce significant reductions in children's externalizing behavior, as reported by teachers, parents, and children (Lochman, Boxmeyer, Powell, Qu, Wells, and Windle, 2009).

Use with Depression Depressed youth have certain common social-cognitive characteristics. Depressed youth display both cognitive distortions and cognitive deficits, evident in their core symptoms of feelings of worthlessness, associated negative beliefs about themselves and their future, attributions of failures, and having an external locus of control (Gladstone & Kaslow, 1995). Depressed children's distorted schemas and internal working models have been found to be linked to insecure attachment to parent figures (Stark, Sander, et al., 2006). In addition to these problems in their habits of thoughts, they often have evident problems in their low rates of social acceptance and high rates of isolation from their peers, caused by poor social skills and poor problem-solving skills.

Common treatment components across different CBT programs include the following:

1. Self-control skills, self consequation (reinforcing themselves more, punishing themselves less), self-monitoring (paying attention to positive things they do), self-evaluation (setting less perfectionist standards for their performance), and assertiveness training
2. Social skills, including methods of initiating interactions, maintaining interactions, handling conflict, and using relaxation and imagery
3. Cognitive restructuring, involving confronting children about the lack of evidence for their distorted perceptions (Stark, Hargrave, et al., 2006)

Meta-analytic reviews indicate that children and adolescents benefit from CBT interventions regardless of severity of depressive symptoms, and that adolescents have larger effect-size improvements from CBT intervention than do children (Stark, Hargrave, et al., 2006). Overall, CBT interventions have had similar effects for mildly to severely depressed adolescents in these reviews, but recent research has suggested that the beneficial effects of CBT may be most apparent with mild to moderate depression in youth (Melvin et al., 2006). Treated youths' reductions in depressive symptoms are maintained over time, and effect sizes at the end of treatment are in the moderate-to-large range across studies (Reinecke, Ryan, & DuBois, 1998).

As an example of CBT with depression, Weersing and Brent (2003) describe the results from a series of CBT studies conducted at the Western Psychiatric Institute Mood and Anxiety Disorders Clinic. In the 1997 clinical trial (Brent et al., 1997), 107 youths were screened for major depressive disorder and were randomly assigned to CBT, to systemic behavioral family therapy (SBFT), or to nonspecific therapy (NST). At posttreatment, CBT had significantly higher rates of youth being diagnosis-free (CBT 83%, SBFT 38%, NST 39%), but these treatment group differences had basically disappeared by the time of a 2-year follow-up (Birmaher et al., 2000).

In the large, multisite Treatment for Adolescents with Depression Study (TADS; March et al., 2004) 351 adolescents who had received primary diagnoses of moderate to severe major depressive disorder were randomly assigned to fluoxetine, CBT, the combination of fluoxetine and CBT, or placebo. CBT was found to be useful in accompaniment to medication, as the combination intervention produced the greatest reductions in symptoms. CBT was also found to produce greater reduction in the likelihood of suicidal ideation and behavior in comparison to the fluoxetine alone. However, CBT alone was less effective than fluoxetine alone in reducing depression symptoms among these adolescents with major depressive disorder. The findings of the lack of intervention effects for CBT alone in TADS may have been due to the use of a less intensive version of CBT than had been used in earlier research.

Use with Anxiety Cognitive-behavioral treatments for anxiety disorders integrate cognitive and behavioral perspectives on the origin and maintenance of anxiety symptoms (Stark, Sander, et al., 2006). There is a focus on the child's internal and external environments, addressing behavioral, cognitive, affective, and social factors. Children with anxiety disorders have been found to have certain information processing and emotional experiencing styles.

The goal of typical CBT programs is not to alleviate anxiety entirely, but to assist the child in learning skills to better manage or cope with anxiety in the future. The following are three of the primary treatment targets commonly addressed:

1. To identify physiological cues related to anxiety and to use relaxation skills to manage this arousal, because anxiety is associated with manifest physiological arousal
2. To identify automatic thoughts and to learn countervailing coping thoughts, because children have cognitive distortions that lead them to

overestimate the chance of negative events occurring and the impact of those events

3. To be exposed to the feared situations as the child learns and actively practices problem-solving skills (Kendall & Suveg, 2008)

Reviews of empirically supported treatments for children with anxiety disorders conclude that behavioral and cognitive-behavioral procedures have more empirical support than do other approaches (Chorpita & Southam-Gerow, 2006; Kazdin & Weisz, 1998). Behavioral techniques (including imaginal and in vivo desensitization) are especially effective for phobias, and cognitive-behavioral procedures have been determined to be well established and probably effective for other anxiety disorders (Kendall & Suveg, 2008).

A well-supported program, the Coping Cat program, has been evaluated in a programmatic series of studies, beginning with Kendall's (1994) study of forty-seven 9- to 13-year-old youths who had been diagnosed as separation anxiety disorder, overanxious disorder, or avoidant disorder. At posttreatment, 64% of those who had received Coping Cat no longer met the diagnostic criteria for one of these disorders, in comparison to a 5% diagnosis-free rate for wait-list controls, and these gains were maintained at a 1-year follow-up. A longer term follow-up of this sample, at a point over 3 years after the end of intervention, indicated that these intervention gains were long-lasting (Kendall & Southam-Gerow, 1996). Similar positive findings were obtained in a second sample (Kendall et al., 1997). In an effort to compare to different forms for delivering the intervention, Flannery-Schroeder and Kendall (2000) randomly assigned thirty-seven 8- to 14-year-old children to group CBT, to individually delivered CBT, or to a wait-list control. At postintervention, both intervention conditions demonstrated significant improvement, but the rate of improvement was stronger in children who had been seen individually (73% diagnosis-free in individual CBT, 50% in group CBT, and 8% in the control condition).

FAMILY THERAPY

Family therapists tend to identify with distinct theoretical models (structural, strategic, Milan systemic, narrative), but in practice, family therapists often integrate ideas from different approaches to address the range of disorders that they face (Eisler & Lask, 2008). Family therapists also generally find it useful to have at least some separate sessions with the child or the parents to assist individuals who are otherwise invisible in family sessions or who have information that will not be readily discussed with all participants present. Thus the boundary lines between different forms of family therapy are often indistinct, and the defining feature of family therapy—working with the whole family—has been dealt with more flexibly over time.

The nature of the models underlying family therapy has also changed over time. Although early family therapy models were based on the assumption that specific dysfunctional family interaction patterns would cause certain disorders in children, the family therapy field has become more nuanced over the years. Few family therapists today believe in a direct, unidirectional causal role for family interactions on child behavior (Eisler & Lask, 2008). Instead, there is emphasis on the reciprocity of influence between parents and children (Scaramella & Leve, 2004), and on the findings that the same family environment can have differential effects on various children in a family (Rutter, Silberg, O'Connor, & Simonoff, 1999) because of complex interactions between the child's temperament and genetic characteristics and the family environment (Rutter, 1999).

The forms of family therapy have been categorized into those that focus on how family interactions and structures maintain problems of family members (e.g., structural family therapy), those that focus on how change can be stimulated in families regardless of the original source of the problems (e.g., strategic therapies, the Milan approach), and those that focus on how new perceptions, hidden meanings, and unexplored stories can emerge in family sessions, with resulting emphasis on beliefs and narratives rather than behaviors (narrative therapies; Eisler & Lask, 2008). These forms of family therapy are briefly overviewed here.

Structural Family Therapy Structural family therapy was originally developed to work with low-income families of delinquent boys and later was applied to anorexia nervosa and other psychosomatic problems (Minuchin, Montalvo, Guerney, Rosman, & Schumer, 1967; Minuchin, Rosman, & Baker, 1978). Problems of children and adolescents in the families were perceived to be part of self-perpetuating dysfunctional family structures. Intervention was focused on transactions between family members within the session to change these family structures. Emphases were placed on strengthening the parental subsystem, by framing and encouraging the parents to work together to assume a role of being in charge of the children, and on making clearer, yet often flexible, boundaries between family members, sometimes by de-triangulating specific family members (Eisler & Lask, 2008).

Although structural approaches have been used in families with children who have a variety of disorders, the best-designed studies with clearest outcomes have been in the areas of eating disorders. Randomized controlled trials have found that structural family therapy has produced significant improvement in youth with anorexia nervosa in hospital settings (e.g., Russell, Szmukler, Dare, & Eisler, 1987) and outpatient settings (Eisler, Dare, Hodes, Russell, Dodge & Le Grange, 2000), and these effects have been maintained at 5-year follow-ups (Eisler, Simic, Russell, & Dare, 2007). Although more recent versions of structural therapy have been adapted in various ways, they retain a focus on empowering parents to assist the child to address the eating problems (Rhodes, Gosbee, Madden, & Brown, 2005).

Strategic Therapies Although the actual practice of strategic therapies (e.g., Haley, 1990) overlaps in many ways with structural and behavioral approaches to family therapy, the defining features of strategic therapy are not on the type of outcome to be achieved but on identifying family interactions that interfere with change and on identifying how change can be induced in the family. There is a focus on identifying the level of motivation to change existing in family members, and, depending on family members' motivational levels (e.g., ready for change, don't see a problem, see a problem but not sure about wanting to change), different strategies are used to alter interactions between family members. These motivational blockages are assumed to be relatively idiosyncratic to each family, and there is no presumption that family structure will need to change in similar ways across families (Eisler & Lask, 2008). The Milan approach to family therapy extended the strategic family therapy model, and was centered around a method of family interviewing in which co-therapists and the family were observed by a team behind a one-way mirror. In the middle of the sessions, the co-therapists met with the team to create hypotheses to explore with the family and to devise in-session interventions to "perturb" the paradoxical bind that was paralyzing the family (Bertrando & Arcelloni, 2006; Palazzoli, Boscolo, Cecchin, & Prata, 1980).

In general, these strategic therapies have not been evaluated in rigorous research. An exception is the brief form of strategic therapy developed by Szapocznik and Kurtines (1989) for use with substance abusing adolescents. This variant of strategic family therapy has been found to be effective in randomized control trials (Szapocznik & Williams, 2000), and has been demonstrated to be particularly effective in engaging resistant families (e.g., Coatsworth, Santisteban, McBridge, & Szapocznik, 2001.

Narrative Therapies Narrative therapy is a form of family therapy that has a clear overlap with cognitive therapies and has evolved from the Milan approach assumption that beliefs shape behavior. Narrative therapies are based on the assumption that children's problems are at least partially the result of how their experiences are filtered through the narratives that people develop about themselves (Parry & Doane, 1994). The family therapist emphasizes new perceptions of events and hidden meanings of behaviors and processes. Although not extensively evaluated, preliminary investigations found that childhood stealing decreased in most cases when families received this treatment (Seymour & Epston, 1989). More rigorously controlled studies have found that narrative therapy had equivalently high remission rates for depressive diagnoses in comparison to brief psychodynamic therapy (Trowell et al., 2007).

Multidimensional Family Therapies In recent years, family therapy has often been delivered as part of a multidimensional intervention program that frequently has included behavioral and cognitive elements. One example is functional family therapy (Alexander & Parsons, 1982), which combines behavioral, structural, and strategic approaches, and conceptualizes problem behaviors as taking on functional roles within families. Therapy works to reinforce the use of appropriate behaviors that can serve the same function within the family.

Another prominent example of this blended type of therapy is multisystemic therapy (MST; Henggeler, 1999), which includes a careful assessment of the delinquent behavior problems of the adolescent, and the contextual factors that serve to maintain the behavior. Integrating evidence-based intervention strategies from several orientations, MST has had replicated effectiveness in reducing adolescent delinquent behaviors. Other research-based multidimensional family approaches include using multidimensional family therapy for substance-abusing adolescents and their families (Liddle & Hogue, 2001) and multidimensional foster care for conduct problem children in foster care settings (Chamberlain, 2003).

Programs for Infants Based on Attachment Theory A newer and specific variant of family intervention involves programs that include parents and infants together. Parents and infants typically interact, and the therapist then goes over video replays of the interactions with the parents, reinforcing instances of sensitive responding by the parent to specific behaviors of the infant (Velderman, Bakermans-Kranenburg, Juffer, van Ijzendoorn, Mangelsdorf, & Zevalkink, 2006). It is assumed that when the parents can appropriately and positively respond to the infant's signs of distress and playful behaviors, then they can provide a secure attachment base for the infant (Scott, 2008). Some of these programs have been developed around specific problems. Dozier, Lindheim, and Ackerman (2005) developed and evaluated a 10-session program to work with birth parents and foster parents when child abuse has occurred. A meta-analysis has found that these attachment-based programs have enhanced parental sensitivity and attachment security, although there were clear differences in the effectiveness of the various programs reviewed with stronger effects for focused, briefer programs (Bakermans-Kranenburg, van Ijzendoorn, & Juffer, 2005.

Culturally Relevant Interventions

As will be described in Chapter 9, it is essential that therapists attend to the cultural diversity of their clients during their delivery of interventions. Through supervision and multicultural training, therapists should learn to sensitively assess for cultural issues that can affect the children's course of disorder and their and their families' responses to intervention.

Some of the programs reviewed earlier have examined whether ethnicity served as a moderator of intervention effects. For example, Lochman and Wells (2003, 2004) conducted intervention research with two samples that included African-American and Caucasian children, and they did not find that ethnicity served as a moderator of intervention effects on children's aggression or delinquency. Hence, it would appear that this cognitive-behavioral intervention can be used effectively with African-American as well as White children. However, because Hispanic children were not included in these original samples, it was not initially clear whether the same positive intervention effects would be evident with Hispanic children. Subsequent research found that a translated and adapted form of this cognitive-behavioral intervention could usefully reduce disruptive behaviors of Puerto Rican children (Cabiya, Padilla-Cotto, Gonzalez, Sanchez-Cestero, Martinez-Taboas & Sayers, 2008), indicating that the intervention approach could be even more broadly applied. Thus, when therapists review the evidence base for a particular intervention approach or program they plan to use, they should especially note whether its effectiveness has been demonstrated with children and families who represent the ethnicity of the client.

Relatively few evidence-based interventions have been developed and tested specially for children and families of specific ethnic groups. However, when such programs do exist, they should be carefully considered by the therapist. For example, the brief strategic family therapy approach described earlier in this chapter was originally developed for use with Hispanic youth, and recognizes the influence of cultural factors in the development and maintenance of behavior problems. This program has been found to effectively increase family functioning and reduce adolescents' substance use and delinquency rates in controlled trials (Robbins, Szapocznik, Santisteban, Hervis, Mitrani & Schwartz, 2003). Malgady and Costantino (2003) described another culturally based approach to working with Hispanic children, and it involves providing narrative therapy through Hispanic parables, historical figures, and family videos to Hispanic children and adolescents. This set of narrative programs has produced reductions in adolescents' conduct disorder symptoms. Several research-based programs have also been specifically developed with African-American children, including attribution retraining (Hudley & Graham, 1993) and anger management (Hammond & Yung, 1991) approaches. It will be important for future intervention development to proactively address the cultural appropriateness of interventions.

Intervention Level and Contexts

It is important to recall that treatment of children with identified diagnoses is only part of a continuum of intervention work that extends into professional prevention and consultation activities. Prevention has been conceptualized as having three levels:

1. Universal (an intervention delivered to all children)
2. Selective (intervention delivered to group of children who are at risk because of contextual factors, such as experiencing a recent divorce in the family)
3. Indicated (intervention delivered to children who are at risk because they are already displaying behaviors that are precursors for later diagnosed psychopathology) (Institute of Medicine, 1994; Vitaro & Tremblay, 2008)

The latter two forms of preventive interventions (often identified as targeted interventions) can often be constructed in similar ways to treatment programs, and can be based on similar conceptual models of the active mechanisms that contribute to problem development. Thus, it is not surprising to see that there are some programs that have been shown to be effective both for prevention and for treatment (e.g., Lochman, Wells, &

Lenhart, 2008). In another example of the clear linkage between treatment and prevention, treatment of a given childhood problem (e.g., overt aggressive behavior in children with ODD or CD diagnoses) might lead to the prevention of a later associated problem (e.g., marijuana use) that would have existed on that child's developmental pathway (Zonnevyille-Bender, Matthys, van de Wiel, & Lochman, 2007).

It is also important to note that psychological interventions for children and adolescents do not always involve formal treatment sessions in outpatient or inpatient mental health settings. Prevention, and treatment itself, can take place in a variety of settings, including schools, hospitals, and the community.

INTERVENTION IN SCHOOLS

With regard to treatment and targeted prevention of identified and diagnosed childhood disorders, school-based mental health services are offered in many communities. Rather than seeing the child for treatment in the psychologist's own office, he or she sees the child for treatment within the school setting. School-based treatment has the advantages of permitting the therapist to consult closely with the school staff (which is important because of the large number of hours the child spends each day in the school setting), to more closely observe the child's peer problems, and to increase the child's likelihood of attendance for therapy sessions (an important issue in cases in which the parent is ambivalent about getting to the clinic for sessions). Primary practical problems inherent in this form of professional work are that it can be difficult to get school approval to provide services on their grounds, and arrangements with third-party payments for services may be more complicated to arrange.

A school base for services also permits the psychologist to plan, develop, and implement universal prevention programs that can attempt to improve the mental health function of all children in a classroom or in a school. Delivery of universal prevention programs often involves training teachers and school counselors to implement the program. An example of a classroom-based universal prevention program is the Good Behavior Game (Barrish, Saunders, & Wolf, 1969). The program focuses on increasing children's acceptance of authority and rules within the school classroom, and is based on operant conditioning. Children in the classroom are divided into teams and a scoreboard is kept to indicate which teams have accrued the fewest "fouls" (i.e., a foul is a rule that is broken). Rewards are given to the team with the fewest fouls, and smaller rewards are given to teams that earned a number of fouls but below an established threshold

(Embry, 2002). In several studies, the Good Behavior Game led to the reduction of aggressive behavior, poor achievement, and shy behaviors, and these results have been evident at follow-up points for the initially most problematic children (Embry, 2002; Ialongo et al., 1999).

The Promoting Alternative Thinking Strategies (PATHS) program is another example of a universal prevention program that seeks to promote general social-emotional competencies and cognitive skill-building in elementary school children (Greenberg & Kusché, 2006). Teachers are trained to use the PATHS curriculum to instruct children in emotion awareness, emotional regulation, and social problem-solving skills (Kusché & Greenberg, 1994). Results at 1- and 2-year follow-ups have indicated that children receiving the PATHS intervention were better at understanding emotions, better at problem solving, and had reported decreases in conduct problems and impulsivity compared to children in a control group (Greenberg & Kusché, 2006).

INTERVENTION IN PEDIATRIC SETTINGS

The psychologist in pediatric settings can be confronted with a range of treatment issues, including working with children whose psychological disorder leads to a medical condition, with children who have psychological sequelae of the medical illnesses or treatments, and with children who are adjusting to chronic or life-threatening illnesses (Abrams & Rauch, 2008). Survival rates for many childhood illnesses have improved in recent years because of medical advances, and that has led to increased interest in the psychological adjustment and quality of life for children with chronic illnesses. Research has identified a variety of factors related to this psychosocial adjustment process, and has resulted in transactional stress and coping models of children's adaptation to medical illness (Thompson & Gustafson, 1996). These models address not only the child's coping processes, but also the impact of pediatric illness on the entire family (Labay & Walco, 2004). Treatment approaches, using cognitive-behavioral and family systems approaches, have been used to address psychological distress in the child and the family who are faced with chronic illnesses such as asthma, diabetes, and cancer (Abrams & Rauch, 2008).

One example of a childhood condition that may require psychological intervention is sickle cell disease (Hocking & Lochman, 2005). Children with sickle cell disease exhibit more depressive symptoms and internalizing behaviors than nondiseased siblings (Brown et al., 1993), and adjustment difficulties have been found to be higher for boys than girls and to increase as children move into adolescence (Hurtig, Koepke, & Park, 1989;

Hurtig & White, 1986). Intervention can target adjustment problems (Hocking & Lochman, 2005), such as children's self-esteem, attributional style, and appraisal of stress and mood (e.g., Gil, Carson, et al., 2003; Thompson, Gustafson, Gil, Godfrey, & Bennet Murphy, 1998). Among the few controlled intervention studies in this area, Gil, Wilson, Edens, Workman, Ready, and Sedway (1997) found that sickle cell children taught to use coping skills (such as calming statements, pleasant imagery, and relaxation skills) had reductions in negative thinking, health care contacts, and school absences, and increases in active coping attempts and physical activity, in comparison to those in the untreated control condition.

Although a psychologist working with children who have conditions like sickle cell will likely focus primarily on how they cope with the disease and its effects, one who works with children with a disease like insulin-dependent diabetes mellitus (IDDM) will also address children's treatment adherence and metabolic control (Hocking & Lochman, 2005). Unlike most childhood chronic illnesses, IDDM requires the child and the family to shoulder much of the management of the disease (Daviss, Coon, Whitehead, Ryan, Burkley, & McMahon, 1995). The child must actively manage blood glucose levels by maintaining a structured diet, exercising at expected levels, and checking glucose levels in school and community settings. Parents must also be involved in these activities (Hocking & Lochman, 2005). Children who have poor adjustment to IDDM can display low motivation and ability to comply with their treatment regimen, and as a result of poor treatment adherence can have poor metabolic control. Intervention with IDDM children should address their feelings of control over events, their feelings of efficacy, their coping methods, and their appraisal of their disease (Edgar & Skinner, 2003; Skinner & Hampson, 2001; Weist, Finney, Barnard, Davis, & Ollendick, 1993). Controlled and uncontrolled intervention studies have found that cognitive-behavioral therapy focusing on social problem-solving and cognitive restructuring have led IDDM youth to have better metabolic control and higher feelings of self-efficacy over their diabetes (Grey, Boland, Davidson, Li, & Tamborlane, 2000; Silverman, Hains, Davies, & Parton, 2003).

INTERVENTIONS IN THE COMMUNITY

Community-based interventions and services are those that are implemented and operated by service professionals in the community (Groark & McCall, 2008), and are often preventive in nature. Psychologists can be involved in the planning, training, evaluation, and overall administration of the community service programs that can be delivered in community recreation centers, neighborhood library branches, local houses of worship, day care centers, or in homes.

An increasingly widely disseminated home visitation program is the Nurse-Family Partnership (NFP), which is directed at low-income, higher risk mothers who are pregnant with their first child (Olds, Henderson, Kitzman, Eckenrode, Cote, & Tatelbaum, 1999). Nurses visit homes during the mother's pregnancy and continue visiting until the child is 2 years old, aiming to reduce maternal adverse behaviors such as smoking, alcohol use, and drug use. In a series of controlled intervention studies, NFP increased the rate of maternal employment, maternal life skills, and improved parenting; the program reduced parental abuse, and the children had improved health, socioemotional, language, and cognitive development and reduced levels of adolescent behavioral problems. However, these positive findings were evident only for subsets of the mothers who were at highest risk (single parenthood, being a smoker, very low income or education).

Another example of a community-based program is one that focuses on early child development. Early Head Start (EHS) provides health care, child care, and family support to low-income families who have children in the birth-to-age-3 period, and services are provided in centers or in homes. At 3 years of age, EHS intervention children had higher levels of cognitive, language, and socioemotional abilities that did comparison children randomly assigned to other community programs. Benefits were greatest for African-American families, families who began the program while the mother was pregnant (instead of after the child was born), and families with moderate levels of risk factors (Administration for Children and Families, 2002). Children who had the EHS intervention had better reading-related skills at age 5, especially if they had transitioned into formal early care and education programs.

Summary

Following collaborative establishment of a treatment plan, a clinical child and adolescent psychologist will consider a range of evidence-based intervention practices and programs designed to address the risk mechanisms that underlie the child's behavioral or emotional psychopathology. This chapter provided a brief overview of prominent intervention approaches, including behavioral therapy, cognitive-behavioral therapy, and family therapy, and the principles serving as a framework for these approaches. This chapter then presented examples of evidence-based programs within these intervention orientations that could then be used with children with internalizing and disruptive behavior disorders. When matching an intervention approach to the specific risk mechanisms that a child and her or his family display, it is essential to consider cultural factors that could affect intervention outcomes. Finally, it is useful to consider that treatment and prevention interventions often operate on a continuum, and that clinical child and adolescent psychologists implement interventions in a variety of settings besides outpatient and inpatient mental health offices, including in school, pediatric, and community settings.

PART IV

Other Functional Competencies

SIX

Consultation in Clinical Child and Adolescent Psychology

Whereas many clinical child and adolescent psychologists provide assessment and therapy directly to children and families, often the specialist works collaboratively with others to deliver the necessary services through consultation. This may take several forms, such as having another professional (physician, nurse, social worker, teacher) conduct an intervention under advice and supervision from the psychologist, providing information about symptoms and screening for behavior problems and how to make a referral, advising juvenile care or detention workers about management techniques, or serving on a collaborative team by offering psychological insights that help create therapeutic interventions for children with certain conditions (e.g., maltreatment, chronic illness).

Consultation is an important core competency and function for clinical child and adolescent psychologists. This is a broad concept that has existed since the earliest years of the specialized psychological services for children. Consultation in clinical child and adolescent psychology has been extended to multiple settings, problems, and people as a critically important activity for the specialist (Hupp, Jewell, Reitman, & LeBlanc, 2010; Johnson, Janicke, & Reader, 2008). This chapter will outline the key concepts of this competency through formal definitions and models of consultation with examples of professional activities in school and pediatric settings.

Consultation Defined

One of the first mental health professionals to write about this core activity was Gerald Caplan, who defined *consultation* as "a process of interaction between two professionals—the consultant who is a specialist and the consultee, who involves the consultant's help in a current work problem. . . . The work problem involving managing or implementing a program to cater to the clients. . . . [T]he consultee will be free to accept or reject all of or part of this help. . . . [T]he consultant exercises no administrative or coercive authority over the consultee" (Caplan & Caplan, 1993, p. 12).

This historical definition, although informative, is not necessarily binding on current professionals serving as mental health consultants in different settings. Although Caplan and others maintained that the relationship is nonhierarchical and the consultant is *outside* the agency or organization of the consultee (Brown, Pryzwansky, & Schulte, 2006), in practice this external consultant status is not often a requirement for successful consultation. (Note that authority may be present, but this factors into the topic of supervision described in another chapter [see Chapter 7] of this book.) Additionally, the psychological consultation is not always between two professionals at similar levels of training or functioning. The clinical child and adolescent psychologist often offers consultation in an egalitarian stance with consultees at different levels of background who might serve the child or family client best. The following are examples of consultees and reasons for the consultation:

- School paraprofessionals and teachers about behavior problems and classroom management
- Nurses, pediatricians, and psychiatrists about proper diagnosis and treatment
- Parents about child management and adjustment issues
- Child welfare workers about child protection and placement
- Attorneys and judges about custody and care placements
- Detention facility officers about behavior management

Clearly, in practice, implementing consultation may not follow the classical consultation definition.

Bergan and Kratochwill (1990) described a model of behavioral consultation that has several defining characteristics: (a) consultation is problem-solving, (b) consultation provides indirect service, (c) consultation is a collegial relationship, and (d) consultation relies on knowledge utilization. Most writers on consultation also emphasize that there is a triadic relationship in consultation involving the consultant, the consultee, and the client, with each playing roles in the process, and outcomes such that "a consultant usually works with a consultee, who in turn provides services to a client" (Bergan & Kratochwill, 1990, p. 16).

In the case of consultation regarding children, adolescents, and their families, the process focuses on enhancing healthy development with a child or adolescent for mental health and educational improvement that is both preventive and remedial (Bergan & Kratochwill, 1990). Erchul and Martens (2010) articulated the conceptual and empirical bases of practice in consultation in the schools where many psychologists provide services by noting that

> consultation is an indirect model of delivering psychological and/or educational services. Within this model, a specialist (consultant) and staff member (consultee) work together to optimize the function of a client in the staff member's setting and to increase the staff member's capacity to deal with similar situation in the future. In schools, for example, a psychologist may consult with a teacher about a student in the teacher's classroom. . . . Consultation can be a powerful tool for delivering psychological services in schools, but only when the consultant possesses a requisite level of skill and sophistication. (p. vii)

As applied to consultation with physicians (e.g., pediatricians, family medicine physicians) and in medical units (another major setting for the specialist psychologist), Drotar (1995) elaborated the multiple considerations, benefits, and obstacles of this professional activity in pediatric settings, while providing examples to serve as definitional concepts. He and others in pediatric psychology combined the concepts of *consultation* and *collaboration* (e.g., Hamlett & Stabler, 1995; Roberts, 1986; Roberts & Wright, 1982), although other fields value a distinction (e.g., Brown et al., 2006).

Psychological consultation lacks a coherent theoretical approach (Gallessich, 1982); considerably less research has been conducted into applications of consultation models and outcomes than for psychological assessment and psychotherapy approaches. Although not as evidence-based as the field might need, there are a number of models or frameworks available to provide guidance to clinical child and adolescent psychologists who wish to develop and practice this competence skill. For the psychologist in this specialty, consultation occurs in school and pediatric settings; psychiatric and child guidance clinics; juvenile justice agencies; and with teachers, pediatricians and nurses, social workers and psychiatrists, and parents and other caregivers.

General Consultation Models

Caplan (1970) approached consultation from a predominantly psychodynamic orientation, but his models require an egalitarian relationship in which the consultee is free to accept or reject the input of the consultant. His taxonomy of consultation approaches includes (a) client-centered, (b) consultee-centered, (c) program-centered, and (d) consultee-centered/administrative.

CLIENT-CENTERED CONSULTATION

In this model, the consultant focuses on a specific client or patient and performs a psychological assessment and writes a report with treatment recommendations that are presented to the consultee. The consultee then uses the information in treatment planning and implementation as he or she chooses. The consultant is not responsible for the treatment, but is responsible for providing information about diagnostic implications for treatment, taking into consideration as many elements as known about the client and the environment in which treatment may take place (Caplan, 1970). This is a rather traditional view of a psychologist as an examiner who assesses, but does not treat, and was much more prevalent in the years in which Caplan was formulating his conceptualizations on consultation than is occurring today. However, some psychologists providing services in schools might find themselves testing and diagnosing educational problems and developing intervention plans to be implemented by others in the school system.

CONSULTEE-CENTERED CONSULTATION

This form of consultation assumes the focus on improving the functioning of the consultee in performing her or his activities. Although individual clients/patients might be discussed in the context of the consultative discussions, the interaction works to enhance consultee competencies or skills. The consultant attends to how the consultee performs with clients and identifies deficiencies that can be remedied. Caplan (1970) indicated that consultees might lack (a) objectivity, (b) confidence, (c) knowledge, or (d) skill. Each of these becomes a potential issue for specific consultation foci. The goal here is to develop the consultee's eventual ability to function independently from the consultant regarding their provision of mental health services.

PROGRAM-CENTERED CONSULTATION

This is a higher level of consultation that is focused on the system in which mental health services are situated. The consultant attends to the organizational or programmatic needs and offers recommendations related to how, for example, administrative or systemic problems might be resolved. This may require assessment within the unit or program with staff at all levels as well as with administrators to gain a comprehensive understanding of how units function; to determine what obstacles might be present that impede program initiatives; and to develop plans or recommendations for improving performance, overcoming the barriers, and developing the abilities and successful outcomes of the professionals while enhancing the overall health and functioning of the unit.

CONSULTEE-CENTERED/ADMINISTRATIVE CONSULTATION

This form of consultation combines other forms to focus the consultant's attention on the administrator (or administrative personnel) as the consultee(s) to enhance effectiveness in their roles. The consultee may be a clinic director (e.g., at a mental health center), unit chief (e.g., at a child inpatient psychiatric facility or outpatient pediatric clinic), or school administrator (e.g., school superintendent or principal). The consultant tries to gain a full understanding of all aspects of the consultee's skills, interactions with subordinates, and the context in which he or she works. The consultant uses this understanding to inform, influence, and enhance the administrator/consultee in her or his capacities and performance of duties.

These general models of mental health consultation are background to what clinical child and adolescent psychologists will do in the typical consultation settings in which they work (i.e., pediatric medicine settings and schools).

Pediatric Consultation Models

> The development of a liaison relationship [between psychology and pediatrics] occurred as pediatricians, by the force of their clinical practice, recognize that the problems they are called upon to treat require more than just medical and physical interventions; there are emotional and psychological aspect of the problems. Concomitantly, psychologists began to discover the varied types of psychopathology related to organic illness and the utility of behavioral interventions for some medical and pediatric entities. (Roberts & Wright, 1982, p. 251)

In describing mental health consultation in pediatric primary care settings, Stancin (2005) articulated important conditions for successful pediatric psychology work depending on collocation (psychologists in physical proximity with medical providers), collaboration ("the practice of providers with separate sets of expertise bringing their work together so as to coordinate treatments between the two," p. 89), and integration ("mental health services are a component of primary care, rather than a specialty service," p. 89). Roberts and Wright (1982) and Roberts (1986) outlined three primary models for consultation in pediatric psychology settings: (a) independent functions consultation, (b) indirect consultation, (c) consultation through a collaborative team. Later writers included a fourth model: (d) systems consultation perspective (Drotar, 1995; Mullins, Gillman, & Harbeck, 1992).

INDEPENDENT FUNCTIONS CONSULTATION

In this pattern of functioning, the clinical child and adolescent/pediatric psychologist performs as a specialist who works fairly independently from the referring physician, much like a cardiologist or radiologist. The psychologist receives a referral for psychological consult, and then conducts assessment as appropriate, develops a diagnosis, and undertakes a psychosocial intervention as indicated. The psychologist and physician exchange information about the case, but they work separately without close collaboration because each takes independent responsibility for the distinctive domains of a patient's treatment. Accordingly, Drotar (1978) called this the "noncollaborative" approach, whereas Stabler (1979) described this as "coordination of multiservices."

This form of consultation likely is the most prevalent interaction between pediatrician and psychologist in that it is similar to how a pediatrician or family medicine practitioner might interact with other specialty professionals. The physician makes a referral for a psychological evaluation or treatment but continues to see the patient and family for medical interventions. The specialty psychologist then works with the child or family and does what is indicated from evidence-based practice in psychology. The key in this interaction is diplomatic communication both about what the psychologist is doing with the patient and how they are progressing, and also about things the physician could do in his or her work with the patient. Often psychologists working with medical personnel need to clarify the reason for the referral initially. Over time, the psychologist will continually provide feedback that will help shape the referrals and improve the referral questions to be more appropriate and focused for what a psychologist consultation can provide (Carter & von Weiss, 2005; Drotar, 1995).

Carter and von Weiss (2005) asserted the necessity of setting "mutually agreed upon and achievable" goals for consultation in pediatric settings

(p. 69). They suggested that referrals for psychological consultation with parents or child patients be framed such that psychological consultation-liaison is "a frequently employed and natural mechanism for helping all parties better understand the patient's or family's problems and to come up with a solution in which all members can play a role, and that will facilitate patient or family functioning in the midst of medical stressors" (p. 69). This may help the family accept psychological assistance and avoid resistance to involvement of the consultant.

The psychologist may need to provide information from the medical and/or psychological literature that helps the pediatrician or family practitioner understand psychological development and children's functioning as well as what interventions are most effective under the circumstances. Communication via reports, letters, and phone calls are important so that patients are not removed from responsibility and reciprocal decision making with the physician. Rarely would in-person contacts be utilized in this consultation model due to the busy nature of practice, and often the psychologist's office would likely be physically in a different place than the medical practice (Roberts & Wright, 1982), although not always (Schroeder, 2005). A strong working relationship with the physician avoids misunderstanding over "turf" issue of areas of concomitant treatment that are considered medical domains. Professionals work optimally to benefit patients with mutual respect for respective expertise.

INDIRECT CONSULTATION

In this model, the pediatrician or family practitioner retains the responsibility for patient care while the psychologist works through the physician and staff to provide psychological services. The psychologist may not have direct contact with the patient or family. This model requires more supervision/collaboration than the independent functions model because psychological concepts and actions are performed by others with training and input from the consulting psychologist. This type of consultation may first occur in medical centers with training of residents wherein the psychologist is teaching. This model requires some educating and supervising of the trainee about psychosocial and mental health issues and activities that are often required in pediatric and family medicine practice. The indirect consultation model has also been described as "process-educative" by Stabler (1979).

As noted by Roberts and Wright (1982), the indirect consultation model may come about when the physician requests brief contact for specific information. When psychologists and physicians are situated in the same clinic, the request may happen in "curbside" interactions for specific problems or questions arising with a particular patient in the clinic at the time. A pediatrician may, for example, ask for information about the appropriateness of a diagnosis or treatment intervention given a developmental or family situation (e.g., anxiety or social skills training, availability of community resources for children with a disability, interpretation of test scores from school assessment relative to a diagnosis of ADHD, or appropriateness of referral for more comprehensive psychoeducational evaluation).

The specialty psychologist may also indirectly consult and affect the psychosocial assessment and treatment of children through presentation of psychological evidence-based practice through pediatric section grand rounds, workshops and seminars, or other continuing education activities. The psychologist may or may not discuss particulars of presenting cases, but offers more general educational information that may be applicable to a range of cases. For example, the specialist may present on diagnosis and treatment of children exhibiting stomach pain or on techniques to enhance adherence to medical regimens. The physicians would then utilize that information in their practice, sometimes consulting with the psychologist over proper implementation and problems arising.

Indirect consultation may also take place when the physician carries out psychosocial interventions (not psychotherapy per se) as recommended by the psychologist. Standardized protocols may be developed for screening or dealing with the psychological concomitants of chronic illness or for using behavioral interventions for medical and behavior problems (Christophersen, 1994). Treatment of enuresis or encopresis, for example, may be treated in this way with indirect psychological involvement through consultation with the pediatrician or family practitioner or their clinic staff (Friman, 2008).

CONSULTATION THROUGH A COLLABORATIVE TEAM

The clinical child and adolescent /pediatric psychologist may work collaboratively with physicians and other professionals through identified teams. These teams may include, in addition to the physicians and psychologists, social workers, nurses, nurse practitioners, education specialists, respiratory therapists, audiologists, speech pathologists, child life specialists, and occupational and physical therapists, depending on the types of disorders and conditions being served. All team professionals function in a relatively coequal status, and each contributes expertise relative to his or her competency areas. Over time, roles may become less distinctive as cooperative service-provision is made repeatedly. Stabler (1979) identified this as "process consultation."

These interprofessional and multidisciplinary teams are often created to deal with common issues or pediatric disorders (e.g., gastrointestinal disorders, burns, organ transplants, renal disease, orthopedic problems, hematology/oncology issues, endocrine disorders and diabetes, asthma, leukemia and cancer, cystic fibrosis) that present in a hospital (including pediatric intensive care and neonatal intensive care units) or outpatient clinic. Not uncommonly, interdisciplinary teams might consider all child maltreatment cases identified in a children's hospital (see Kees & Bonner, 2005) or evaluations and treatment planning for developmental disabilities (Campbell, Herzinger, & James, 2008).

The pediatric and clinical child and adolescent psychologist may function within a unit in a children's hospital devoted to both inpatient and outpatient responsibilities (Carter & von Weiss, 2005; Stancin, Perrin, & Ramirez, 2009), or an outpatient clinic for pediatric and family medicine (e.g., Kleinsorge, Roberts, Roy, & Rapoff, in press; Schroeder, 2005; Wu, Messner, & Roberts, in press), or a developmental and behavioral pediatrics clinic (Stancin, 2005), or an outpatient pediatric psychology (behavioral pediatrics) clinic (Sobel, Roberts, Rayfield, Barnard, & Rapoff, 2001). Davis and Vuong (2005) described services for children with chronic illness and effects on patient and parents at different stages of the process of diagnosis and ongoing treatment. A systematic approach to these issues through collaborative teams for evaluation and treatment is likely more comprehensive and competent.

These teams feature mutual responsibility and shared decision making among the professionals (Drotar, 1995; Roberts, 1986). These types of teams are most likely to function within institutions such as children's hospitals because of the resources (that are not typically available in pediatric office practice). Often these teams evolve as part of interactions, sharing, and reciprocal respect for disciplinary contributions. Additionally, demands for effective and efficient care require multiple and coordinated services; these are facilitated by teams.

Drotar (1995) highlighted the value of collaborative teams for conjoint mental health and physical health interventions, while also noting that that organization and leadership are critical. He indicated that the major disadvantage to teams is the amount of time that is often required for proper functioning, which may be too expensive to maintain. He also suggested that "team consultation makes taxing personal demands on sharing of responsibilities, communication, and flexibility of role functioning" (p. 26).

SYSTEMS CONSULTATION

Assessment and treatment of pediatric patients necessarily occurs in a complicated system involving several different change agents and intervention strategies (Mullins et al., 1992). Within these systems and subsystems are social, cultural, medical, family, institutional, intrapersonal, and ethical considerations. Mullins et al. (1992) noted how pediatric psychology practice often requires multiple-level actions. Multiple professionals and caregivers also play roles that interface even more systematic considerations. Thus, systems models have become important conceptualizations applied to child development for pediatric and clinical child and adolescent psychologists (Kazak, 2006; Kazak et al., 2010; Steele & Aylward, 2009). Mullins et al. (1992) summarized the conceptual contributions of a book on systems consultation by Wynne, McDaniel, and Weber (1986) that the systems consultant takes "what is referred to as a 'meta-' position, from which he or she can selectively evaluate the multiple subsystems related to a given problem, can shift professional roles between and among such subsystems, and can establish multiple-level treatment interventions" (p. 382). The specialty psychologist working within pediatric settings may need to effect change within these different levels.

The systems approach to psychological consultation requires a metaconceptual consideration of the context or systems in which medical and psychological services are provided (Drotar, 1995; Mullins et al., 1992). Different levels of systems have effects on quality and organization of services. For example, systems consultation might consider how outpatient clinics schedule patients and families, how pediatricians and mental health professionals interact over psychosocial issues, and how all unit staff, including receptionists, aides, and custodial personnel are trained in psychosocial supportive behaviors.

This systems approach may also require consideration of how higher organizational levels are structured and function, such as the organization of children's hospitals or how pediatric units are combined or separated for optimal effectiveness (e.g., to be patient-oriented, developmentally appropriate, and culturally sensitive). Special units or clinical services might be developed through systems interventions. For example, pain treatment teams can be created that take referrals from other units that may be organized according to medical condition (e.g., gastrointestinal disorders; hematology/oncology).

In describing an ecological model of pediatric pain in particular, Cohen, MacLaren, and Lim (2008) presented a conceptualization of systems surrounding the child in pain (including age, biology, coping, health, and experience) that includes systems of (a) family, health services, hospital policies, peers, and schools; (b) media, health care, and public policy, (c) attitudes, cultural ideologies, and societal values, and (d) sociohistorical conditions, and life transitions and patterns. This systems model offers indications of where psychosocial consultation might be effectively offered.

Systems consultation might utilize psychological principles and evaluation expertise to develop more community based problem prevention and health promotion efforts. For example, clinical child and adolescent psychologists can help create and maintain community projects for the promotion of safe behaviors that prevent childhood injuries or obesity (both critical concerns for healthy development of children and adolescents; Kirschman, Mayes, & Perciful, 2009; Wilson & Lawman, 2009).

A systems orientation also empowers the clinical child and adolescent psychologist to consider how society and its socioeconomic disparities might impact healthy development and create initiatives to remedy financial and physical obstacles that limit access to health care or to educational and psychosocial services. Psychologists advocate changing systems to benefit others. In the case of clinical child and adolescent psychologists and pediatric psychologists, this means advocating on behalf of a vulnerable part of the population that cannot advocate for themselves.

Often the specialty psychologist will flexibly move among these various consultative models as needs and situations dictate. Schroeder (2005) reported that the psychologist in pediatric medical settings may take on interactive and sometimes simultaneous roles of educator, advocate, treatment provider, and case manager. The psychologist needs to be flexible in application of these consultation models, adapting for the particular situation and perhaps utilizing different models as circumstances dictate.

Examples of Specialty Psychological Consultation in Pediatric and Family Medicine Settings

Carter and von Weiss (2005) described consultation-liaison (C-L) activities in inpatient pediatric units (e.g., diabetes, cystic fibrosis, renal disease, and cancer and leukemia), noting that many referrals are made for

> differential diagnosis of organic versus psychogenic contributors to symptom presentation; adherence problems to medications and treatment; coping and adjustment to chronic illness and trauma; pain management; decision making for organ transplantation; behavior problems that present management difficulties in the

> hospital; assessment and disposition of suicidal ideation or attempt; end-of-life issues; difficulties with parents or family members that impact on the child's care and adjustment; and arranging for post-hospitalization follow-up. (pp. 67–68)

They presented critical issues in developing C-L relationships and the developing research base for these services.

Providing details on consultation in a pediatric gastroenterology clinic, Cunningham (1995) described how she developed roles dealing with psychological concerns associated with inflammatory bowel disease, recurrent abdominal pain, and feeding problems. In her daily work, she coordinated care with the pediatric services and collaborated through problem solving, consultation, and education on specific issues for different clients, and created policies for general management of patients presenting with GI symptoms. As an example of her consultation practice, she developed a treatment protocol for a child who refused to go to school because of repeated episodes of stomach pain for which no organic cause could be discerned. A more complicated case involved a teenager with severe ulcerative colitis, requiring repeated surgeries, which necessitated conjoint sessions with the physician and psychologist.

Rosenthal (1995) presented a consultation service for psychosocial problems presenting in an adolescent medicine clinic in which the psychologist provided training to enhance the physicians' knowledge of adolescent development. In addition, she developed a clinical care model of collaboration between professionals over such concerns as patients' risk behaviors, chronic fatigue syndrome, and physical symptoms of gynecological conditions. Psychological services for the prevention of sexually transmitted diseases derive from such collaboration (Auslander, Short, & Rosenthal, 2005).

In an exemplar practice, Schroeder (1996, 2005) not only developed a consultation model for clinical child and adolescent psychologists and pediatric psychologists and pediatricians, but also conducted research on psychologists working in an outpatient pediatric clinic. Primary care clinics such as the offices in pediatrics and family medicine offer opportunities for psychology specialists to consult with physicians, nurse practitioners, physician assistants, and nurses (Stancin, 2005). For example, frequent mental health problems presenting during well-child visits include negative behaviors of disobedience, tantrums, and aggression, and school-related problems. The psychologist may consult to help identify and screen psychosocial problems, and make referrals, and develop standardized protocols for handling cases that might be implemented by other professionals.

Pediatric psychology is not formally recognized as a specialty, as clinical child and adolescent psychology is more generally (through the CRSPPP procedures outlined earlier in this book or through ABPP credentialing), although pediatric psychology is often considered a well-developed part of clinical child and adolescent psychology. Those seeking to provide psychological services, especially in consultant roles, will want to prepare themselves to be competent in the evidence-based literature, assessment and intervention techniques, and the unique ecological roles and functions of psychology in the medical setting (Brown, 2004; Drotar, 1995; Roberts & Steele, 2010).

School Consultation Models

Erchul and Martens (2010) defined the term *school consultation* as follows:

> School consultation is a process for providing psychological and educational services in which a specialist (consultant) works cooperatively with a staff member (consultee) to improve the learning and adjustment of a student (client) or group of students. During face-to-face interactions, the consultant helps the consultee through systematic problem solving, social influence, and professional support. In turn, the consultee helps the client(s) through selecting and implementing effective school-based interventions. In all cases, school consultation serves a remedial function and has the potential to serve a preventive function. (pp. 12–13)

The school consultant may be a clinical child and adolescent psychologist or school psychologist, and the consultee might include schoolteachers, principals, counselors, support staff, school social workers and nurses, parents, and educational specialists (Marks, 1995). In contrast to other models, "school consultation rarely involves a collaborative, nonhierarchical relationship between coequal professionals but is more accurately described as a cooperative relationship in which the consultant leads by directing the process and the consultee, in turn, follows" (Erchul & Martens, 2002, p. 208).

Erchul and Martens (2010) provided an excellent detailed conceptualization with multiple illustrations of school consultation activities by the psychologist. They schematically outlined the competencies needed to deliver psychological and educational services in schools, the tasks within the consultation process, and the outcomes that are intended. There are multiple precursors or competencies essential to providing consultation services in schools and with personnel such as teachers, paraprofessionals, and principals. For example, the consultant must have an understanding of the school and educational system, its organization, the formal and informal role structures and functions, and legal and ethical nuances (e.g., confidentiality, contracts), in addition to having technical competencies in assessment and interventions. Furthermore, Sheridan and Kratochwill (2008) emphasized that the consultant needs communication and interpersonal skills to be effective with ability to build trust and manage conflict. To achieve this, Erchul and Martens (2010) presented an "integrated model of school consultation" that is "client-centered, problem-solving" (p. 110).

The consultation process involves three reciprocally interacting tasks:

1. The *problem-solving task* includes identifying the problem and gathering data to focus on what is the target for behavior change. This may involve interviews, observation, and functional assessment.
2. The *support and development task* involves the consultant providing social and emotional support as well as assistance in learning how to carry out the consultant's recommendations.
3. The *social influence task* recognizes that the consultant-consultee relationship requires social interactions in which the consultee perceptions and behavior are influenced by the consultant to increase appropriate action. Erchul and Martens recommended noncoercive strategies to accomplish this social influence in the consultation process.

Although school consultants (whether coming from outside the school district or from within through special education or school psychology units) may have little formal control over the consultees, they do have the power to persuade and influence through a variety of means. Rarely, however, will advice giving or simple instruction through in-service training suffice to change teacher behavior. Other strategies are often needed such as establishing goals (for teacher and student behavior), arranging demonstrations and practice with corrective feedback and reinforcement, and implementing scripted protocols. Furthermore, as outlined by Erchul and Martens, the consultant will need to provide assistance and support in implementing outlined interventions. The consultation outcomes include improved learning and adjustment for the children in the classroom with improved skills and performance of the consultees/teachers.

Although school consultation may be made by specialists trained in school psychology per se, many clinical child and adolescent psychology specialists are actively engaged in consulting from within school systems and from outside (e.g., Jackson, Alberts, & Roberts, 2010; Johnson et al., 2008; Roberts, Jacobs, Puddy, Nyre, & Vernberg, 2003). For this form of consultation activity, specialists in clinical child and adolescent psychology will seek to achieve knowledge and competence through educational resources to enable them to be effective consultants (e.g., Dougherty, 2009; Erchul & Martens, 2010; Sheridan & Kratochwill, 2008; Weist, Evans, & Lever, 2003). Additionally, clinical child and adolescent psychologists with pediatric psychology expertise frequently are called upon to consult and collaborate with school staff on issues of transition and reintegration of children with chronic medical conditions, adjustment, and behavioral management (see Brown, 2004; Drotar, Palermo, & Barry, 2004; DuPaul, Power, & Shapiro, 2009; Lescano, Plante, & Spirito, 2004).

Other Consultant Roles for the Clinical Child and Adolescent Psychologist

The clinical child and adolescent psychology specialist often provides services and consultations to personnel and programs in mental health service delivery settings other than medicine and schools. The specialty psychologist might establish independent or group practice for outpatient mental health services (e.g., Landolf, 2005). In this role, the specialist would provide direct psychological services to clients (children, adolescents, and families), and the roles would not be considered consultation per se. These independent practitioners also may be called upon to provide diagnostic assessments and treatment planning for inpatient and residential treatment facilities as a consultant (Vargas & Brambila, 2005). Furthermore, the specialty practitioner may provide consultative services to community mental health centers regarding training, diagnostic procedures, and psychotherapeutic interventions with center staff (Smith-Boydston, 2005; Smith-Boydston & Nelson, 2008). Psychologists may also consult with a variety of agencies and programs in their communities. These may include consulting with other professionals in programs for substance abuse treatment and prevention (Pringle & Flanzer, 2005), sex offenders (Murphy, Page, & Ettelson, 2005), homeless persons (Walsh & Jackson, 2005), and children who are maltreated (Kees & Bonner, 2005).

Summary

Clinical child and adolescent psychologists will find multiple roles in which to apply the consultation models described in this chapter, adapting for types of settings and other consultation arrangements. Consultation competencies allow the clinical child and adolescent psychologist to extend services often in efficient and effective ways beyond what could be accomplished in one-on-one psychological contacts. These competencies may be especially important for this specialty given the large number of systems and people affecting the lives of children, adolescents, and their families.

SEVEN

Supervision and Teaching

In this chapter we will discuss two competency areas that are important for some, but not all, clinical child and adolescent psychologists: (1) providing clinical supervision to trainees or subordinate employees, and (2) teaching students and trainees in college, university, or other educational settings. Depending on psychologists' work settings, they may be expected to spend some of their professional time in these activities. In both cases, the clinical child and adolescent psychologist will be placed in the role of providing information and facilitating learning, and in both cases there is a relationship between an authority figure (the psychologist) and a mentee (the clinical trainee or student) that must be carefully managed. This chapter will discuss these two areas of professional activities, with reference to models of supervision and teaching and to research on these topics.

Supervision

Supervision has been used by mental health professionals since at least the early 1900s (Goodyear & Bernard, 1998), starting with social workers supervising paraprofessionals. Supervision is regarded as separate from training (Goodyear & Bernard, 1998). Training refers either to teaching of new clinical skills or to the broad graduate training programs for the trainees. Both of these concepts are different from supervision, which refers to the monitoring of services provided to actual clients. Precise and empirical definitions of supervision have been elusive, however (Milne, 2007).

In their book on competency-based supervision, published by the American Psychological Association, Falender and Shafranske (2004) defined *supervision* as follows:

> Supervision is a distinct professional activity in which education and training aimed at developing science-informed practice are

> facilitated through a collaborative interpersonal process. It involves observation, evaluation, feedback, the facilitation of supervisee self-assessment, and the acquisition of knowledge and skills by instruction, modeling, and mutual problem solving. . . . Supervision ensures that clinical consultation is conducted in a competent manner in which ethical standards, legal prescriptions, and professional practices are used to promote and protect the welfare of the client, the profession, and society at large. (p. 3)

Supervision has been recognized as a distinct practice related to clinical work, and in the past decade has been identified by the American Psychological Association Committee on Accreditation (2002b) and by the Association for Counselor Education and Supervision (1995) as a specific competency area. Effective supervision has multiple characteristics, and is believed to include a focus on developing useful *supervisory relationships*, methods to assist the supervisee to become aware of the *therapeutic process*, and *education* about therapy techniques and skills through instruction, observation, and role-playing (Falender & Shafranske, 2004).

What is it that we expect from effective professional supervision? Supervision can have important outcomes at the level of the client being served, as clinical care is monitored during supervision, and at the level of the supervisee, as the psychologist's training and education is enhanced (Falender & Shafranske, 2004, 2007). Of these two areas of focus, the most important is a positive outcome for the client, and this is accomplished through the monitoring of the supervisee's clinical work. Thus, the supervisor's primary ethical responsibility is the quality of clinical care that the supervisee provides. This monitoring aspect of supervision is more complicated in most instances of child and adolescent therapy than in adult therapy because the clinical child and adolescent psychologist must work effectively with individuals who are at quite different developmental stages: a child or adolescent (client) and an adult (a parental caregiver).

The supervisor's responsibility for client care is more critically important than the supervisor's role as an educator, trainer, and evaluator to the supervisee. However, the latter is a significant secondary function for the supervisor. In supervision, the supervisee learns how to apply knowledge and theory gleaned from other sources in his or her education, and leads to his or her ability to function in an increasingly competent way. The supervisor evaluates and verifies the supervisee's competence, provides clear feedback to the supervisee, and heightens the supervisee's awareness of ethical concerns (Robiner, 2008). In this way, supervision complements academic and research training. Supervision also provides an opportunity for the supervisor to socialize the supervisee into the profession, and to indirectly model how supervision itself can be done.

SUPERVISION MODELS

An important early source for the development of supervision came from Freud's efforts in the early 1900s to teach young doctors about the practice of psychoanalysis; psychoanalytic supervision became formalized by the 1920s (Goodyear & Bernard, 1998). As a variety of treatment approaches began to be developed, supervisors began to train new therapists in these skills. However, most supervisors were not trained in how to supervise, and they used implicit models of supervision, based on their experience of being supervised by others (Falender & Shafranske, 2004; Tipton, 1996).

Early supervisors emphasized the supervisors' authority and used a master-apprentice model of the supervisory relationship (Binder & Strupp, 1997). Although the initial focus was on teaching the supervisee about the client's psychodynamics and behavior, starting in the 1950s some supervisors became more experiential and focused more on the anxieties, defenses, and problems of the supervisee. In more recent years, as psychology has focused more on evidence-based practice (Chambless & Hollon, 1998), the field has begun to focus more on research on the process and outcomes of supervision. Using the framework of Falender and Shafranske (2004), at least two prescriptive approaches to supervision have evolved, one being an extension of psychotherapy theory and the other being process-based and developed specifically for supervision.

Psychotherapy-based approaches to supervision incorporate into the supervisor-supervisee relationship some of the mechanisms and procedures from the particular form of psychotherapy being used. A supervisor who has a cognitive-behavioral treatment orientation tends to focus on the supervisee's cognitions and behavior, and may incorporate therapy-related practices such as agenda setting and homework into supervision (Liese & Beck, 1997). Supervisors who are training supervisees from a rational-emotive framework aim to have the clinician monitor and dispute their own irrational cognitions (Woods & Ellis, 1997). Supervisors of family therapists tend to think of the supervisory process and roles as being part of the larger systemic context around the client. Although there are advantages for psychotherapy-based supervisory approaches, in that supervisors can model and demonstrate procedures directly to the clinician, these approaches do not address all of the functions of supervision (Falender & Shafranske, 2004).

Process-based approaches to supervision address the roles of the supervisor and supervisee, and the tasks and procedures that occur in supervision. These approaches address that aspect of supervision that focuses on the development of the clinical competence of the trainee. One example of a process-based approach is the discrimination model described by Bernard (1997). This model distinguished three focus areas in supervision (the intervention skills to be used by the clinician; skills to conceptualize the clients' presentation of background information and problems; and the trainee's personality and cultural experiences), from three general roles that the supervisor can assume (teacher, by assuming responsibility for assisting the trainee to become more competent; counselor, by facilitating the trainee's exploration of her or his own cognitions, emotions, and behaviors; and consultant, who serves as a resource by encouraging the trainee to rely on his or her own thoughts about how to proceed).

Another example of a process-based approach is the systems approach articulated by Holloway (1995). This approach identifies seven interrelated factors that are part of supervision (e.g., supervision relationship, client, supervisor, trainee), and has been studied by use of the systems approach to supervision (SAS) on transcripts of supervision. Using the SAS, supervision has been found to be a mutual and shared interaction that can contribute to building the supervisee's clinical competence and enhance the supervisor's experience.

At a more descriptive, less theoretical level than these prescriptive models of supervision, developmental models of supervision (e.g., Stoltenberg, 2005; Stoltenberg et al., 1998) have been advanced that describe developmental sequences that a therapist moves through to become an experienced, seasoned therapist. Trainees' developmental levels affect their expectation for supervision style and focus, with beginning trainees expressing the need for greater amounts of support, structure, and encouragement and for training that is directive, didactic, and focused on technical skills, whereas advanced trainees are more focused on their personal issues that affect their clinical care, on theory-based conceptualizations, and on learning higher order skills (Goodyear & Bernard, 1998; Magnuson, Wilcoxon, & Norem, 2000). Stoltenberg's integrated developmental model (IDM) suggests that trainees become increasingly autonomous, then begin shifting awareness from self to client, and finally begin to function independently. The supervisor is expected to adjust his/her behavior to match the trainee's changing developmental level. Stoltenberg et al. (1998) and others have suggested that, in a parallel way, the supervisor moves through a developmental sequence. These developmental stages for the supervisor can include the degree to which they feel competent to be a supervisor, the degree of autonomous independence as a supervisor, and the degree that they feel confusion with supervisory roles (Watkins, 1993).

SUPERVISION COMPETENCIES

What areas of competency should an effective supervisor acquire? In 2004, Falender et al. identified six interrelated categories of supervision competencies for entry-level psychologists. This preliminary list generated by this workgroup can serve a heuristic function in outlining possible supervisory competencies, some of which could be attained by the end of graduate training.

1. The supervisor acquires *knowledge* about the area in which he/she is providing supervision; learns about models and research on supervision; learns about how supervisees develop; and acquires and uses knowledge about ethical, legal, and diversity issues.
2. The supervisor displays adequate *skills,* building appropriate supervisory relationships, managing the multiple roles inherent in being a supervisor, assessing the clinical developmental level of the trainee, providing feedback to the supervisee, and assessing one's own supervisory performance.
3. The supervisor's *values* should include a belief that the supervisor is responsible for the client, should be respectful and empowering when interacting with the supervisee, should strike a balance between being supportive versus challenging the supervisee and a balance between clinical and training needs, and should be committed to lifelong professional growth as a supervisor.
4. The supervisor must consider the *social context* (e.g., training setting, accrediting agencies, government policies) that shapes the supervisory interaction, and should have the goal of creating a climate within this context in which honest feedback, both supportive and challenging, occurs.
5. The *education and training* of the supervisor should include coursework in the relevant knowledge and skills noted earlier, and can provide for supervision of supervision. In this context, it is very important that a supervisor of a clinical child or adolescent psychologist also have substantial experience themselves in working directly with both children and parents.

6. Competency to provide supervision should be *assessed* in transparent ways, such as completion of a course on supervision, direct audio- or videotaped observation of the supervisor's supervision sessions, summaries of self-assessment and supervisee feedback, and assessment of supervision outcomes at the supervisee and client levels.

PROCEDURES IN COMPETENCY-BASED SUPERVISION

Falender and Shafranske (2004) identify several procedural steps that are important in providing a foundation for competency-based supervision. The first step is to establish supervision goals and objectives. The knowledge, skills, and values that will be the focus of supervision are identified, recognizing that it will be important to adjust these to the developmental level of the specific trainee. Thus, the goal setting process should be collaborative, and should permit the supervisor to tailor the supervision to meet the individual needs and preexisting competencies of the trainee. The training objectives and learning processes can be included in a formal supervision contract. The use of videotaping or audiotaping of sessions, live supervision (behind a one-way mirror, or in the room), and demonstration by the supervisor can enhance supervisory effectiveness.

The second step involves case management of the trainee's clinical work, and addresses client care as well as the supervisee's learning. The supervisor provides on-site instruction to complement the trainee's preexisting skills and training. The on-site instruction can include teaching, demonstrations, live observation, and practice activities, and helps the supervisee to reflect on her or his perceptions of the therapeutic interaction and how he/she contributed to these interactions. Effective supervision assists the supervisee to nondefensively examine what has occurred in sessions, and provides the supervisee with a conceptual framework and readings related to the client's psychopathology and to the nature of the intervention to be provided. As noted earlier, the primary responsibility for the supervisor is to ensure quality care to the client.

This process of supervision of the trainee's clinical work assists the trainee to reflect on his or her actions, within relevant conceptualizations of the intervention plan and process for the particular client. Milne and James (2002) suggest that trainees acquire skills and understanding through four modes of learning: reflection, conceptualization, planning, and practical experience. In this framework, the supervisor assists the trainee to participate in an experiential learning cycle through didactic teaching, role-playing and modeling. After the trainee reflects on the prior clinical experience, the trainee then experiments with new strategies and behaviors.

RESEARCH ON SUPERVISION

In contrast to the rapidly emerging literature on evidence-based intervention strategies, there is a striking relative lack of efficacy and effectiveness research on supervision (Ellis & Ladany, 1997). The research that exists addresses trainee reports of supervisors, but rarely links these perceptions of supervisors to objective outcomes related to treatment efficacy, and has only begun in recent years to document the ways in which supervision training programs can facilitate clinical trainees' acquisition of therapeutic skills (Sundin, Ogren, & Boethius, 2008). Goodyear and Barnard (1998) suggest that this condition exists for several reasons, including the lack of supervision manuals or protocols, and the difficulty in designing a rigorous supervision study that could adequately protect the interests and rights of clients. However, research in the past 10–15 years has begun to identify characteristics of higher quality supervision (Falender & Shafranske, 2004). This research has particularly addressed the supportiveness of the supervisory relationship, the working alliance, disclosure, conflict resolution, and mentoring (Falender & Shafranske, 2004).

Supportive Relationship Facilitating attitudes and behaviors in supervision permits the creation of teamwork between supervisor and supervisee (Henderson, Cawyer, & Watkins, 1999). Factors that facilitate the development of a supportive supervisory relationship include supervisor empathy (Nerdrum & Ronnestad, 2002), supervisor approachability, attentiveness and respect for autonomy (Henderson et al., 1999), and supervisor warmth and validation (Wulf & Nelson, 2000). Highly rated supervisors are flexible, genuine, experienced, currently conducting therapy, and have a sense of humor. Specialized expertise and conceptual knowledge are also highly prized, along with encouragement of trainee experimentation and strategic self-disclosure to normalize trainee's concerns (Worthen & McNeill, 1996). Supervisors who impart in trainees a sense of accomplishment and imagination are also perceived well (Guest & Beutler, 1988).

Working Alliance The working alliance in supervision involves a bond, agreement on goals, and agreement on tasks (Bordin, 1994). Supervisors and supervisees with a respectful and caring relationship experience less role conflict, and work through conflicts more readily. Supervisees who have a behavioral orientation prefer task-oriented supervisors, whereas supervisees with a psychodynamic or humanistic orientation preferred supervisors who were warm and supportive (Lochner & Melchert, 1997). When this issue about orientation is addressed, cognitive-behavioral supervisors are rated by trainees as being more task-oriented, but psychodynamic and humanistic supervisors are rated as being more interpersonally sensitive and less task-directed (Ladany & Lehrman-Waterman, 1999).

Self-Disclosure The supervisory alliance has been described as being affected by the supervisee's ability to disclose to the supervisor (Ladany & Walker, 2003). Forty percent of supervisees have reported that they have failed to inform supervisors of their own perceived clinical errors at least periodically, and 30% rarely disclosed to supervisors when they thought the supervisors were wrong (Yourman & Farber, 1996). Fifty percent of the supervisees reported to the supervisors only what they thought the supervisor wanted to hear, and 59% reported that they did not feel comfortable disclosing their negative feelings toward the supervisors. These rates of nondisclosure are likely to reduce the likelihood of establishing effective supervisory alliances, although research has not yet explored this question. It is anticipated that supervisor self-disclosures may model and facilitate trainee self-disclosures, and most supervisors typically do provide at least some self-disclosures. Trainees have reported that 73% of supervisors have provided at least one self-disclosure about personal issues, counseling experiences, and counseling struggles (Ladany & Lehrman-Waterman, 1999).

Conflict Resolution Moskowitz and Rupert (1983) conducted a survey of 158 practicum students, and 38% reported having a major conflict with a supervisor, and reported wide variability in how these conflicts were broached and resolved. Most trainees (86%) preferred that the supervisor take the lead in discussing the conflict situations. In general, conflicts over the directness of supervisory style were easier to resolve than differences about theoretical orientation or about personality issues. Supervisors were able to effectively resolve conflicts best when they initiated the discussion of the identified conflicts, and when the supervisors responded to the supervisees' concerns in a nondefensive, nonaccusatory way.

Mentoring Although supervision is distinct from mentoring, because mentoring is usually initiated by the recipient, some supervisors do become mentors to their supervisees (Falender & Shafranske, 2004). Someone functioning in the mentoring role provides knowledge and advice to assist the trainee to become a professional in their discipline. Trainees who have received mentoring advance more rapidly in their careers and have stronger development of their professional identity.

Negatively Perceived Supervision Practices Much can be learned about perceived negative aspects of supervision, and research has provided some focus on specific aspects of supervision that has led some trainees to perceive supervision negatively (Allen, Szollos, & Williams, 1986). In a sample of predoctoral interns and practicum students, Ramos-Sanchez et al. (2002) found that a fifth of the sample reported negative events such as harsh criticism and judgmental attitudes in supervision, and that these trainees had weaker supervisory alliances. Other supervisor behaviors that have been linked to negative experiences by trainees are supervisor dismissal of trainee's conceptualizations, supervisors' inappropriate self-disclosure, lack of preparation for supervision by the supervisor, and focus on trainee deficiencies rather than improvements (Gray, Ladany, Walker & Ancis, 2001).

SUMMARY: SUPERVISION

Despite sparse research to date, especially in connecting trainee and supervisor perceptions of supervision to client outcomes, certain aspects of supervision appear important. Supervisors who are perceived as effective attempt to establish supportive and trusting supervisory alliances, identify and nondefensively discuss apparent conflicts between supervisor and supervisee, provide titrated amounts of self-disclosure, and adjust their supervisory style to the developmental level of the trainees. More novice trainees require more concrete and directed training about therapeutic planning and therapeutic strategies in a supportive manner, but more advanced trainees need opportunities to create their conceptualization of cases more independently. Supervisors of clinical child and adolescent psychologists should be sensitive to the widely varying developmental issues involving the child clients and adult parents, and should have substantial experience working directly with children and parents.

Teaching

As noted previously, there are certain functional similarities between supervision and teaching. Supervision assists trainees in learning how to directly apply psychological processes to clients, but teaching is typically considered to address a more basic task that assists students to understand psychological processes. Teaching of college students or other trainees is often described by those who are intensely involved in this activity as an adventure, in which the teacher is an explorer who helps students discover new insights about themselves and the world around them. Teachers often develop a teaching philosophy that addresses key teaching outcomes.

Because of the personal nature of the teaching experiences that teachers have experienced themselves and have provided to their students, these teaching philosophies are often highly individualized. However, they can contain common elements, such as the importance of conceiving teaching as an active (for both the students and the teachers) and bidirectional (between students and teachers) process, and of creating a community of learners in which students teach and learn from each other. To pursue this learning process, models of learning and of teaching styles have been articulated.

MODELS OF LEARNING

Effective teaching is based on having a coherent model of how students learn that then leads to certain teaching styles and strategies. Several decades ago, models of student learning began focusing increasingly on students' cognitive processing and motivation. For example, King (1992) described how students understand new material best when they elaborate on that material, by adding details, clarifying an idea, examining the relationship between several concepts, making inferences, and associating the material to information already known (Wittrock, 1990). Efforts to elaborate new information make it more meaningful to the individual and easier to remember. Unfortunately, learners are often not motivated to engage in this elaborative activity spontaneously, and yet self-generated elaborations have been found to be more useful in the learning process than elaborations provided by teachers (Pressley et al., 1987, 1992). Thus, both cognitive and motivational processes were perceived to be important, and led to useful teaching strategies.

Other examples of models of learning, such as the model articulated by Vermunt and Vermetten (2004), address regulative and metacognitive facets of learning as well as cognitive and motivational facets. At the cognitive level, three main cognitive processing strategies have been identified: deep processing (e.g., relating and structuring pieces of information), stepwise processing (e.g., memorizing and analyzing), and concrete processing (e.g., finding applications for the information) (Vermunt, 1998). Students' affective processes can influence learning in positive and negative ways, through students' subjective appraisals of tasks and through their ability to block interfering emotions. Cognitive and affective processes are controlled through regulatory processes.

Three regulation strategies include self-regulation, as children engage in regulation themselves; an externally regulated strategy, in which teachers lead learning; and a lack of regulation, when unregulated students lack supportive controls from teachers or their learning environment. According to Vermunt (1998), these cognitive, affective, and regulatory elements combine to create one of four learning styles: unidirected, reproduction-directed, meaning-directed, and application-directed, with the latter two styles representing higher level learning styles. In this model, higher quality learning styles are believed to be promoted by certain teaching functions (Vermunt & Vermetten, 2004). Teaching functions involve *processing* of material (e.g., presenting and clarifying subject matter), creating a positive *affective* and motivational climate for students, and *regulating* and steering students' learning. Attention to teaching functions leads to a consideration of teaching styles.

TEACHING STYLES

Teachers develop and use a teaching style based on their beliefs about education, their personal preferences, and their abilities. Teaching styles can range from being teacher-oriented, in which the focus is on information and the content to be acquired, to being learner-centered, in which the focus is on the learning process. At the extremes of this continuum, a teacher who has a highly teacher-oriented style uses traditional lectures and serves as an expert, while a teacher who is highly learner-centered will use collaborative learning techniques such as group work and peer review and will serve as a coach or facilitator.

Teachers who are learning-centered often use process-oriented teaching to promote students' thinking strategies and self-directed learning (Bolhuis, 2003) and the meaning-directed and application-directed learning patterns identified by Vermunt and Vermetten (2004). This type of teaching fosters more reflective thinking through interactive working groups of students, and, after initially slowing down the study pace of students, can improve students' performance on examinations. Students' self-directed learning involves setting learning goals, engaging in learning activities such as direct experience and reflection, and monitoring the results of the learning to determine whether new learning activities are required.

Bolhuis (2003) suggests that there are four principles in process-oriented teaching designed to stimulate self-directed learning:

1. Teaching moves gradually from teacher-regulation to student-regulation, and recognizes that individual differences in students influence the timing of this shift. Students with a high tolerance for uncertainty and well developed regulation skills can move more quickly to student-regulated learning. Process-oriented instruction assists students' self-regulation with teachers initially thinking aloud

and modeling how to identify and monitor goals for a learning task, followed by activating students to practice using learning activities on their own.

2. The teacher focuses on students' acquisition of content and knowledge by having students critically assess their prior knowledge on a given topic, and then acquire new content through experiential learning and by using newly acquired general principles in applied ways.
3. Process-oriented teaching attends to emotional aspects of teaching by providing positive feedback to students, and by assisting students in recognizing their anxiety and frustrations about learning, and how to deal with these concerns.
4. Classrooms are social learning environments. Process-oriented teaching focuses on assisting students to observe and learn from others' actions, to understand other students' perspectives on information, and to relate one's ideas to others'. Cooperative learning, in which students learn from each other, is promoted through teachers' clear instructions about how cooperation would concretely operate, and reinforcement of positive interdependence and cooperative behaviors.

Educational research continues to examine how variations in cooperative teaching styles influence students' acquisition of knowledge. King (1992) examined a guided student-generated questioning strategy, which involved students posing and answering their own thought-provoking questions to the content of a lesson. In this procedure, teachers provide generic question stems (e.g., "What are the strengths and weaknesses of . . .?"). This approach has been used by individuals and by groups, using guided peer questioning in small cooperative groups. Research has compared guided student-generated questioning to lecture presentations, and college students using student-generated questioning had better, more elaborated comprehension of lecture content. Guided peer questioning produced better outcomes than guided self-questioning.

In another example of student-generated learning, undergraduate students were randomly assigned to either a traditional didactic lecture format (with a question-and-answer period at the end of formal lectures) or to interactive discussion sessions in which the specific content was derived primarily by students (Costa, Van Rensburg, & Rushton, 2007). Although both student groups reported high teacher satisfaction, the students in interactive discussion groups were more highly satisfied with the presentations in class and had significantly better knowledge retention on end-of-course tests.

Social constructivist teaching methods, in a related way, emphasize problem-based learning, case-based collaboration, and collaborative student projects (Hanson & Sinclair, 2008). By focusing on the applications of knowledge, undergraduate students are expected to gain a deeper and more practical understanding of theoretical concepts. Teachers step out of the didactic roles, and as co-inquirers, model collaborative inquiry through carefully selected problem-solving activities. In survey research, faculty who use social constructivist teaching methods with preprofessional undergraduates reported that their students acquired knowledge and profession-specific skills more rapidly, but that this approach had less effect on students' acquisition of knowledge of theories.

TEACHING TEACHERS

Historically, little attention was paid to formally preparing new teachers to teach, and training didactic-oriented teachers to be more process-oriented. Teachers developed teaching practices and teaching styles largely based on their own experiences. However, an increasing number of psychology training programs have begun to offer graduate students the opportunity to teach course modules, course sections, or full classes while they take graduate courses on teaching (McElroy & Prentice-Dunn, 2005).

In one course that trains graduate students to teach a section of introductory psychology (McElroy & Prentice-Dunn, 2005), students attend a weekly seminar in which they share ideas for lectures and for handling student issues, receive peer feedback from other graduate students who have observed their teaching, receive ratings from the undergraduate students in the class, and periodically meet with the faculty instructor to review videotapes of class sessions. McElroy and Prentice-Dunn (2005) reported on 48 graduate students who taken these courses, and found that the graduate students rated the feedback about the videotaped sessions as being especially useful, and that undergraduate narrative feedback obtained in the early weeks of a course were helpful in improving the graduate students' teaching. Although fewer than half of teacher training courses in psychology departments include video review of class sessions (Buskist, Tears, Davis, & Rodrigue, 2002), these findings suggest that this is an important element of new teachers' teaching.

SUMMARY: TEACHING

Teachers should use a teaching philosophy to guide their teaching style, and they should be able to tailor their teaching style to meet the developmental needs of their students. An optimal strategy can involve moving gradually from teacher-oriented to learner-centered, increasing students' responsibility for self-generated learning. In doing so, process-oriented and social constructivist teaching styles emphasize the importance of using and developing collaborative and applied student activities to enhance student learning and retention of information. Research suggests that effective teaching styles can be taught in graduate school courses, especially when there are opportunities for consultation and videotape reviews of sessions.

PART V

Foundational Competencies

EIGHT

Ethical Issues When Working with Children and Adolescents

A man without ethics is a wild beast loosed upon this world.
—Albert Camus

Clinicians working with children have challenging tasks requiring them to be especially attentive to ethical issues. While working with the child as a patient, they may be dealing with the parents, school officials, court officials, and numerous other professionals. Assuming that the parents have the child's best interest at heart, the child's treatment path may take fewer twists and turns; however, the clinician frequently has to intervene in the various systems in which the child lives. Because the clinician must grasp the complex ethical-legal issues surrounding privacy, confidentiality, informed consent, research, assessment, and record keeping, it is essential for the clinician working with children to be well versed in professional ethics.

This chapter will review the Ethical Principles of Psychologists and Code of Conduct adopted by the American Psychological Association (APA; 2002a) in their meeting on August 21, 2002, amended in February 2010, and approved June of that year. It will focus on some of the very basic questions and definitions in areas of the code as they apply to working with children. It will also identify potential risks associated with working with children as related to the professional code of ethics and to provide suggestions to aid in minimizing these risks. The goal of this chapter is to provide a helpful dialogue for the child clinician when ethical issues arise. Hopefully it will assist the child and adolescent psychologist in navigating the complicated maze woven by all the interested parties tied to the child in treatment. However, it is not meant as a substitute for the code, and psychologists should refer that as the primary source. Although this chapter will be focused primarily on clinical practice, some discussion on issues about conducting research with children will be mentioned.

The word *ethics* is derived from the Greek word *ethos*, which means "character." The Greek philosophers were some of the first to study ethics. For Aristotle, ethics was more than a moral, religious, or legal concept. The most important element in ethical behavior for him was the knowledge that actions were accomplished for the betterment of the common good. He asked whether actions performed by individuals or groups were good both for an individual or a group and also for society. To determine what is ethically good for the individual and for society, Aristotle said, it is necessary to possess three virtues of practical wisdom: temperance, courage, and justice (*Black's Law Dictionary*).

Ethics law is the branch of philosophy that defines what is good for the individual and for society. It establishes the nature of obligations, or duties, that people owe themselves and one another. In modern society, ethics define how individuals, professionals, and corporations choose to interact with one another. Numerous examples of lapses in ethical behavior have been presented in the media, and these failures appear to be an area of increasing public interest.

The American Psychological Association (APA) attempts to provide its members with guidelines for ethical behavior in their professional life. The APA first established an ethics committee in 1938 and published its first code of ethics in 1953. We currently adhere to the most recent version that was adopted in 2002 and amended in 2010. According to Weithorne and McCabe (1987), ethical codes generally refer to basic philosophical beliefs and professional expectations about the morality of human behavior. Most professional organizations (e.g., the American Psychiatric Association, the American Psychological Association, and the National Association of School Psychologists) have codes of conduct for their members.

Hadjistavropiulos and Koocher (2009) point out that codes of ethics are typically divided into two parts: (1) ethical principles and (2) ethical standards. The principles are designed to guide behavior and give the clinician a goal to strive toward while recognizing that actual behavior will not meet the suggested principle. Principles are the overarching concepts behind the standards. The standards, however, are the benchmark that the clinician must meet to stay within the guidelines of the rules enforced by formal professional regulatory organizations. They are similar to laws that are not to be broken.

According to Koocher and Keith-Spiegel (1990) the value of professional associations' ethics codes as applied to everyday practice with children may be limited. Many have little to say about working with children, and some may conflict with federal and/or state regulations. In addition, they state that some groups with ethics codes may not have a monitoring or enforcement capability and are essentially educational and consciousness-raising documents for the members.

It is important to understand why our field has a code of ethics. According to Hadjistavropiulos and Koocher (2009), psychologists' high standards of ethical conduct serves not only to protect clients, research subjects, and the public but also to safeguard the reputation and public image of our discipline. To build trust with the public, a high level of ethical behavior is required. The public has come to be skeptical and distrustful of groups whose members obviously engage in questionable behaviors. A number of examples can frequently be found in the national media. In order to build trust with our clients, we as psychologists have to respect their privacy and recognize the importance of confidentiality. The nature of the problems with which psychologists deal makes it essential that clients trust that their private information will remain private. Hadjistavropiulos and Koocher state that children and adolescents especially require both respect and assurance about their privacy. Conversations with adults have frequently seemed like the inquisition to many children, and the psychologists must overcome these experiences by offering respect, acceptance, and confidentiality.

There have been times when our ethics codes and legal requirements have not been congruent. In situations in which there is a discrepancy between ethics and law, the ethical code requires psychologists to state their commitment to ethical principles and attempt to resolve the conflict. However, if a resolution to the conflict is not possible, psychologists should adhere to the legal requirements and/or regulations in such a fashion as to uphold basic human rights (APA, 2002a).

General Principles

The APA code explains that general principles, as opposed to ethical standards, are aspirational in nature and are intended to guide and inspire psychologists toward the highest ethical ideals of the profession. General principles do not represent obligations and do not form the basis for imposing sanctions. Rather, the general principles are overarching guidelines for conducting professional interactions. We will now turn to these general principles.

GENERAL PRINCIPLE A

General Principle A has to do with beneficence and nonmaleficence. This principle is generally attributed to the concept proposed by Hippocrates and the Pythagorean philosophers before him (Hergenhahn, 2009). Basically, it warns against doing any harm while encouraging that we attempt to maximize the good that we do for our clients and/or subjects. When working with children and adolescents and the various systems in which the child is involved, the psychologists should try to improve the interactions of the systems: to better the situation for the child without making things worse. At times, psychologists may find themselves in a situation in which the intervention seems initially to make the situation worse with the intent that things will improve at a later date. For example, it is possible at times that the reporting of abuse will initially make the family situation worse and make the child feel guilty for disclosure. However, such a temporary worsening of the situation is required by the law and is supported by the data demonstrating long-term benefits.

In addition, General Principle A deals with the relationship between professionals and encourages psychologists to be responsible in their interactions with others while attempting to resolve any conflicts that arise. Furthermore, psychologists should be careful to ensure that their own issues do not interfere with their ability to work with others. For example, a psychologist who is having a difficult time in his own family would need to exercise care that his own issues did not interfere with his ability to work with other distressed families.

GENERAL PRINCIPLE B

General Principle B deals with fidelity and responsibility. This principle has to do with the obligation that psychologists have to accept responsibility for their professional behavior; for setting and following high professional standards; for building relationships of trust; and for consulting with colleagues about both their own behavior and that of other psychologists. Also falling under this principle is pro bono work or work for reduced fee. Psychologists working with children and adolescents frequently find themselves in a position in which they have to devote time consulting with schools or other organizations. Much of this time is unlikely to be reimbursed or compensated but is necessary for effective intervention with their patients.

Another issue that the clinical child psychologists has to struggle with under this principle is how to deal with colleagues who may be providing services to children, adolescents, and families without specific training in that area. How do you question a colleague about her practice without appearing to be attempting to limit her livelihood? Clinical child and adolescent psychologists have strong convictions about what type and how much training is needed to provide services to this population. Where do we draw the line without appearing pompous? On the other side of the issue, when do we seek consultation when we find ourselves dealing with a parent whose difficulties push our intervention skills with adults? Both of these situations frequently arise.

GENERAL PRINCIPLE C

General Principle C has to do with integrity. Psychologists are obligated to be truthful and honest in all of their professional work. The major issue that might arise around this principle for the practicing clinician has to do with how much information to share with a child or adolescent client about events that might not be the psychologist's responsibility to disclose to the child. For example, if the parents are considering divorce and have talked about this with the therapist but have not yet discussed the issue with the child, there might be issues that come up in therapy in which the clinician cannot be completely truthful with the child. Similarly, if a pediatric psychologist is working with a family whose child has a very poor medical prognosis but the physician has not discussed this with the family, the psychologist may find herself in a difficult situation.

GENERAL PRINCIPLE D

Justice is covered in General Principle D, which has to do with the fairness and justice entitled to all people. It is designed to ensure that individuals have access to and benefit from competent and unbiased psychologists' contributions. Psychologists take care to keep their own biases out of their dealings with others and to recognize their limitations and competences. Everyone has biases and maybe even prejudices. These characteristics are part of being human. The important point here is for the psychologist to be sufficiently aware of these biases in order to recognize if and when they become an issue in their professional life. Similarly, we all have our weaknesses and should be aware of them so as not to practice in those areas.

GENERAL PRINCIPLE E

Principle E has to do with respect for the rights and dignity of others. Under this principle comes the importance of respect for the worth and dignity of all persons and the rights to self-determination, confidentiality, and privacy. People have the right to self-determination even when the psychologist may disagree with them. As long as it does not violate the law or ethical guidelines, the psychologists respects the right of the individual to make their own decisions.

APA Ethical Code Standards: The Rules

In this section the actual ethical code standards will be discussed. Many of the issues raised in the various standards are the same regardless of whether one is working with a child, adolescent, or adult. For these standards, limited issues will be addressed. More attention will be paid to those standards in which specific problems related to working with children and adolescents may present particular challenges.

STANDARD 1: RESOLVING ETHICAL ISSUES

Under Standard 1 falls a group of potential issues that might arise between the psychologist and other groups (e.g., when the ethical code seems to be in conflict with the law or other legal authorities). Varieties of potential conflicting situations fall under this standard and may be potential issues when working with children and adolescents. At times, psychologists may find conflict between the ethical code and the demands of the organization. For example, in some settings there may be institutional rules such as zero drug tolerance and an expectation that violations will be reported. However, if during a therapy session an adolescent mentions having experimented with drugs, there is a perceived conflict between institutional regulations and the confidentiality of the patient. In a number of such situations, prevention is the best approach. Discussions about such potential conflicts with representatives of the organization may take place before the psychologist begins to provide services. In most instances, some resolution of this potential conflict can be avoided by sharing the need for confidentiality during therapy with members of the organization. However, when such conflict cannot be resolved (e.g., in the juvenile justice system), the psychologist should fully disclose to the child or adolescent the limits of confidentiality up front as they are extended in the institution. Just as the duty to warn should be explained prior to therapy with all patients, the institutional restrictions to confidentiality should be discussed prior to treatment.

Actual or perceived ethical violations are other potential issues that fall under Standard 1. Informal resolution of perceived violations is the first step when the psychologist suspects that there may be a violation. For example, if a clinical child and adolescent psychologist believes that a colleague is providing services for which he or she is not qualified, the psychologist might attempt to informally raise this issue with the individual. If the informal approach does not work and the psychologist continues to believe there has been an ethical violation that could potentially harm the patient, he or she is expected to take appropriate actions. According to the code, the appropriate action involves reporting the violation to some administrative body such as the licensing board. This action can result in considerable expense and distress for the reported psychologist, and the code also warns against the filing of improper complaints. The decision of when to report can be a very stressful one to the psychologist who observes the potential violation. Frequently confidential consultation with a colleague can be helpful in the decision-making process.

Another part of this standard is the requirement that psychologists cooperate with the ethical committee when a complaint is filed against them. It is easy to immediately become defensive and even angry when a complaint is filed. However, the response to the complaint needs to be rational and objective. Consultation with an experienced colleague can be an important first step when preparing to respond.

There are certain areas in the practice of clinical child and adolescent psychology that are more likely to result in a patient the filing of a complaint. For example, custody evaluations are well known to be high-risk practice. Divorce and custody are highly emotional issues, and when psychologists become involved in the process, they are at risk to become the recipient of these feelings. When practicing in this area, extreme care needs to be taken to ensure that practice guidelines are followed and clearly documented. This is even more important in custody cases. When the inevitable complaint is filed, having followed approved procedures and having them clearly documented is one of the first things that the investigator will request (Andrew, Benjamin, & Gollan, 2003; Practice Directorate, American Psychological Association, 1994; Stahl, 1999).

When dealing with a complaint, the psychologist should be fully cooperative and forthcoming. Failure to respond is in and of itself a violation. However, if a lawsuit is involved, the psychologist may request that the complaint be resolved after the legal proceedings. Cooperation and thoroughness in responding are keys to the resolution of the complaint. Provide documentation of the procedures or techniques employed and references to support your procedures. Rarely can the psychologist be too thorough. More often they tend to attempt to dismiss the complaint or respond in an overly emotional manner.

The final portion of this standard prohibits the use of a filed and unresolved complaint as a reason to deny the psychologist employment or advancement solely on the basis of the complaint itself. For the psychologist who is in a position of authority, this point is an important one to keep in mind. Some decisions can be delayed until the complaint is resolved, but others cannot. What questions are appropriate during the process? Sanctions against a psychologist are frequently public information, but complaints are most likely not.

STANDARD 2: COMPETENCE

The standard of competence states that the psychologist knows and practices within the boundaries of her or his competence. This competence is usually self-declared and based on the appropriate education, training, supervision, consultation, and/or experience. This issue has been a touchy area and the subject of considerable discussion among many clinical child and adolescent psychologists. When does a psychologist have the competence to provide services to children and their families? Guidelines and training recommendations have been made (see Chapter 1), but there are no hard-and-fast rules. It is the responsibility of the psychologist to determine and limit his or her areas of practice.

When a certain presenting problem or skill set falls outside the psychologist's competencies, an appropriate referral is made. The exceptions to this rule are based on either emergency situations or lack of availability of appropriate services. Under these circumstances, the psychologist may provide the services until the emergency passes or until she or he can obtain the necessary competencies. Consultation or supervision with a colleague is always advisable and can be obtained electronically if no local resource is available.

Also under this standard is the requirement that the psychologist maintain his/her level of competencies. Finch (2009) has laid out some suggestions for the professional psychologist for maintaining and expanding competencies. In addition to maintaining their own competencies, psychologists are responsible for ensuring that those who work for them are competent to accomplish the tasks that they are given and for providing supervision for those tasks. At times, the clinical child and adolescent psychologist will have students or technicians administer tests during evaluations. When this is the case, the psychologist is responsible for the quality of these services and for their supervision.

Also falling under the competence standard is the issue of the personal problems and conflicts of the psychologist him/herself. All of us, even psychologists, experience some personal problems and conflicts as part of our being human. It is the responsibility of the psychologist to recognize when these issues reach a level that they interfere with the ability to function in a competent manner. When a psychologist determines that the problems have reached this level, she or he is responsible for taking the appropriate action, such as seeking professional help or limiting the practice.

Personal and family problems may arise in the life of the clinical child and adolescent psychologist that prevent the clinician from being objective or even competent at certain times. For example, a psychologist may be having particular difficulty with her adolescent daughter and find that this conflict colors her objectivity in dealing with adolescent female patients and their families. It is the psychologist's responsibility to deal in a professional manner with these issues, and it may even be necessary for her to not take referrals of this type until she has resolved her own issues.

The final issue covered under competency has been of interest in recent years. Psychologists base their work on established scientific and professional knowledge. There has been considerable attention devoted to evidence-based treatments in clinical child and adolescent psychology (see Chapters 2 and 5). Although most psychologists see this emphasis as a positive move, others raise the issues of the potential reduction in flexibility that the clinician may have in tailoring treatment to the needs of the individual child (Spirito, 2010b). On one hand there have been discussions of whether or not it is ethical to employ any treatment other than evidence based ones, whereas on the other hand there are concerns about throwing the baby out with the bathwater. Many of these debates reflect the rich blending of science and practice that exists in clinical child and adolescent psychology.

STANDARD 3: HUMAN RELATIONS

The first sections of this standard are related to how the psychologist interacts with others regardless of whether or not we are talking about a clinical child and adolescent psychologist. The psychologist does not discriminate against others regardless of age, gender, gender identity, race, ethnicity, culture, national origin, religion, sexual orientation, disability, socioeconomic status, or any basis proscribed by law. Where the psychologist might have some conflict in this area might have to do with certain beliefs. For example, some psychologists may hold strong religious beliefs that homosexuality is wrong and therefore might not be able to be objective in dealing with clients or families with this orientation. Is it discrimination to decline such a referral? In this case, it would most likely not be discrimination but rather recognition by the psychologist that due to their own biases, they could not provide the treatment.

Sexual harassment and other types of harassment are prohibited. In this area, some situations are clearly harassment (i.e., sexual advances) whereas others may be less clear (i.e., language). At times the appropriateness of jokes and comments falls under the harassment category but may not be seen by the individual making them as harassment or creating a hostile environment. However, if the other person perceives them as offensive, they are generally seen as a form of harassment. It is better to refrain from any comments that might be offensive and to maintain a more professional approach. Sometimes psychologists working with adolescents find themselves in a culture in which their patients employ quite colorful language. In these situations, there may be a tendency for the psychologist to fall into using some of the same language. Such a practice is not advisable because it may be offensive to colleagues or to family members of the adolescent.

Doing no harm and multiple relationships are covered in the next sections of Standard 3. Of these, the issue of multiple relationships has presented the most conflict and is generally related to potentially doing some harm through the relationship. We all have multiple relationships in our professional and nonprofessional lives. The major issues about multiple relationships for the clinical child and adolescent psychologists have to do with the relationship impairing the psychologist's ability to behave objectively and competently and with the potential harm that may be inflected on the client and/or family. The issue is not to avoid all multiple relationships, but rather avoid them if there is any potential harm to the client or any comprise to the psychologist's ability to function professionally. For example, we may be asked to see the son or daughter of someone with whom we have frequent professional contact. Can we be totally objective in working with that family? In addition, is the person with whom we have frequent contact going to be able to interact with us as both a colleague and as a patient? It is generally best to give careful consideration to the implications before entering into any multiple relationships. If it seems necessary to enter into a multiple relationship (i.e., lack of other resources) the psychologist should discuss the implications and develop a game plan with the individual with whom he or she is entering the relationship. If the nature of their relationship becomes an issue, plans of how to resolve them need to be established prior to treatment.

Closely related to multiple relationships is the standard against entering into relationships that are exploitative. For example, a clinical child and adolescent psychologist might be seeing adolescent patients as part of his private practice and conducting research on adolescent problems at the local university. The psychologist might be seen as exploiting his relationship with his patient if he requested that the patient participate in the research project because of the power the psychologist might hold over him.

Issues of conflict of interest fall under this standard and must be avoided. Some potential areas of conflict might arise with the clinical child and adolescent psychologist who provides consultation or evaluations for a school district and also sees private patients. It might be seen as a conflict of interest in such a situation for the person to make referrals to him/herself. Similarly, it might be seen as a conflict of interest for the consulting psychologist to attempt to sell the school products when there is a financial benefit for the consultant.

At times, the clinical child and adolescent psychologist might be asked to provide services to an individual at the request of a third party. For example, a psychologist might be asked to provide treatment (as part of an employee assistance program) to an adolescent dependent of one of her employees. The psychologist needs to clarify, before entering into the therapeutic contract, the nature of the relationship with the patient and the organizations involved. What is the role of the psychologist? Who is the client? What information is the agency expecting, and what are the limits to confidentiality? The issues here are very similar to those faced by psychologists who provide services through organizations.

Psychologists are expected to cooperate with other professionals. This issue can be complicated when working with children and adolescents due to the large number of individuals who may be involved in the systems surrounding the patient. For example, a high school student may have five or six different teachers, a guidance counselor, a social worker, a minister, and a principal all involved in the case. Another example might be a clinical child and adolescent psychologist being asked to do a custody evaluation and the father is in therapy with another professional. If the evaluation is to be independent, should the psychologist contact the father's therapist? If she does not contact the therapist, is this likely to be seen as being uncooperative?

Next is the issue of informed consent, which presents one of the most unique issues for the clinical child and adolescent psychologists. According to O'Donohue and Ferguson (2003), the major area of concern about informed consent with children is the child's competency to make an informed decision. Informed consent implies that the person understands the options being presented, is capable of competent decision making, and then independently agrees to the option(s) chosen. In other words, informed consent requires that decisions are informed, competent, and voluntary. Of major concern here is whether children can give informed consent. Koocher and Keith-Spiegel (1990) suggest that informed consent implies that the information has been presented in a manner that the child can fully understand and that the person meets legal requirements to make a binding and valid decision. This legal requirement is usually 18 years of age. Even if there were no legal restrictions, children's cognitive development may make it very difficult or impossible for them to fully understand what is being asked and what they are agreeing to. Are they competent to make an informed decision? Typically the answer is "no."

Generally children are assumed to be incompetent to make decisions about participation in treatment and research because of their limited cognitive development, independence, and previous experience (O'Donohue & Ferguson, 2003; Pagliocca, Melton, Weisz, & Lyons, 1995). Adults are assumed to be competent in making decisions about their own treatment and that of their children. However, children's and adolescent's behavior problems may be the symptoms of family issues and dysfunction. Sometimes the child or adolescent may be serving as the "ticket" to treatment. The psychologist may also have to evaluate whether or not the parents are competent to provide consent for their child's treatment. It is good practice to document the parents' consent and also to document the child's assent before evaluation and/or treatment.

What if the child does not want treatment? When should the child's input override the adult's? Koocher and Keith-Spiegel (1990) state that there is a general lack of agreement as to when and how the child's input should be used in the decision-making process. This debate is ongoing, and there are not clear guidelines in most cases. For a more extended discussion of this issue, see Kendall and Suveg (2008), Stines and Feeny (2008), and Vitiello (2008).

At what age is the child at a developmental level to understand various issues about which she or he is being asked to assent? Drotar (2008) points out the need for additional research into such issues as the nature of the information the child needs to know to consent, the influence of the child's developmental level and understanding on assent, the child's ability to understand placebo treatments, and so forth.

The other issue of concern about consent has to do with the voluntary nature of the process. For a child to say "no" to a request of an adult is difficult and takes a degree of courage. In addition, children rarely volunteer for evaluation or treatment—they are brought. The same is true of most adolescents. How does the clinical child and adolescent psychologist deal with this issue? Nelson and Finch (2008c) provide a discussion about the development of an agreement with children and adolescents for the provision of psychological treatment.

The final area of discussion under this standard has to do with the interruption of treatment. Psychologists need to have a plan for the provisions of psychological services if there is an interruption due to their illness, death, unavailability, relocation, or retirement or by the patient's relocation or financial limitations. Most psychologists in practice develop some system for "on-call" handling of brief periods of being away or even illness. However, more elaborate plans might be needed in the case of a prolonged illness or death. Some psychologists have developed "psychological wills," or plans for dealing with their practices in case of their deaths. In group practices, there may be informal agreements about how to deal with such issues, but in many cases no plans have been developed.

More common events falling under this standard have to do with clients moving or being unable to meet their financial obligations. In the case of the client moving, the psychologist should attempt to locate a clinical child and adolescent therapist in the new location. Typically the psychologist will ask an acquaintance in the area for a recommendation or search some database (i.e., APA directory, ABPP directory, National Register) to find a list of potential providers. Sometimes this process is relatively simple, and at other times it is practically impossible.

It may become impossible for the client to meet the financial obligation of therapy. Psychologists are expected to provide some pro bono services, but they are also humans and need to make a living. One solution is to agree to see the patient at a reduced rate, which may help, or the psychologist can agree to make a referral to a public sector provider. Both of these solutions may present some problems. For example, seeing a client for a reduced fee may present issues with insurance companies that focus on typical fees. On the other hand, the availability of public sector providers is very limited, and some may not be well qualified. Another solution might be to continue to bill the patient at the customary rate, and write the balance off after a period of time. All of these solutions present potential problems, but all are employed.

STANDARD 4: PRIVACY AND CONFIDENTIALITY

It is the responsibility of psychologists to take all reasonable precautions to protect confidential information given to them by their patients and to ensure that their records remain confidential to the extent limited by law or established by institutional rules or professional or scientific relationship.

Under this standard falls the provision of information to insurance companies, reports, and/or correspondence, and so forth and the need to limit the amount of information to the amount necessary while not disclosing more information than is germane.

The limits of confidentiality should be discussed at the initial meeting with the client, and written consent should be obtained before any information is disclosed. The issues of confidentiality with children and adolescents present challenges to confidentiality. According to Melton, Koocher, and Saks (1983), informed consent is assumed to be from the parents and not from the child. As a result, the psychologist obtains consent from the parents and assent from the child. Due to this unique characteristic of the agreement, the psychologist is required to inform the parents about the treatment. Because of this requirement, there are limitations to the degree of confidentiality provided to the child (O'Donohue & Ferguson, 2003). These limits need to be discussed with both the parents and the child at the beginning of treatment/assessment. Parents will usually respect the need for some privacy by the child and the need for the development of trust with the psychologist. A written contract about the nature and limits of confidentiality should be obtained. Nelson and Finch (2008c) present a useful model and guidelines for such an agreement with children and adolescents. The psychologist needs to be familiar with state laws regarding the age at which at individual can provide consent. This age is typically 18, but there are exceptions.

As with all patients, the limits of confidentiality need to be addressed. For example, parents and children need to know that the reporting of abuse is not covered by confidentiality but is rather mandated by law. Similarly, children and adolescents need to be informed that threat of suicide or homicide will not be confidential. As previously mentioned, any limits placed on confidentiality need to be made clear to all parties.

STANDARD 5: ADVERTISING AND OTHER PUBLIC STATEMENTS

The guidelines provided under Standard 5 basically state that psychologists represent themselves accurately and honestly. This requirement has to do with their training, experiences, skills, and the services provided. In addition, they are responsible for correcting any statements made by others that might be misleading or false. When advertising, they will provide only information that is accurate and not seek endorsements or testimonies.

Clinical child and adolescent psychologist may discuss their specialized education, training, supervision, and experiences that have prepared them to provide the services to this population. Care should probably be taken not to target the perceived deficiencies in the training of others because such comments are likely to create ill will. Statements such as being board certified in clinical child and adolescent psychology are appropriate when the certification is by a nationally recognized certifying body such as the American Board of Professional Psychology.

STANDARD 6: RECORD KEEPING AND FEES

It is the responsibility of psychologists to create, to control as closely as possible, to maintain, to disseminate, to store, to retain, and to properly dispose of all records and data of the patients they serve. These records are designed to facilitate the provision of later services by the psychologist herself or by other professionals. In the case of research data, the records should be recorded in such a fashion as to protect the identity of the subjects yet be complete enough to facilitate replication. The psychologist also needs to ensure that the records are complete enough to meet the institutional requirements and to be in compliance with the law. In addition, the records should be designed to facilitate accurate billing and payment records. Each psychologist needs to have a preestablished plan for what will be done with the records if the psychologist takes another position of stops practicing.

Because the records are the patient's, the psychologist cannot refuse to provide the patient with his or her records simply for failure to pay the bill. With regard to billing, psychologists should make their billing practices know up front and should engage in billing practices that are consistent with the law. If a copay is required by the insurance company, the psychologist should collect or bill it. If there is a question about the client's ability to pay the bill, the psychologist should discuss options regarding other services or regarding what arrangements can be made if it becomes an issue. Although bartering is not against the standards, it creates a number of potential problems, and these should be discussed prior to entering into such an agreement. The psychologist needs to make sure that the patient and family understand that the psychologist can bill only for those services provided and cannot provide inaccurate information to third parties.

For the clinical child and adolescent psychologist, there is the added confusion of who owns the records. Frequently the parents, the patient, and even siblings are involved in sessions. How is the psychologist to ensure the confidentiality of all involved? This question can become a major issue if the parents decide to separate and divorce. Unless consent is obtained from both parents, there is an issue with commingled records. Some clinical child and adolescent psychologists maintain separate records on each parent. However, most do not. In some states, the psychologist does not have to release records in compliance with a lawyer's subpoena. The psychologist should explain the issue to the lawyer, and if the records are necessary, advise the lawyer to get consent from the other spouse through her or his lawyer. Lawyers will attempt to intimidate, but this is simply part of our legal system. If the judge believes that the records are essential, she can subpoena them, and then the psychologist must provide them. When separate records for each parent are kept, the psychologist can release the relevant ones to the lawyer.

STANDARD 7: EDUCATION AND TRAINING

Standard 7 has to with education and training activities. Psychologists involved in education and training programs attempt to ensure that the programs are so designed as to provide the appropriate instruction and experiences for the type of training provided. The students should be prepared to meet the requirements for licensure, certification, or other special training that the program states that it offers. With regard to training in clinical child and adolescent psychology, there are guidelines for the educational preparation (Roberts, Carlson, et al., 1998; Roberts, Erickson, & Tuma, 1985), predoctoral internship (Finch & Robbins, 1985), and postdoctoral training (Ollendick, 1984). Descriptions of the training program should be accurate, and the instruction and supervision provided should also be correct and up-to-date.

Issues of self-disclosure and mandatory therapy for students are addressed. Self-disclosure of personal information regarding personal history can be obtained from students as part of the program only when they have been informed in the program description that such information will be required or when it seems necessary for the student's progress. Similarly, if individual or group therapy is a program requirement, it is the responsibility of the program to provide this information to potential students before they apply. Individuals who are responsible for evaluation of the student(s) should not provide the therapy.

Training programs develop an evaluation process for all their students and inform students regarding the nature of this feedback prior to the process. Evaluation should include both strengths and weaknesses in terms that are clear and preferably behaviorally based. Suggestions for improvement should be provided also.

Finally, faculty members do not engage in sexual behavior with students and supervisees who are in their institution or whom they are likely to evaluate. How far this prohibition extends outside of the individual's department or line of supervision is not clear. For example, is it appropriate for a psychologist in the psychology department to have a sexual relationship with a student in the English department at the same university? This is the same agency.

STANDARD 8: RESEARCH AND PUBLICATION

Psychologists conducting research are required to seek institutional approval. Most institutions have institutional review boards that follow specified guidelines in reviewing and approving research. Informed consent is required, and the same issues that have been previously discussed regarding children apply. Children and adolescents cannot give informed consent; this must be obtained from the parents or guardians. However, children and adolescents can provide assent—an agreement to participate (implying less ability to be fully informed). O'Donohue and Ferguson (2003) state that children and adolescents have the right to assent or dissent to participate in research and treatment, but that their decision can be overridden by the parents, guardians, and courts. Psychologists conducting research with children and adolescents should obtain parental or guardian permission in writing and assent in writing from the child.

Particular care is needed when conducting research with children due to the fact that they are vulnerable and are not competent to provide consent. In addition, their participation can be seen as involuntary. A parent's consent may not always represent the best interest of the child. For example, if compensation is provided for participation in research, some parents might coerce their children to participate. For this reason, it is recommended that the compensation not be so great as to lead the parents to make unwise decisions.

As with other records, psychologists maintain the confidentiality of information obtained from research participants and ensure that research assistants understand and respect this confidentiality. In addition, when recording of voice or image is involved, the psychologists take extra precaution to ensure the subject's privacy. This need for confidentiality also applies to situations in which the psychologist serves as a reviewer of projects or publication submissions.

When deception is necessary and approved, care is taken to explain the nature of the deception soon after the subject has participated. Trust is a major issue in psychological research with children due to their vulnerability, and particular care needs to be exercised in this area.

In reporting psychological research findings, data are not fabricated, and if accidental errors are found, every effort is taken to correct them.

Similarly, psychologists take and assign research credit only to the extent that it is deserved. Sometimes when working with children, the question arises about the inclusion of individuals without whom the project could not have taken place. For example, if a principal has been particularly helpful, should research credit be given? Certainly an acknowledgment in a footnote is always appropriate, but what about authorship? The decision of authorship depends on the degree of scientific or professional contributions of the individuals involved and is not given simply because of their positions. The psychologist needs to discuss the authorship of any publications from a research project prior to the beginning of the process.

Closely related to publication credit is the sanction against plagiarism and claiming another's work as one's own. Although this standard appears straightforward, there can be issues raised about the role of research assistants. If they provide written records of their literature reviews, for example, whose property are the written records? Certainly the psychologist should not simply include an assistant's review as her own, but where is the line drawn? What about a master's thesis in which the idea is basically the professor's? Clear guidelines for dissertation credit are provided, but other areas are less clear.

Another part of this standard may be less clear than initially thought. The publication of duplicate data can be an issue in large research projects and data sets. The intent of this standard is for the psychologist not to publish the same study in more than one source. At times the same data might be used as part of more than one study addressing more than one question. Does this practice run counter to the standard? It is generally best to report the data as part of a larger study and to mention that some of the data has been previously reported.

If another investigator requests copies of published data for the purpose of verification of findings, the psychologist should provide the data and be as cooperative as possible. Sometimes the initial inclination is to be defensive or not respond; this reaction, however, should be avoided. At times this request may create some problems when the data are part of a larger data set. The psychologist is only required to provide that part of the data reported in the study of interest.

STANDARD 9: ASSESSMENT

The use of assessment techniques has a long history in clinical child and adolescent psychology. As Koocher and Keith-Spiegel (1990) point out, children were among the first beneficiaries of psychological testing and as a result were probably among the first victims of its misuse. The history of misuses of psychological testing has resulted is some fairly specific guideless for assessment in the APA code of conduct.

Psychologists base their reports and testimony on sufficient data to support their findings and provide their opinions only after conducting an examination or, when requested, only after a careful review of the records. Psychologists employ appropriate psychological tests and instruments with established reliability and validity. For clinical child and adolescent psychologists, there is the added concern about the long-term effects of their assessments. Critical decisions that can have an effect on the child for the rest of his or her life may be influenced by the results of the report. Care should be taken to ensure that the recommendations are well thought out and that they are based on best practices.

The question of empirically supported methods comes up in assessment. Many of the traditional psychological methods have limited data supporting their reliability and validity. This issue is one not only for projective techniques but also for entire diagnostic groups. For example, there is no universally accepted operational definition of learning disabilities based on psychological testing. In addition, a close look at the diagnostic labels applied to children reveals that they have some of the lowest reliability of any of the psychiatric diagnoses. Given the fact that validity directly relates to reliability, what does this imply for the clinical child and adolescent psychologist? Certainly particular care is needed in providing the most accurate evaluations possible, and it is probably better to err on the side of caution.

Related to reliability is an issue that frequently arises in assessment of children. What if children do not understand what is required of them? How much additional probing and modification of the standard questions can the psychologist provide? We know that the reliability and validity data reported for the test instrument are based on the standard instructions provided in the test manual. Do we stick strictly to the provided instructions, or do we modify or simplify them? Some clinical child and adolescent psychologists would tend to reasonably modify the instructions slightly and then describe the amount of modification needed in the report; others would argue against this practice.

Also related to the comprehension of instructions is the use of language in the assessment process. Certainly the psychologist working with children needs to use language that is appropriate for the developmental level of the child. What if the child's first language is not English? An interpreter is permitted if informed consent is given by the parents and assent is obtained from the child. However, psychological tests are based on norms that assume a certain level of shared experiences and if a child grows up under different experiences, it would seem that extreme caution needs to be exercised. The code states that psychological assessments are conducted in the individual's preferred language unless the use of the alternative language is important to the assessment issue. For example, part of the evaluation question might be whether or not the child adequately understands the majority language or if additional classroom support might be needed in the native language. Given the increasing multicultural nature of our population, such issues are likely to become increasingly common.

Also under the standards related to assessment is the issue of informed consent. The issues related to the difficulty of obtaining informed consent that were previously discussed apply here. It is necessary to obtain written consent from the parents or guardians and obtain assent from the child or adolescent. The same precautions should be followed regarding the release of assessment findings to a third party.

Psychologists are responsible for maintaining test security. The validity of the testing results rests on the secure nature of the test material, and as a result, extra care needs to be taken to maintain this security. One clinical child and adolescent psychology colleague tells of beginning an intellectual evaluation with a child who recognized the testing kit and reported that his mother had bought one at a yard sale for him to play with. Needless to say, any information obtained by using that instrument would not be valid.

When assistants or students are employed to conduct part of the examination process, the psychologist is responsible for ensuring their qualifications for administering the tests. The psychologist also needs to ensure that the use of such assistants is part of the consent and assent agreement, and that the practices employed meet legal standards. Some insurance companies limit the use of such assistants for billed services, and it is the responsibility of the psychologist to ensure the accuracy of their billing.

Psychologists are responsible for explaining their assessment results to responsible individuals unless specifically prohibited by the nature of the evaluation (i.e., forensic). How about the child or adolescent patient? If appropriate, the clinical child and adolescent psychologist might provide the child with an individual feedback session that is developmentally geared toward him or her.

STANDARD 10: THERAPY

The final standard has to do with therapy. Again, the psychologist seeing children needs to deal with the issue of obtaining consent and assent. Obtaining consent and assent represents one of the most consistent of the ethical issues faced, and care should always be exercised to ensure that the consent is provided by the appropriate individual. Does the parent bringing the child to treatment have custody; is there joint custody; or is there a legal guardian? Rarely are these issues present when working with adults, but these questions have to be asked with child patients.

Another issue that was previously raised had to do with the involvement of the parents and even siblings in treatment. The psychologist clearly identifies who the patient is and explains his role with each of the people involved. It is also important to determine the nature of the therapy that is being provided. Although insurance companies often cover therapy for the identified patient, some may not provide coverage for the patient's family members in family therapy. The psychologist needs to be sure that the services provided are those that are being billed.

One of the more frequent dilemmas faced by the clinical child and adolescent psychologist is the potential for conflicting roles. A typical situation might involve the psychologist providing primary services to the child, and then the parents decide to seek a divorce. Role definition should be an essential part of any therapeutic contract, but no matter how carefully this role is described at the beginning of therapy, it may arise again in the heat of the divorce. The psychologist is treating the child and should not be involved in conducting a custody evaluation because these are different responsibilities. The other complication that may arise, and has been previously mentioned, is related to records. If the records of the child also include confidential information about the parents, they cannot be released without written consent from all parties or a judge's orders in most states.

Another issue that frequently arises for the psychologist providing therapy to children and adolescents has to do with one or both parents being involved in therapy with another therapist. The treatment issue and any potential conflicts need to be considered carefully and discussed with the family members as appropriate. In most cases, in order to minimize any potential conflict or confusion, it is wise to obtain permission from the parent(s) receiving therapy to contact his or her therapist.

As was previously mentioned, arrangements need to be made to deal with any interruption of treatment. In addition, issues of termination need to be discussed from the beginning. When it becomes clear that the child no longer needs services, is not likely to continue to benefit from treatment, or is being made worse by treatment, it is the responsibility of the psychologist to terminate therapy. Nelson and Politano (1993) provide useful guidelines about termination with children and adolescents.

Typically the psychologist will assure the family and child that he or she will remain available if the need for additional treatment arises.

Potential sexual misconduct is the other part of this standard. Certainly sex with a minor patient is not only unethical but is also illegal under all circumstances. The standard also applies to a family member of a current patient. It is prohibited. What about former patients or their families? The code suggests that a minimum of 2 years must have passed, and even then only under the most unusual of circumstances. It seems that the best decision is to avoid sexual contact with former patients and their families altogether because such behavior simply presents more risks than benefits.

Summary

The same ethical principles and codes of conduct apply to all psychologists whether or not they work with children. However, a number of unique issues arise when working with children and their families. This chapter has attempted to address these issues, raise some questions, and discuss some conflicts about which the psychologist needs to be aware. Children and even adolescents are more vulnerable that are adults, and they are involved in numerous systems that increase the potential for ethical issues. If there is one final message, it would be to be aware and alert to potential issues and to do no harm.

NINE

Interpersonal and Cultural Competencies

In this chapter we will discuss two separate competency areas that are important for all clinical child and adolescent psychologists: (1) providing clinical work with sufficient interpersonal competence to facilitate the effectiveness of the clinical work, and (2) providing clinical work with knowledge of, and sensitivity toward, the cultural factors that affect children's and families' behaviors and that affect the therapist-client interaction. These represent two very different competencies in some ways. However, both are considered in this chapter because they require finely tuned sensitivity to clients' worldviews. Both sets of competencies require an empathic awareness of children's and families' feelings and concerns, and the contextual factors that influence them. This chapter will discuss literature and practice issues related to these two distinct areas of professional competency.

Interpersonal Competency

Efforts to define psychological practitioners' professional competency have grown substantially in recent years (Rubin et al., 2007). Professional competency has been defined by Epstein and Hundert (2002) as "the habitual and judicious use of communication, knowledge, technical skills, clinical training, emotions, values and reflections in daily practice for the benefit of the individual or community being served" (p. 227). Based on an American Psychological Association Task Force on the Assessment of Competence in Professional Psychology (Kaslow, Rubin, et al., 2006), certain foundational competencies have been identified. Foundational competencies are core knowledge areas that support the psychologist's functional competencies (e.g., in assessment, in intervention), and one important foundational competency is believed to be the psychologist's competency to engage in satisfactory interpersonal interactions. *Interpersonal competency* has been referred to as "interpersonal interactions" in the literature on professional competency. The competency of a clinical practitioner's interpersonal interactions will be evident in how the practitioner communicates and relates in effective and meaningful ways with individuals, groups, and communities.

The assessment of competency has been advocated and conducted in varying degrees in different health disciplines. Leigh et al. (2007) have described how communication and interpretive abilities are defined and noted within a variety of health disciplines such as dentistry, medicine, and psychology. For example, interpersonal and communication skills have been identified as one of six key competence areas for physicians (Epstein & Hundert, 2002).

Leigh et al. (2007) noted that professionals' interpersonal skills could be assessed via questionnaires or essays (tapping knowledge), via observation of decision-making skills with clients, and via clinical case descriptions or use of simulated patients. For example, O'Sullivan, Chao, Russell, Levine, and Fabiny (2008) have described how physicians' communication and interpersonal skills were assessed by preceptors' ratings of physicians' responses to scenarios of cases, rating the physicians on clarity of explanations and communication and on their ability to elicit appropriate information.

In medicine, it has long been recognized that difficulties in the effective delivery of health care can be due, in many cases, to poor communication between patient and health-care provider, rather than to failings in the technical aspects of health care (Teutsch, 2003). Because the quality of physician-patient communication can affect health-care outcomes, clinicians are expected to gain an understanding of the patients' perspectives on their illnesses; to explore patients' values, cultures, and preferences; and to avoid being judgmental or scolding. When factors related to patients' satisfaction with their health care have been reviewed, some of the factors with the clearest relationship to patient satisfaction include the clarity of physicians' communication to patients, the patients' ability to retain this information, and the affiliative and supportive nature of the physicians' behavior (Lochman, 1983).

Physicians judged to be highly empathic typically ask fewer closed and biased questions, and have less nonverbal tension and withdrawal in their videotaped interactions with patients (Lochman & Dain, 1982). When physicians' interview styles were more collaborative and less controlling, participants who had an internal health locus of control reported greater satisfaction (Lochman, Dain, & Babick, 1984); thus an interpersonally astute physician should adjust her or his interview style to match the expectations that patients have for maintaining or not maintaining high degrees of personal control over their health-care behaviors.

A psychologist's levels of interpersonal competence have long been considered to be important for becoming skillful as a therapist (Loo, 1979), and a therapist's empathy, acceptance, and openness were found to be predictors of therapeutic skill (D'Augelli, 1973; Rappaport, Chinsky, & Cowen, 1971). Interpersonal competency has been described by the American Board of Clinical Child and Adolescent Psychology (ABCCAP) as having certain key components: (a) a level of self-awareness exists that promotes effective performance in the functional competencies (e.g., assessment, intervention, consultation); (b) an awareness of the needs, feelings, and reactions of others; and (c) sensitivity to the welfare, rights, and dignity of others.

When candidates are examined by the ABCCAP for professional certification, failing-level examples of problematic interpersonal interactions include the following: (a) poor self-awareness, evident in inappropriately personalizing, discounting, or misunderstanding clients' reactions, with an inability to manage countertransference reactions; (b) poor awareness of others, evident in the ignoring of clients' feelings; and (c) failure to be sensitive to the welfare, rights, and dignity of others, evident in not being compassionate and understanding, being disrespectful, and acting in ways that are harmful to the client. Thus, having a capacity to accurately be aware of emotional reactions within oneself and within clients, and having an ability to self-regulate one's emotional and behavioral reactions, are considered to be essential elements of a competent practicing psychologist.

THERAPEUTIC ALLIANCE

One important aspect of a clinician's interpersonal competence can be evident in the types of therapeutic alliances that she or he can create (Lochman & Pardini, 2008). Historically, the therapeutic relationship has been viewed as a key change mechanism in child psychotherapy (Shirk & Karver, 2003), and the development of a therapeutic relationship may be especially critical when working with children and families from a variety of cultures (Welch, 2003). Therapeutic alliance has been found in a meta-analysis to be significantly, albeit modestly, associated with outcomes in child and adolescent therapy (Shirk & Karver, 2003). Currently, a majority of child psychologists and psychiatrists report in surveys that the therapeutic alliance and other nonspecific processes are critical for change in child treatment (Chu et al., 2004; Kazdin et al., 1990). Therapeutic alliance can be conceptualized as follows: (1) as a means to an end, such as the working alliance in psychoanalytic therapy, (2) as a necessary and sufficient mechanism for therapeutic change, as in play therapy and client-centered therapy, or (3) in cognitive-behavioral therapy, the therapist serves as an active "coach," with an emphasis on a collaborative process (Chu et al., 2004). Thus therapeutic alliance is assumed to be necessary but not sufficient in cognitive-behavioral therapy. Therapeutic alliance may be especially important in child intervention, because children don't initiate treatment. The affiliative bond between client and therapist and the agreement and involvement in intervention tasks may be key in child interventions. These dimensions are expected to be interrelated (Shirk & Saiz, 1992), and are assessed in one of the few therapeutic alliance measures available for children (Shirk & Russell, 1996).

There is minimal research to date, but a meta-analysis (Shirk & Karver, 2003) and literature review (Green, 2006) indicate (1) a small but significant effect for therapeutic alliance (0.21), with somewhat greater effect for externalizing (0.30) than internalizing (0.10) problems; (2) measures of therapeutic alliance taken late in treatment are more strongly associated with outcome than measures taken early in treatment; and (3) there is little support for the *predictive* effect of therapeutic alliance. However, recent research has found that a positive alliance between parents and therapists in parent management training for antisocial children has predicted improvements in parenting practices (Kazdin & Whitley, 2006), and positive child-therapist alliance has predicted improvements in children's behavior (Kazdin, Whitley, & Marciano, 2006).

To address a lack of examination of therapeutic alliance in group forms of cognitive-behavioral therapy, Lochman, Barth, and Mager (2005) examined therapeutic alliance in a sample of 80 children screened as being in the top 30% of children in behavioral problems according to fourth-grade teachers. The children received the Coping Power group CBT program. Findings indicated that children's baseline behavior problems predicted poor therapeutic alliances, and weak therapeutic alliances are related to higher levels of children's problem behaviors at the end of intervention. However, the therapeutic alliance was not a very good predictor of *change* in children's externalizing behavior during intervention, suggesting that therapeutic alliance was not the primary mechanism accounting for CBT effects in group interventions with children.

Cultural Competency

Cultural competency, also referred to as *individual and cultural diversity*, is another foundational competency that is related to clinicians' abilities to interact in interpersonally competent ways with their clients, and to successfully be able to perceive their clients' perspectives and to communicate clearly with them. Competency to respond to clients' individual and cultural diversity involves clinicians' awareness of, and sensitivity to, factors such as gender, ethnicity, sexual orientation, and spirituality that can influence clients' presentation. Attention to multicultural issues is especially important with clients in the child and adolescent age range (Asamen, Ellis, & Berry, 2008). Children from visibly different racial groups are likely to be faced with stereotyped attributions of their cognitive, academic, and social abilities, leading to limited acceptance by their peers and possibly their teachers (Graves & Graves, 2008), and making the adjustment of minority children with behavioral and emotional problems doubly difficult. Culturally competent clinicians are those who can anticipate culturally related appropriateness of, and obstacles to, the use of common assessment or intervention procedures for children and families.

Culture and ethnicity are sometimes used interchangeably, but they are qualitatively different constructs (Jones, Kephart, Langley, Parker, Shenoy, & Weeks, 2001). Culture involves the norms and values, influenced by society, that influence how someone thinks, feels, and behaves, whereas ethnicity is a set of genetic, morphological, and anthropological characteristics (Parron, 1994). Culture can be as large as a nation and as small as a rural town, whereas ethnicity is based on cultural heritage, race, religion, language, and so forth. Thus, individuals' behaviors are influenced by acquired cultural beliefs rather than by ethnicity, and because cultural beliefs are open to environmental influence, the behavior and beliefs of ethnic groups are not static and homogeneous (Jones et al., 2001).

Provision of culturally competent mental health services has become a central aspect of mental health reform in the United States (Department of Health and Human Services, 2005). Appreciation of diversity is a core foundation for psychologists' respect for people's rights and dignity. The American Psychological Association states this principle clearly:

> Psychologists respect the dignity and worth of all people, and the rights of individuals to privacy, confidentiality, and self-determination. Psychologists are aware that special safeguards may be necessary to protect the rights and welfare of persons or communities whose vulnerabilities impair autonomous decision making. Psychologists are aware of and respect cultural, individual, and role differences, including those based on age, gender, gender identity, race, ethnicity, culture, national origin, religion, sexual orientation, disability, language, and socioeconomic status, and consider

> those factors when working with members of such groups. Psychologists try to eliminate the effect on their work of biases based on those factors, and they do not knowingly participate in or condone activities based upon such prejudices. (APA, 2002a, Principle E)

The emphasis on cultural competency for professional psychologists is especially important as the United States becomes more racially and ethnically diverse and thus requires more culturally responsive practices and services (APA, 2002b). Disparities in mental health care based on race and ethnicity have been well documented (Stanhope, Solomon, Finley, Pernell-Arnold, Bourjolly & Sands, 2008). Diverse racial and ethnic populations experience poor access to care, inaccurate assessments and diagnoses, reduced amounts of psychosocial and medication treatments, high dropout rates, low satisfaction and poor outcomes with services, and underrepresentation in clinical research studies (Stanhope et al., 2008). These disparities suggest that there may be basic biases in the mental health system at the organizational and provider levels. At the organizational level, Western values may be embedded in care planning, although some goals for psychiatric rehabilitation, such as emancipation from one's family, are not appropriate for all cultures (Barrio, 2000; Pernell-Arnold & Finley, 1999).

At the level of the clinical provider, clinicians' appreciation for diversity permits them to more effectively understand the experiences of the clients, and to more accurately assess the appropriate use of psychological assessment and intervention procedures (Falender & Shafranske, 2004). Clinicians working with minority children may be challenged to earn the trust of the child and the family, which is essential for a strong viable relationship (Jones et al., 2001). Cultural competence inherently involves the development of strong self-awareness abilities by the clinician, and ensures that culturally appropriate practices inform applied clinical services.

Cultural competency has been described by the ABCCAP as having certain key components: (a) knowledge about individual and cultural diversity, (b) sensitivity and responsivity to individual and cultural diversity in each functional area of professional competency (e.g., testing, intervention, consultation), and (c) awareness of the interaction between the clinician's own diversity characteristics and those of the people with whom the clinician is working professionally. When clinical child and adolescent psychologists are examined by the ABCCAP for professional certification, failing-level examples of problematic cultural competence include (a) failing to convey adequate or correct knowledge about individual and cultural diversity, and (b) selecting assessment tools or research measures not normed for individuals with demographic characteristics similar to the client being tested, or not including a cultural formulation in case conceptualization or recommendation. Thus, culturally competent clinicians attend to the cultural values of individuals in various ethnic groups and to culturally relevant factors such as clients' ethnic identities.

CULTURAL VALUES VARY BY ETHNICITY

In general, research on children of varying ethnicities in the first half of the 20th century was directed by white researchers and examined differences between white and minority children on cognitive and psychological tests, often concluding that minorities were inferior in certain ways. Such claims, based on faulty data, have reduced confidence in the psychological assessment process among minority families (Jones et al., 2001). In recent decades, more minority researchers have become involved in cross-cultural research, and there has been more emphasis on topics such as how resiliency and protective cultural attributes help minority individuals handle stressors related to racism and poor socioeconomic conditions (Council of National Psychological Associations for the Advancement of Ethnic Minority Interests [CNPAAEMI], 2009).

African-American Children When working with African-American children and families, clinicians should attend to how contextual variables may have an effect on the expression of psychopathology and on the level of impairment involved (Jones et al., 2001). For example, according to 2008 U.S. Census reports, about a third of African-American children under the age of 18 live in poverty (CNPAAEMI, 2009). Although not all African-American families are poor, poverty may be the risk factor that contributes to the development and maintenance of psychopathology among some African-American children. Attention to an Afrocentric worldview can assist the clinicians' understanding of strengths in African-American children and families. Some of the following Afrocentric values and beliefs may be important:

1. Spirituality, involving a belief in a being or force greater than self
2. Collectivism, interdependence, and cooperation, which motivate a person to work for the well-being of the group rather than oneself
3. Time orientation, as time is viewed as subjectively flexible rather than being bound concretely by clocks, and as being more focused on the past and present rather than the future

4. Sensitivity to affect and emotional cues (e.g., "I am well if you are well")
5. Balance and harmony with nature. (CNPAAEMI, 2009)

As will be noted, some of these worldviews—such as collectivism, spirituality, and harmony with nature—are found among other minority groups in the United States as well.

Native American Children When working with Native American children and adolescents, clinicians should be sensitive to the heterogeneity among Native American peoples (there are 562 federally recognized American Indian and Alaska Native tribes in the United States), and to the difficult contextual risk factors that affect the families (the highest poverty rate of any ethnic group in the United States) (CNPAAEMI, 2009). The learning experience of Native American children is different from that of children of the majority culture because Native Americans value noninterference and minimize the power differential among individuals, and adults view even young children as autonomous individuals capable of making their own decisions (Jones et al., 2001). Thus, Native American parents could be perceived as neglectful when they are simply following cultural norms.

The following Native American values and beliefs are relatively common across tribal groups and may be important to clinicians:

1. Close connection to all forms of life, because all living things share the essence of the Creator, and to relatives who have died, and thus relationships with ancestors help to guide present-day actions
2. Relationships among extended, multigenerational family members are close and defined (e.g., a woman's sisters may be considered as "mothers" to her children)
3. Respect is given to elders because of their experience, knowledge, and wisdom, and children are respected and considered sacred because they are the future of the tribe
4. Spirituality is a way of living (there is no separate word for *religion* in most Native American languages because spirituality is not considered to be separate from the rest of life) rather than merely what one believes, and each tribe has its own spiritual cosmologies and ceremonies integrated into all aspects of social and cultural life
5. Balance within the self and harmony and interdependence with the environment (healing involves reestablishing harmony within the

physical, mental, emotional, and spiritual parts of the self, as well as with others and the environment)

6. Community well-being, because tribes are collectivistic societies and decisions are made by consensus
7. Generativity, and responsibility to promote the next generation's well-being (Native elders teach that each present decision must be considered with respect to its impact on the next seven generations) (CNPAAEMI, 2009)

Latino Children When working with Latino children and adolescents, clinicians should be aware of the notable diversity among the rapidly growing Latino groups in the United States (Mexican Americans, Puerto Ricans, Cubans, Salvadorans, Dominicans, and other Central and South Americans), including variations in the degree of acculturation of the youth and family. The following common Latino values and beliefs may be important to clinicians:

1. *Familia*, involving loyalty, solidarity, cooperation, and reciprocity among family members, living in extended kinship systems that emphasize interdependence
2. *Communidad*, involving responsibility to the community (e.g., coparentage of children by godfathers and godmothers)
3. Core values of *personalismo* (an orientation in which people are more primary than tasks or events, and in which personal warmth and genuineness guide interpersonal interactions), *simpatia* (engendering respectful and harmonious interpersonal behaviors), and *confianza* (trustworthiness, intimacy, loyalty)
4. *Respeto* (friendship based on respect, mutual understanding, and appreciation; respect within relationships acknowledges the personal power one has)
5. Allocentrism, involving the worldview that all persons and things are interrelated, including how the family or group helps to maintain the balance between the individual and the larger world and the supernatural, and how belief in a higher spiritual power is fundamental (CNPAAEMI, 2009)

Because of these varying key cultural factors, interventions for children and families of diverse cultural backgrounds should be tested for their appropriateness. In addition, as noted in Chapter 5, interventions should be developed to specifically address important aspects of the sociocultural context and perceptions of African-American, Native American, and Hispanic children (e.g., Hammond & Yung, 1991; Hudley & Graham, 1993; Malgady and Costantino, 2003; Robbins, Szapocznik, Santisteban, Hervis, Mitrani, & Schwartz, 2003).

ETHNIC IDENTITY

Ethnic and racial identity are part of children's social identity (Blackmon & Vera, 2008), and social identities are formed through children's interactions with others in family, school, and peer settings. Ethnic identity involves developing a self-identification with one's ethnic group, and this in turn leads to a stronger social and psychological connection with other group members. Feelings of closeness to a particular ethnic group increase the likelihood that values associated with that group will be internalized (Hogg, 2003). Ethnic identity for ethnic minority children is important not only as one aspect of identity development in general, but also it instills a sense of pride and positive feelings toward one's ethnic group (Phinney, 1990); provides a self-protective method for coping with prejudice, discrimination, and stigmatization (Crocker & Major, 1989); and may have implications for children's achievement, educational attitudes, adjustment, and behavior (Lochman, Holmes, & Wojnaroski, 2008). Ethnic identification has been found to be positively related to children's academic performance (Wong, Eccles, & Sameroff, 2003) and feelings of academic efficacy (Oyserman, Harrison, & Bybee, 2001). Adolescents who have stronger ethnic identification also are more positive about education and their schools and believe education is useful for their future (Fuligni, Witkow, & Garcia, 2005).

Ethnic identity is also related to children's behavioral adjustment. Paschall and Flewlling (1997) found that African-American adolescent males who have higher levels of ethnic identity have less violent behavior. Ethnic identity has been negatively associated with aggressive behavior among children (McMahon & Watts, 2002) and positively associated with nonfighting attitudes among African-American and Latino youth ages 10 to 13 (Arbona, Jackson, McCoy, & Blakely, 1999).

Holmes and Lochman (2009) investigated the relations among schematic variables (ethnic identity, self-worth, and social goals) and aggression for European-American and African-American aggressive preadolescents (ages 9–13). A primary goal of the study was to determine the extent to which self-worth and social goals mediated the relation between ethnic identity and aggressive behavior. Ethnic identity emerged as important for both groups, but in different ways. Different patterns of influence of ethnic identity and of mediation were found for the European- and African-American preadolescents. Ethnic identity was found to mediate the relation between self-worth and preadolescents' aggressive behavior for European Americans. For African Americans, ethnic identity was significantly negatively correlated with dominance and revenge-oriented social goals, and ethnic identity and dominance/revenge-oriented social goals tended to be positively associated with children's aggression. Thus, African-American aggressive preadolescents with high ethnic identity place less value on dominance and revenge and have lower levels of aggressive behavior.

ASSESSMENT AND CULTURAL COMPETENCY

Assessment has been a particular area of concern related to cultural competence (Erdley, Nangle, Burns, Holleb, & Kaye, 2010). Assessments of individual children must take into account their race, ethnicity, and sociocultural context (Pumariega, 2001). Concerns about the use of nondiscriminatory assessment for ethnic minority children began in the 1970s, leading to debates that still exist in school psychology about the utility of tests such as IQ measures with minority children (Frisby, 2009). Individually administered tests of academic and cognitive ability have been found to measure planned constructs and to predict academic progress equally well for minority and nonminority children, as long as they are English-speaking and American-born (Reynolds & Kaiser, 2003), but skepticism remains in some quarters about the appropriateness of intelligence tests with culturally diverse groups (Ortiz & Dynda, 2003). These concerns have been due, in part, to the lack of norms for minority groups such as African Americans for many of the popular psychological tests, leading to the possibility of erroneous interpretation of test results by psychologists (Jones et al., 2001).

Jones et al. (2001) have noted that though few instruments have been designed for assessment of general psychological functioning in African Americans, promising strategies, such as the Culturally Informed Functional Assessment interview (Tanaka-Matsumi, Seiden, & Lam, 1996), have emerged. As a result of these concerns, Jones et al. (2001) note that culturally competent clinicians should be wary of relying solely on results from a single assessment tool. In addition, clinical child and adolescent psychologists must become knowledgeable about the developmental norms and child-rearing patterns of multicultural populations to adequately assess minority children and their families (Pumariega, 2001).

Given the concerns about cultural appropriateness of assessments and psychological practices of school psychologists, Rogers and Lopez (2002) conducted a study of what school psychology programs should be doing in multicultural training. Using a national sample of school psychology faculty, practitioners, and school administrators, the importance of 14 domains of cultural competencies were rated, and the importance of culturally competent assessment practices and interpretation was especially prominent. The following cultural competencies were rated in order as the five most critical:

1. Assessment (nonbiased assessment, and adaptation of available instruments to assess linguistically and culturally diverse children)
2. Report writing (integration of cultural and language background and proficiency of the child and family into the report)
3. Laws and regulations designed to protect culturally diverse children from bias and discrimination
4. Working with interpreters (competencies needed by interpreters, and assessing children and interpreting information through interpreters)
5. Working with parents while taking into account differences in family structure, authority, hierarchies, and communication patterns across cultures

Other training topics that would facilitate cultural competency were as follows: strengths and limitations of theoretical paradigms, counseling, reduction of psychologists' biased beliefs and behaviors, norms of cultural groups, academic interventions with culturally diverse youth, research methods, working with organizations to eliminate biases, prejudices and discriminatory practices, and the second language acquisition process (Frisby, 2009).

MULTICULTURAL TRAINING

Attention needs to be paid to the cultural diversity of child and adolescent psychologists, and how they interface with the culturally diverse children they serve. The cultural "fit" between the child and therapist can affect the therapeutic alliance and children's motivation in therapy. The establishment of a therapeutic alliance may be the most critical factor in treatment success with culturally diverse youth and families (Bernal, Bonilla, Padilla-Cotto, & Perez-Prado, 1998). Child and adolescent psychologists' preexisting biases and stereotypes of multicultural groups can adversely affect minority children's and families' perception of the therapeutic process

(Abreu, 1999). Clinicians need to become aware of how their previously acquired perceptions of diverse cultural and racial groups, and their own racial status, can interfere with treatment progress.

Regardless of specialty area, psychologists must be grounded in research in specific cultural and ethnic perspectives (CNPAAEMI, 2009). Education and training in multicultural issues must be provided prior to psychologists beginning to practice, and should be part of the lifelong learning mandate for professional psychologists. Multicultural training, such as outlined and advocated by CNPAAEMI (2009), should aim to improve provider awareness, knowledge, and skills in relation to diverse populations (Stanhope et al., 2008).

Training providers to be culturally competent can be challenging because of the complexity of the concept of culture. Training would address not only race and ethnicity, but also gender, age, sexual orientation, religion, and physical ability. Training in cultural competence addresses the providers' own worldviews as well as increases the providers' understanding of the role that culture plays in clients' lives. Thus, Stanhope et al. (2008) note that training professionals in cultural competence involves both a personal transformation for the provider as well as gaining a broad range of culturally specific knowledge and skills. These trainings vary in intensity and depth, ranging from a half-day session to 6-week intensive courses (Beach et al., 2005). When trainings are limited in time and scope, providers may only make superficial gains in cultural competence (Vega, 2005).

Although few multicultural training programs are evaluated, Stanhope et al. (2008) surveyed providers and clients after the providers had received an intensive 18-session multicultural training lasting 9 months. Although clients generally did not feel that they needed a provider who was ethnically matched to them, clients did rate themselves as being satisfied with their providers' focus on the clients' cultural background and rated their providers as culturally competent. It is not clear whether the training led to the generally positive ratings from the clients, but the survey results are suggestive of the value and potential importance of this type of focus on the cultural competence of clinicians.

Summary

Two critically important competencies for clinical child and adolescent psychologists are (1) their ability to competently handle complex interpersonal interactions with their child clients and their families, and (2) their ability to address multicultural issues that affect assessment and the course of treatment. A central feature of these two areas of clinical competence is the therapist's ability to sensitively and accurately understand the child and adolescent client's perspectives, emotions, and needs, and the sociocultural context that surrounds the child. Related to this is the therapist's own ability to develop productive therapeutic alliances with children from a range of cultural backgrounds. To be effective, therapists must attend to their own cultural biases and expectations and take advantage of multicultural training and supervision.

TEN

Professional Identification in Clinical Child and Adolescent Psychology

The clinical child and adolescent psychologist forms an identity as a psychologist with specialized competencies and skills to provide services to children and adolescents and their families and to conduct research into issues of development, psychotherapy, assessment and diagnosis, and treatment. This identity is partially achieved through membership in professional organizations, personal continuing efforts to maintain competences and develop new skills, and advanced credentials or board certification in clinical child and adolescent psychology.

Although membership in professional organizations does not automatically bestow competencies or credentials on a specialty psychologist, it does permit the clinical child and adolescent psychologist to monitor changes in the field, remain current with evidence-based practice and scientific advances, seek counsel on clinical challenges and ethical dilemmas, and gain support from the specialty community of practitioners and scholars.

American Psychological Association

The largest and oldest scientific and professional organization in psychology is the American Psychological Association (APA). This is an organization of 150,000 members representing the breadth of the discipline and profession of psychology. Within the structure of the APA are governance groups for considering policy and practices in education, professional practice, science, and public issues of psychology. The APA Practice Organization provides information for advocacy to advance psychological science and practice. Through its constituent groups and governance, the APA supports a range of activities and prepares practice-relevant documents. These include, for example, a model act for state licensure of psychologists and the Ethical Principles of Psychologists and Code of Conduct.

The APA also develops and publishes guidelines for practitioners on such topics as record keeping, psychological practice with girls and women, multicultural practice, psychological evaluations in child protection matters, and child custody evaluations in family law proceedings. Most of the resources are available on the APA website (http://www.apa.org). The organization also is moving toward development of treatment guidelines that may outline approaches for psychological assessment and treatment of specific disorders based on the available scientific evidence base.

There are 54 divisions within the APA, each centered on similar interests and activities, sharing information and providing forums for interaction and education. These divisions frequently publish journals and newsletters, maintain websites, and offer educational resources, conferences, and convention events to psychologists in the specialized interest area of the division. Later subsections in this chapter describe the activities of these divisions most relevant to the clinical child and adolescent psychologist.

The APA publishes a range of general and specialty scholarly journals, many with direct relevance to the clinical child and adolescent psychology specialty (e.g., *Professional Psychology: Research and Practice*, *Clinician's Research Digest*, *Journal of Consulting and Clinical Psychology*). Additionally, the APA publishes books and monographs providing significant information for psychologist practitioners and scientists.

SOCIETY FOR CLINICAL CHILD AND ADOLESCENT PSYCHOLOGY (SCCAP; DIVISION 53 OF THE APA)

This scientific and professional society is often considered one of two primary homes for those identifying as clinical child and adolescent psychologists. It started as a section within the clinical psychology division, but over time it became large and active enough to warrant development into a full division. The society articulates as its mission as serving children, adolescents, and families with the best possible clinical care based on psychological research.

The division publication, *Journal of Clinical Child and Adolescent Psychology* (previously *Journal of Clinical Child Psychology*), is a highly regarded scientific journal whose purpose is to publish "original contributions on development and evaluation of assessment and intervention techniques, clinical child and adolescent and cross-cultural and sociodemographic issues, training and professional practice in clinical child and adolescent psychology, and child advocacy" (SCCAP, 2010). In addition to a subscription to this journal, membership in SCCAP entitles the member to a newsletter, listserv membership, and free membership to Quest BehavioralPro (a web-based behavioral information service with access to journals and other documents relevant to practice, research, and education). The Division cosponsors two national conferences (the Kansas Conference in Clinical Child and Adolescent Psychology and the Niagara Conference on Evidence-Based Practices) as well as programming at the APA annual convention.

There are often task forces developed to address important concerns for scientist-practitioner psychologists with position papers and resources developed on special topics. SCCAP also cosponsors a website with the Association for Behavioral and Cognitive Therapies for promulgation of information about evidence-based mental health treatment for children and adolescents (http://www.effectivechildtherapy.com/). This website provides information for the public, professionals, and educators about effective interventions for specific child and adolescent diagnoses.

SOCIETY OF PEDIATRIC PSYCHOLOGY (SPP; DIVISION 54 OF THE APA)

Similar to the development of SCCAP, the Society of Pediatric Psychology (SPP) has a long history of existence and contribution to the scientific understanding and application of psychological principles for children, adolescents, and families, but with a primary focus on pediatric health. SPP serves those with a primary identity to science and clinical services in the areas of

> psychosocial, developmental and contextual factors contributing to the etiology, course and outcome of pediatric medical conditions; assessment and treatment of behavioral and emotional concomitants of illness, injury, and developmental disorders; prevention of illness and injury; promotion of health and health-related behaviors; education, training and mentoring of psychologists and providers of medical care; improvement of health care delivery systems and advocacy for public policy that serves the needs of children, adolescents, and their families. (SPP, 2010)

As noted earlier in this book, pediatric psychology is intrinsically related to clinical child and adolescent psychology, but SPP provides a special focus on promoting health and alleviating the impact of disease, illness, and injury for children and their families. As the organizational home for pediatric psychology and child, adolescent, and family health psychology, SPP publishes the flagship journal of the area, *Journal of Pediatric Psychology*. SPP also maintains a website with information about the organization's activities, evidence-based practice in pediatric psychology, educational and training opportunities, professional development, diversity issues, and mentorship (http://www.societyofpediatricpsychology.org/). SPP sponsors a biennial national conference on pediatric psychology and presents programming at the APA convention. The organization publishes the *Handbook of Pediatric Psychology* (Roberts & Steele, 2010) and monographs from its task forces.

SOCIETY FOR CHILD AND FAMILY POLICY AND PRACTICE (SCFPP; DIVISION 37 OF THE APA)

The focus of this division provides an identity for psychologists who are interested more generally in improving mental health services and organizational structures for children and their families. Frequently, this division serves as a "second home" for clinical child and adolescent psychologists and pediatric psychologists (who may join either Division 53 or 54 as a primary identity). Psychologists from other backgrounds, such as from developmental and school psychology or clinically oriented psychology, come together in this society to deal with significant social policy issues affecting children and their families. The society regularly deals with such topics as preventing and treating child maltreatment, meeting the psychosocial needs of ethnic minorities, investigating and influencing children's media, and the treatment of juvenile offenders. The society states as its mission "to advance research, education, training, and practice and relate psychological knowledge to other fields such as anthropology, law, and pediatrics in such areas as employment, education, recreation, and family planning" (SCFPP, 2010).

The society publishes a substantial newsletter, *Child and Family Policy and Practice Advocate*, and frequently develops task forces on emerging issues. It often partners with other organizations, such as the Society for Research in Child Development and the Interdivisional Task Force on Children's Mental Health, for advocacy, service, and research. For example, the society was a lead group in an important conference and resulting report on *Healthy Development: A Summit on Children's Mental Health* (Society for Research in Child Development, 2010) with public policy and services implications.

Other Organizations Related to the Clinical Child Psychology and Adolescent Specialty

There are numerous other professional groups with activities in scientific and professional domains that are related to this specialty. These will be briefly noted with their significant foci.

INTERNATIONAL SOCIETY FOR RESEARCH IN CHILD AND ADOLESCENT PSYCHOPATHOLOGY

ISRCAP provides a forum for exchanging information regarding "the nature and treatment of childhood mental disorders" (http://isrcap.org/). The society holds a biennial conference in different locations worldwide and sponsors the publication *Journal of Abnormal Child Psychology*, an influential journal in psychopathology and clinical child and adolescent psychology. Members have research interests in a range of psychopathological conditions involving basic and applied approaches.

SOCIETY FOR RESEARCH IN CHILD DEVELOPMENT

SRCD has a long history of involvement in basic research in development of children and adolescents, with some activities in applied developmental psychology (related to clinical child and adolescent psychology). The organization publishes an esteemed scientific journal, *Child Development*, and other monographs on basic and applied developmental issues. SRCD publishes commentary on public policy in the *Social Policy Report* and other briefs on concerns related to children and families (recent issues have explored children's lead exposure, autism spectrum disorder, early education, home visitation, and evidence-based programming). The society sponsors a biennial meeting and multiple other information and professional resources (http://srcd.org).

ASSOCIATION FOR BEHAVIORAL AND COGNITIVE THERAPIES

ABCT is an interdisciplinary organization that focuses on scientific applications for "the understanding and amelioration of problems of the human condition. These aims are achieved through the investigation and application of behavioral, cognitive, and other evidence-based principles to assessment, prevention, and treatment" (ABCT, 2010). ABCT publishes scientific and professional journals, including *Behavior Therapy* and *Cognitive and Behavioral Practice*, and holds an annual conference. Not all members of this organization are clinical child and adolescent psychologists, although many in the specialty find consonance with the cognitive-behavioral orientation and find an identity within this group. As noted earlier, ABCT cosponsors a website with SCCAP/Division 53 on evidence-based treatments for children (see http://www.effectivechildtherapy.com/).

SOCIETY OF BEHAVIORAL MEDICINE

SBM is another interdisciplinary organization; its mission is to promote "the study of the interactions of behavior with biology and the environment, and the application of that knowledge to improve the health and well being of individuals, families, communities and populations" (SBM, 2010). Although oriented not just to children, adolescents, and families, the society does have activities and interest groups for psychologists with special interests in child and family health. SBM promotes evidence-based behavioral medicine, including psychological applications. The organization sponsors an annual convention and produces scientific publications.

SOCIETY OF CLINICAL PSYCHOLOGY (SCP; DIVISION 12 OF THE APA)

Division 12 has been a primary home for those whose professional identity is more as a clinical psychologist, recently with an adult clinical psychology emphasis (given the rise of SCCAP and SPP as Divisions 53 and 54 in the APA). The organization does not exclude child and adolescent psychology interests, and the website states a large mission of the field of clinical psychology "focuses on the intellectual, emotional, biological, psychological, social, and behavioral aspects of human functioning across the life span, in varying cultures, and at all socioeconomic levels," and notes that clinical psychologists "work directly with individuals at all developmental levels (infants to older adults), as well as groups (families, patients of similar psychopathology, and organizations), using a wide range of assessment and intervention methods to promote mental health and to alleviate discomfort and maladjustment" (SCP, 2010). Thus, some of the organization's activities might encompass clinical psychology issues related to children. The society publishes a book series with some child-oriented titles (*Advances in Psychotherapy: Evidence-Based Practice* by Hogrefe) and a respected scholarly review journal, *Clinical Psychology: Science and Practice.*

SOCIETY FOR FAMILY PSYCHOLOGY (DIVISION 43 OF THE APA)

Many clinical child and adolescent psychologists participate in the Society for Family Psychology (Division 43 of the APA) given the intrinsic interest in family and systems issues and evidence-based practice in a broad focus. The American Board of Professional Psychology provides board certification in family psychology; CRSPPP and the APA Council of Representatives approved the recognition of family psychology as a distinctive specialty. For more information, see the Division 43 website (www.division43apa.org/).

Professional Licensure

In all states in the United States and provinces in Canada, in order to practice professionally as a psychologist and provide services to children and families, the psychologist must be licensed by a state regulatory board under laws enacted by the state. These laws and regulations are designed, as summarized by Rae (2003), to protect the welfare of the populace so that "only those individuals with the appropriate credentials are able to provide psychological services within that state or province. The legal basis for licensure is to protect the citizens of that state or province from unqualified practitioners and to remove incompetent or/and unethical psychologists from practice" (p. 343). Licensure is designed to protect the public, not the profession, although licensure does bestow some privileges as well as responsibility on the licensed psychologist. Candidates for licensure in the state in which they practice must have received a doctorate (PhD/PsyD/EdD) with defined requirements for education and training experiences, including internship and postdoctoral work. Passing the Examination for Professional Practice in Psychology is required, and states may add additional requirements and examinations for their jurisdictions.

The state licensure laws and regulations are available in each state in which the psychologist might wish to practice; these can be easily accessed through the Association of State and Provincial Psychology Boards (http://www.asppb.org) with links to the websites of individual state boards and to specific licensure requirements by state, province, and territory. Practitioners working in more than one state need to obtain a license from each state. State/provincial psychology boards also are charged with regulating practice and enforcing relevant laws that involve investigating psychologists' potential violations of professional conduct standards, including unethical behavior and incompetence, with disciplinary action as necessary.

Clearly, a psychologist's identity as a practitioner and the legal ability to provide services rest on professional licensure. Specialty licensure is not required by the state psychology boards, although an applicant for licensure and a renewing practitioner often must indicate areas of competence within which he or she is able to demonstrate education and training experiences and supervised clinical work in assessment and treatment that prepared the candidate for practice. This would be especially important with psychological services for children, adolescents, and families in which specialized training and competencies are absolutely essential for quality assessment and treatment.

Board Certification: American Board of Clinical Child and Adolescent Psychology

Because licensure is generic to psychology in the sense that specialty expertise is not indicated in a license, the most essential way a clinical child and adolescent psychologist identifies as a specialist at an expert level is through the advanced credentialing process. The American Board of Clinical Child and Adolescent Psychology (ABCCAP) is a member board of the American Board of Professional Psychology (ABPP), which is an overseeing organization with an illustrious history of certifying specialists in different specialties. (Others include, for example, clinical, school, counseling, clinical health, and forensic psychology.) ABCCAP is responsible for establishing criteria for board certification in the specialty of clinical child and adolescent psychology through stated definitional criteria, education and training requirements, clinical competencies, and examination. As noted on the ABCCAP website (http://www.clinicalchildpsychology.com), the primary objective of the board certification process is to recognize, certify, and promote competence in the specialty of clinical child and adolescent psychology. As defined earlier in this book, the practice specialty involves the provision of diagnostic/assessment; evaluation; and psychological treatment and consultation for psychological, emotional/behavioral, and psychiatric disorders. By definition, to be identified as a specialty psychologist at the doctoral level requires advanced levels of preparation and practice of doctoral degree in psychology with competencies "discriminately higher than the basic level of competence certified by state licensure" (ABCCAP brochure). Board certification provides identification as a specialist in clinical child and adolescent psychology and assures the public and profession that the psychologist has had her or his advanced competences assessed through a rigorous check of credentials and individualized peer-reviewed examination.

For specialty certification in clinical child and adolescent psychology, the candidate must present the following:

1. A doctoral degree from an accredited training program in professional psychology (accredited by the APA, Canadian Psychological Association, or listed in the directory "Doctoral Psychology Programs Meeting Designation Criteria")

2. A license for independent practice at the doctoral level in the United States, its territories, or Canada
3. Completion of a clinical internship in which two-thirds of the experience was with child, adolescent, and family clinical populations
4. Completion of 1 year of postdoctoral supervised experiences in the specialty or a formal postdoctoral residency training program in clinical child and adolescent psychology

The evaluation process for certifying clinical child and adolescent psychologists as specialists includes assessment of knowledge and skills in the following areas:

a. Assessment and intervention specific to children, adolescents, and family functioning
b. Interpersonal self-awareness to enhance effectiveness of services ("sensitivity to the welfare, rights, and dignity of all clients is critical for a clinical child and adolescent psychologist")
c. Knowledge and application of the scientific bases relevant to professional practice
d. Knowledge and application of ethical and legal standards and those for professional practice
e. Commitment to and involvement in psychology through professional identification and knowledge of the critical issues facing the specialty
f. Competencies in supervision and consultation

The specialty candidate presents practice samples to ABCCAP and, after review and approval to proceed, undergoes an oral examination that emphasizes current issues in professional psychology; professional practice experience and clinical judgment; knowledge of the scientific basis of clinical child and adolescent practice; sensitivity to diversity issues; and responsivity to ethical, professional, and legal standards of practice. Only after these standards have been met can the candidate claim that he or she is board certified in the specialty and include ABPP (or ABCCAP) after his or her name and doctoral degree.

National Register (NR) of Health Service Providers in Psychology

The National Register (NR) provides credentialing for doctoral-level psychologists but does not credential practitioners in a specific specialty such as clinical child psychology. Through its "Find a Psychologist" search registry (see http://www.nationalregister.org/), NR presents information for consumers about psychologists in regional searches and by expertise in advanced search mode. For example, with the register, the psychologist does not claim a specialty, but can name "areas of expertise" in childhood disorders and services and "ages served" for children (3–12 yrs.) and adolescents (13–17 yrs.).

Maintaining Competence Is a Specialty Identity

Clinical child and adolescent psychologists practice in a variety of settings with a multitude of problems and client characteristics. Although specialty practitioners may eventually focus their work with a smaller number of problems and in particular settings, competent psychologists will seek not only to become knowledgeable of developments in their focused areas but also to remain broadly aware of advancements in psychological research and practice. Continuing education requirements exist in many states for maintenance of knowledge over time in diagnosis and treatment of psychopathology and professional ethics.

The clinical child and adolescent psychologist can also readily access useful resources through a diversity of outlets. The professional organizations noted earlier provide information that is directly relevant to professional practice and provision of services in ways that are competent and effective, developmentally appropriate, culturally sound, evidence-based, and ethical. The SCCAP (Division 53 of the APA) regularly provides up-to-date publications on evidence-based psychosocial treatments for children and adolescents (see *Journal of Clinical Child and Adolescent Psychology*, Silverman & Hinshaw, 2008; *Journal of Clinical Child Psychology*, Lonigan, Elbert, & Johnson, 1998, special issue on empirically supported treatments). These include articles on autism, eating disorders, depression, phobic and anxiety disorders, obsessive-compulsive disorder, trauma, attention deficit/hyperactive disorder, disruptive behavior, and substance abuse. Also as noted earlier, SCCAP cosponsors a website with ABCT for the public and professionals providing detailed information about evidence-based treatments for psychological disorders such as anxiety and school refusal, social phobia, depression, autism, and ADHD (http://www.effectivechildtherapy.com/).

Professional and scientific information is available to members of Division 53 through its contract with Quest BehavioralPro to provide online access to journal articles and databases for psychological and medical information. This resource contains guides to psychotropic medication, diagnosis and treatment of behavioral disorders, as well as information on practice concerns such as billing and diagnostic coding. Continuing education opportunities, case conferences, and consultations are planned to be available through this system.

The *Journal of Pediatric Psychology* (published by SPP) also presents evidence-based practice and empirically supported treatments for psychosocial interventions for problems presenting in pediatric settings. The SPP website presents pages for evidence-based practice, including information on psychological diagnosis and treatment of such disorders as asthma, cancer, disease-related pain, obesity, diabetes, and recurrent abdominal pain (http://www.societyofpediatricpsychology.org/evidence/).

Books on evidence-based treatments and professional practice provide reviews and summaries of therapies and approaches (e.g., Steele, Elkin, & Roberts, 2008; Goodheart, Kazdin, & Sternberg, 2006; Shriver & Allen, 2008; Weisz & Kazdin, 2010). A book by Spirito and Kazak (2006), *Effective and Emerging Treatments in Pediatric Psychology*, has a companion website with manuals and appendices on specific treatments in pediatric psychology (http://www.oup.com/us/companion.websites/0195156153/?view=usa).

A task force of the APA published its report on evidence-based practice for children and adolescents with attention to a meta-systems approach including families; cultural norms and values; and service delivery in schools, pediatric clinics and hospitals, mental health centers and child guidance clinics, and other settings (Kazak et al., 2010).

New online and print resources are being created almost daily to provide information on evidence-based practice and effective treatments for conditions treated by specialists in this field. Clinical child and adolescent psychologists need to utilize their scientist-practitioner background to critically evaluate the source and content. Whereas highly respected organizations may provide scientifically based materials, not all resources meet explicitly stated criteria for evaluating effectiveness and utility. The specialist may wish to remain updated by frequently accessing listings of reviews and programs:

National Registry of Evidence-based Programs and Practices (Substance Abuse and Mental Health Services Administration): http://www.nrepp.samhsa.gov/

California Evidence-Based Clearinghouse for Child Welfare: http://www.cebc4cw.org/

The Cochrane Collaboration (Reviews): http://www.cochrane.org/about-us/evidence-based-health-care

Evidence-Based Behavioral-Practice http://www.ebbp.org/

Evidence-Based Mental Health Treatment for Children and Adolescents http://www.effectivechildtherapy.com/

Summary

The various organizations and information resources mentioned in this chapter are available for the clinical child and adolescent psychologist in developing his or her expertise and, thus, one's professional identity. Not everybody who has good intentions and interests in helping children should be allowed to provide psychological services to this special and vulnerable population. Training and education leading to recognizable competencies and skills are necessary for high-quality and effective services. Those who pursue the professional identity as a clinical child and adolescent psychologist will find a rewarding and vibrant specialty of practice and research when they aim to become competent, remain current, and develop their skills as this new evidence-based practice emerges.

Appendix A

Collaborative Problem-Solving Work Sheet

1. Problem-solving grid ______________________
2. Client/family names ____
3. Defining the problem
   a. Case conceptualization (see Chapter 4)
4. Setting treatment goals collaboratively
5. Generating solutions/intervention strategies with child/adolescent and his/her family
6. Choosing the best one with input from all parties. (Ratings: 0 = neutral; 1 = very poor; 2 = poor; 3 = fair; 4 = good; 5 = very good)
7. Intervention strategies

Intervention strategies	rating
a. ________________________________	a. ____
b. ________________________________	b. ____
c. ________________________________	c. ____
d. ________________________________	d. ____
e. ________________________________	e. ____
f. ________________________________	f. ____
g. ________________________________	g. ____

8. Trying it out.
9. Did it work?

(Adapted from Spiegler & Guevremont, 2010)

Appendix B

Case Formulation Summary Form for Children and Adolescents: Behavioral Version

Child/Adolescent's Name: ____________________

Date: ____________________

Educational Level: ____________________

Diagnosis: ____________________

Axis I ____________________ Axis II ____________________

Axis III ____________________ Axis IV ____________________

Axis V ____________________

Relevant Developmental History							
Weaknesses/Risk Factors				Strengths/Protective Factors			
Child	Family	School	Social	Child	Family	School	Social

Problem List and Other Issues to be Addressed				
Self	Family	School	Peers	Other
1.	1.	1.	1.	1.
2.	2.	2.	2.	2.
3.	3.	3.	3.	3.

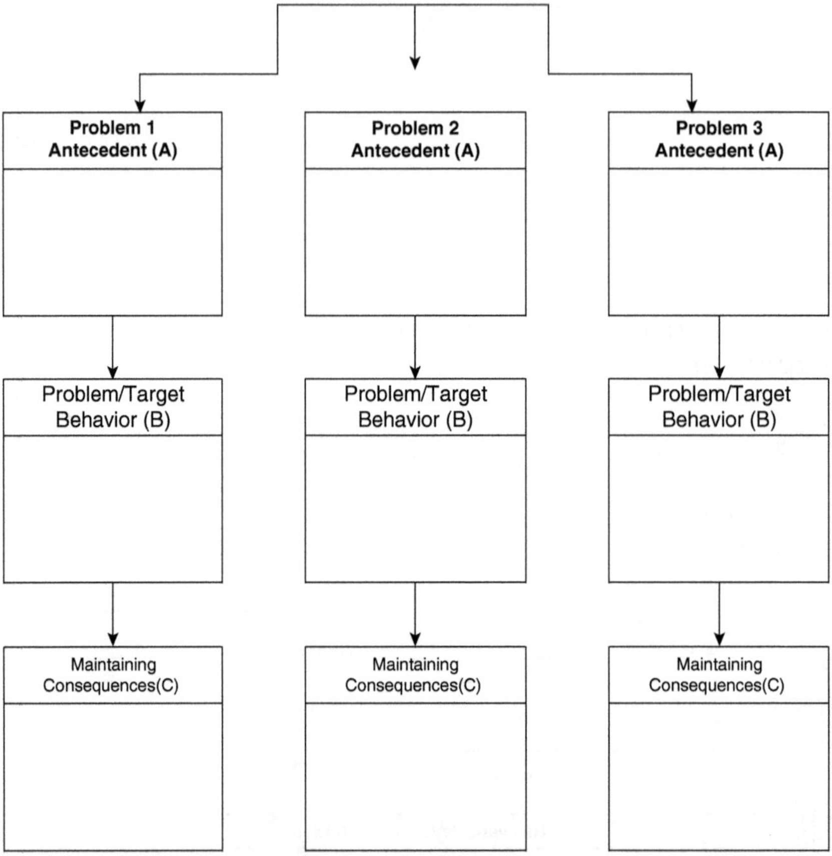

Origins/hypotheses about how the problem/target behavior(s) was (were) learned and is (are) being maintained:

In infancy/childhood/adolescence, ________________, was ______________. Within
(name of client) (origins/culture)

this context, ________________ learned to __________________________. This was
(name of client) (problem or target behavior[s])

__________________ [MECHANISMS] and has resulted in a(n) __________________
(e.g.,reinforced/punished) (e.g.,increase/decrease)

in the frequency/intensity/duration of the ________________ behavior.
(problem/target)

Problem 1
Therapy Strategies/Interventions:

1.____
2.____
3.____

Problem 2
Therapy Strategies/Interventions:

1.____
2.____
3.____

Problem 3
Therapy Strategies/Interventions:

1.____
2.____
3.____

____________________	____________________
Date	Therapist's Name

Appendix C

Case Formulation Summary Form for Children and Adolescents: Cognitive-Behavioral Version

Child/adolescent's name: ______________________________

Date: ______________________________

Educational level: ______________________________

Diagnosis: ______________________________

Axis I ____________________ Axis II ____________________

Axis I ____________________ Axis II ____________________

Axis V ____________________

Relevant Developmental History					
Weaknesses/Risk Factors			Strengths/Protective Factors		
Child	Family	School	Child	Family	School

Developing Schema/Core Beliefs			
About Self:	About Family:	About School:	About Peers:

Problem List and Other Issues to be Addressed				
Self	Family	School	Peers	Other
1.	1.	1.	1.	1.
2.	2.	2.	2.	2.
3.	3.	3.	3.	3.

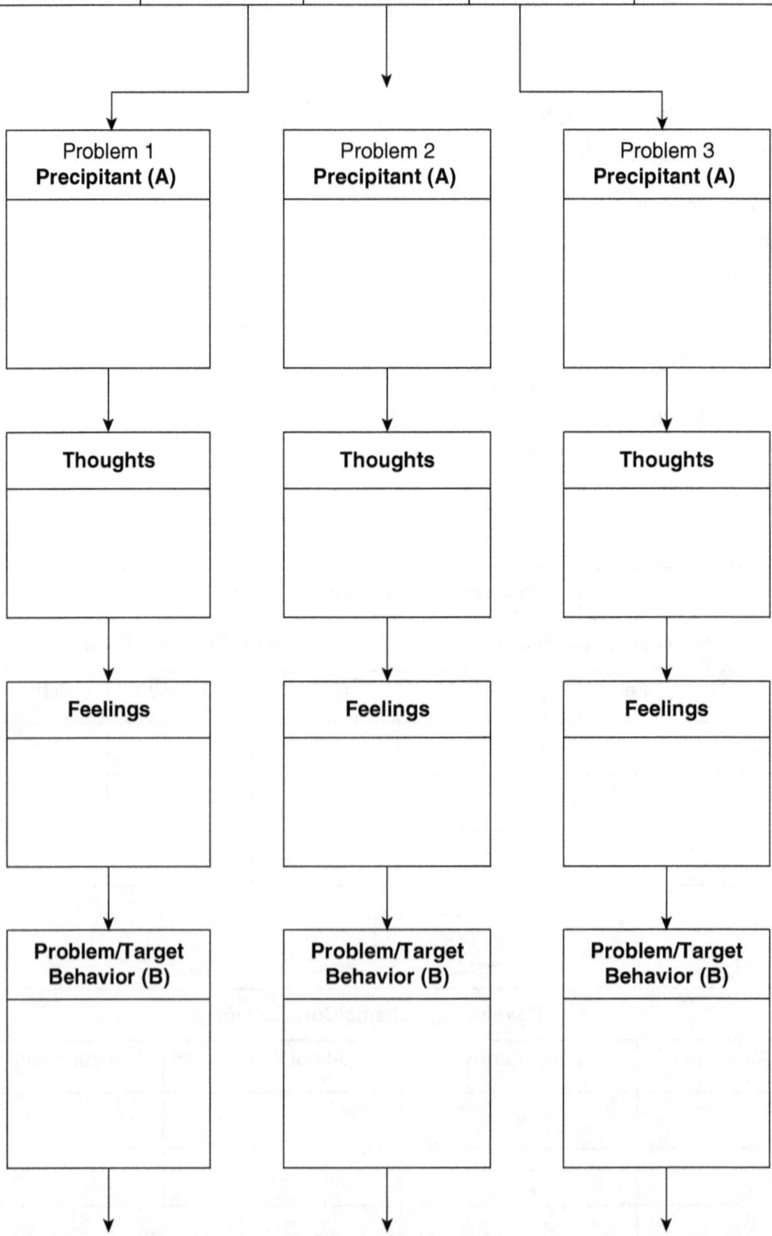

Maintaining Consequences (C)	Maintaining Consequences (C)	Maintaining Consequences (C)

Origins/hypotheses about how the problem/target behavior(s) was (were) learned and is (are) being maintained:

In infancy/childhood/adolescence, ________________, was ______________

(name of client)

[ORIGINS]. As a result, ________________ is learning (or has learned) these schemas:

(name of client)

____________; ____________; ____________; ____________ [MECHANISMS].

(about self) (about family) (about school) (about peers)

These schemas are currently activated by precipitants or Activating events that results in these emotions (___________; ___________; ___________), which have two components:

cognitive (___________; ___________; ___________), and physiological (___________);

___________; ___________); [MECHANISMS]. These problem/target behaviors then are

manifested: ___________; ___________; ___________ [PROBLEMS/SYMPTOMS

or Emotional/Behavioral Consequences].

Problem 1
Therapy Strategies/Interventions:

1.____
2.____
3.____

Problem 2
Therapy Strategies/Interventions:

1.____
2.____
3.____

Problem 3
Therapy Strategies/Interventions:

1.____
2.____
3.____

______________________ ______________________

Date Therapist's Name

REFERENCES

Abrams, A. N., & Rauch, P. K. (2008). Pediatric consultation. In M. Rutter, D. Bishop, D. Pine, S. Scott, J. Stevenson, E. Taylor, et al. (Eds.), *Rutter's child and adolescent psychiatry* (5th ed., pp. 1143–1155). London: Blackwell.

Abreu, J. (1999). Conscious and nonconscious African-American stereotypes: Impact on first impression and diagnostic ratings by therapists. *Journal of Consulting and Clinical Psychology, 67,* 387–393.

Achenbach, T. M. (1974). *Developmental psychopathology.* New York: Ronald Press.

Achenbach, T. M. (1990). Conceptualization of developmental psychopathology. In M. Lewis & S. E. Miller (Eds.), *Handbook of developmental psychopathology* (pp. 3–13). New York: Plenum.

Achenbach, T. M. (1991a). *Manual for the Child Behavior Checklist 4–18 & 1991 Profile.* Burlington, VT: University of Vermont Department of Psychiatry.

Achenbach, T. M. (1991b). *Manual for the Teacher's Report Form & 1991 Profile.* Burlington, VT: University of Vermont Department of Psychiatry.

Addis, M. E., & Krasnow, A. D. (2000). A national survey of practicing psychologists' attitudes toward psychotherapy treatment manuals. *Journal of Consulting and Clinical Psychology, 68,* 331–339.

Administration for Children and Families. (2002). *Making a difference in the lives of infants and toddlers and their families: The impacts of Early Head Start.* Washington, DC: U.S. Department of Health and Human Services.

Akhutina, T. V. (1997). The remediation of executive functions in children with cognitive disorders: The Vygotsky-Luria neuropsychological approach. *Journal of Intellectual Disability Research, 41,* 144–151.

Alexander, J., & Parsons, B. (1982). *Functional family therapy.* Monterey, CA: Brooks Cole.

Allen, G. J., Szollos, S. J., & Williams, B. E. (1986). Doctoral students' comparative evaluations of best and worst psychotherapy supervision. *Professional Psychology: Research and Practice, 17,* 91–99.

American Board of Clinical Child and Adolescent Psychology. (2007). Examination manual for board certification in clinical child and adolescent psychology for the American Board of Professional Psychology. Retrieved from http://www.abpp.org/files/page-specific/3352%20Clinical%20Child/16_Examination_Manual.pdf

American Psychiatric Association. (2000). *Diagnostic and statistical manual of mental disorders* (4th ed., text rev.). Washington, DC: Author.

American Psychological Association (2002a). *Ethical principles of psychologists and code of conduct 2002.* Retrieved from http://www.apa.org/ethics/code2002.html

American Psychological Association, Committee on Accreditation. (2002b). *Guidelines and principles for accreditation of programs in professional psychology.* Washington, DC: American Psychological Association.

American Psychological Association. (2002c). *Guidelines for multicultural education, training, research, practice, and organizational change for psychologists.* Washington, DC: Author.

Andrew, G., Benjamin, H., & Gollan, J. K. (2003). *Family evaluation in custody litigation.* Washington, DC: American Psychological Association.

Arbona, C., Jackson, R. H., McCoy, A., & Blakely, C. (1999). Ethnic identity as a predictor of attitudes of adolescents toward fighting. *Journal of Early Adolescence, 19,* 323–340.

Asamen, J. K., Ellis, M. L., & Berry, G. L. (2008). *Child development, multiculturalism, and media.* Los Angeles: Sage.

Association for Behavioral and Cognitive Therapies (ABCT). (2010). Our mission. Retrieved from http://www.abct.org/Home/

Association for Counselor Education and Supervision. (1995). Ethical guidelines for counseling supervisors. *Counseling Education and Supervision, 34,* 270–276.

Auslander, B. A., Short, M. B., & Rosenthal, S. L. (2005). Services to prevent sexually transmitted diseases in adolescents. In R. G. Steele & M. C. Roberts (Eds.), *Handbook of mental health services for children, adolescents, and families* (pp. 167–179). New York: Kluwer Academic/Plenum.

Axline, V. M. (1964). *Dibs: In search of self: Personality development in play therapy.* Boston: Houghton Mifflin.

Axline, V. M. (1969). *Play therapy.* New York: Ballantine.

Axline, V. M. (1989). *Play therapy.* Edinburgh and New York: Churchill Livingstone.

Axline, V. M., & Carmichael, L. (1947). *Play therapy: The inner dynamics of childhood.* Boston: Houghton Mifflin.

Bakermans-Kranenburg, M. J., van Ijzendoorn, M. H., & Juffer, F. (2005). The importance of parenting in the development of disorganized attachment: Evidence from a preventive intervention study in adoptive families. *Journal of Child Psychology and Psychiatry, 46,* 263–274.

Bandura, A. (1969). *Principles of behavior modification.* New York: Holt, Rinehart & Winston.

Bandura, A. (1977). Self-efficacy: Toward a unifying theory of behavioral change. *Psychological Review, 84*(2), 191–215.

Bandura, A., Ross, D., & Ross, S. A. (1963). Vicarious reinforcement and imitative social learning. *Journal of Abnormal and Social Psychology, 67,* 601–607.

Barker, R. G. (1965). Explorations in ecological psychology. *American Psychologist, 20,* 11–14.

Barlow, J. (1999). *Systematic review of the effectiveness of parent-training programmes in improving behaviour problems in children aged 3–10 years* (2nd ed.). Oxford: University of Oxford, Health Services Research Unit.

Barrett, P., Healy-Farrell, L., & March, J. S. (2004). Cognitive-behavioral family treatment of childhood obsessive-compulsive disorder: A controlled trial. *Journal of the American Academy of Child and Adolescent Psychiatry, 43,* 46–62.

Barrett, P. M., & Ollendick, T. H. (2004). *Handbook of interventions that work with children and adolescents: Prevention and treatment.* Hoboken, NJ: Wiley.

Barrio, C. (2000). The cultural relevance of community support systems. *Psychiatric Services, 53,* 1547–1555.

Barrish, H. H., Saunders, M., & Wolf, M. M. (1969). Good Behavior Game: Effects of individual contingencies for group consequences on disruptive behavior in a classroom. *Journal of Applied Behavior Analysis, 2,* 119–124.

Beach, M. C., Price, E. G., Gary, T. L., Robinson, K. A., Gozu, A., Palacio, A., et al. (2005). Cultural competence: A systematic review of health care provider educational interventions. *Medical Care, 43,* 356–373.

Beauchaine, T. P., Webster-Stratton, C., & Reid, M. J. (2005). Mediators, moderators, and predictors of 1-year outcomes among children treated for early-onset conduct problems: A latent growth curve analysis. *Journal of Consulting and Clinical Psychology, 73,* 371–388.

Beck, A. (1963). Thinking and depression. *Archives of General Psychiatry, 49,* 681–689.

Beck, A. T., Emery, G., & Greenberg, R. L. (1985). *Anxiety disorders and phobias: A cognitive perspective.* New York: Basic Books.

Beck, J. S. (1995). *Cognitive therapy: Basics and beyond.* New York: Guilford Press.

Beidas, R. S., & Kendall, P. C. (2010). Training therapist in evidence-based practice: A critical review of studies from a systems-contextual perspective. *Clinical Psychology: Science and Practice, 17,* 1–30.

Beidel, D. C., & Turner, S. M. (1986). A critique of the theoretical bases of cognitive behavioral theories and therapy. *Clinical Psychology Review, 6,* 177–197.

Bergan, J. R., & Kratochwill, T. R. (1990). *Behavioral consultation and therapy.* New York: Plenum Press.

Bernal, G., Bonilla, J., Padilla-Cotto, L., & Perez-Prado, E. (1998). Factors associated to outcome in psychotherapy: An effectiveness study in Puerto Rico. *Journal of Clinical Psychology, 54,* 329–342.

Bernard, J. M. (1997). The discrimination model. In C. E. Watkins, Jr. (Ed.), *Handbook of psychotherapy supervision* (pp. 310–327). New York: Wiley.

Bergan, J. R., & Kratochwill, T. R. (1990). *Behavioral consultation and therapy.* New York: Plenum Press.

Bertrando, P., & Arcelloni, T. (2006). The evolution of family interventions for schizophrenia: A tribute to Gianfranco Cecchin. *Journal of Family Therapy, 28,* 4–22.

Berwick, D. M. (2003). Disseminating innovations in health care. *Journal of the American Medical Association, 289,* 1969–1975.

Bettelheim, B. (1967). *The empty fortress: Infantile autism and the birth of the self.* New York: Free Press.

Binder, J. L., & Strupp, H. H. (1997). Supervision of psychodynamic therapies. In C. E. Watkins, Jr. (Ed.), *Handbook of psychotherapy supervision* (pp. 44–62). New York: Wiley.

Birmaher, B., Brent, D. A., Kolko, D., Baugher, M., Bridge, J., Iyengar, S., et al. (2000). Clinical outcome after short-term psychotherapy for adolescents with major depressive disorder. *Archives of General Psychiatry, 57,* 29–36.

Blackmon, S. M., & Vera, E. M. (2008). Ethnic and racial identity development in children of color. In J. K. Asamen, M. L. Ellis, & G. L. Berry (Eds.). *Child development, multiculturalism, and media.* Thousand Oaks, CA: Sage.

Black's Law Dictionary (9th ed.) (2009). Washington, DC: Thomson Reuters.

Bolhuis, S. (2003). Towards process-oriented teaching for self-directed lifelong learning: A multidimensional perspective. *Learning and Instruction, 13,* 327–347.

Bollard, J. (1982). A 2-year follow-up of bedwetters treated by dry-bed training and standard conditioning. *Behavioral Research and Therapy, 20*(6), 571–580.

Bordin, E. S. (1994). Theory and research in the therapeutic working alliance: New directions. In A. O. Horvath & L. S. Greenberg (Eds.), *The working alliance: Theory, research and practice* (pp. 13–37). New York: Wiley.

Brent, D. A., Holder, D., Kolko, D., Birmaher, B., Baugher, M., Roth, C., et al. (1997). A clinical psychotherapy trial for adolescent depression comparing cognitive, family, and supportive treatments. *Archives of General Psychiatry, 54,* 877–885.

Brestan, E. V., & Eyberg, S. M. (1998). Effective psychosocial treatments of conduct-disordered children and adolescents: 29 years, 82 studies, and 5,272 kids. *Journal of Clinical Child Psychology, 27,* 180–189.

Brinkmeyer, M. Y., & Eyberg, S. M. (2003). Parent-child interaction therapy for oppositional children. In A. E. Kazdin & J. R. Weisz (Eds.), *Evidence-based psychotherapies for children and adolescents* (pp. 204–223). New York: Guilford.

Bronfenbrenner, U. (1977). Toward an experimental ecology of human development. *American Psychologist, 32,* 513–530.

Bronfenbrenner, U. (1979). *The ecology of human development.* Cambridge, MA: Harvard University Press.

Bronfenbrenner, U., (1986). Ecology of the family as a context of human development: Research perspective. *Developmental Psychology, 22,* 723–742.

Bronfenbrenner, U. (1989). Ecological systems theory. In R. Vasta (Ed.). *Annals of child development* (Vol. 6, pp. 187–251). Greenwich, CT: JAI.

Bronfenbrenner, U. (2004). *Making human beings human.* Thousand Oaks, CA: Sage.

Bronfenbrenner, U., & Morris, P. A. (1998). The ecology of developmental process. In W. Damon (Ed.). *Handbook of child psychology* (5th ed., Vol. 1). New York: Wiley.

Bronfenbrenner, U., & Morris, P. A. (2006). The ecology of developmental process. In W. Damon (Ed.). *Handbook of child psychology* (6th ed., Vol. 1). New York: Wiley.

Brown, D., Pryzwansky, W. B., & Schulte, A. C. (2006). *Psychological consultation and collaboration* (6th ed.). Boston: Pearson Education.

Brown, R. T. (2004). (Ed.). *Handbook of pediatric psychology in school settings.* Mahwah, NJ: Erlbaum.

Brown, R. T., Kaslow, N. J., Doepke, K., Buchanan, I., Eckman, J., Baldwin, K., et al. (1993). Psychosocial and family functioning in children with sickle cell syndrome and their mothers. *Journal of the American Academy of Child and Adolescent Psychiatry, 32,* 545–553.

Buskist, W., Tears, R. S., Davis, S. F., & Rodrigue, K. M. (2002). The teaching of psychology course: Prevalence and content. *Teaching of Psychology, 29,* 140–142.

Cabiya, J. J., Padilla-Cotto, L., Gonzalez, K., Sanchez-Cestero, J., Martinez-Taboas, & Sayers, S. (2008). Effectiveness of a cognitive-behavioral intervention for Puerto Rican children. *Interamerican Journal of Psychology, 42,* 195–202.

Campbell, J. M., Herzinger, C. V., & James, C. L. (2008). Evidence-based therapies for autistic disorder and pervasive developmental disorders. In R. G. Steele, T. D. Elkin, & M. C. Roberts (Eds.), *Handbook of evidence-based therapies for children and adolescents* (pp. 373–388). New York: Springer.

Caplan, G. (1970). *The theory and practice of mental health consultation.* New York: Basic Books.

Caplan, G., & Caplan, R. B. (1993). *Mental health consultation and collaboration.* San Francisco: Jossey-Bass.

Carlson, C. I. (2003). Assessing the family context. In C. R. Reynolds & R. W. Kamphaus (Eds.), *Handbook of psychological and educational assessment of children: Personality, behavior, and context* (2nd ed., pp. 473–492). New York: Guilford Press.

Carmichael, K. D. (2006). *Play therapy: An introduction.* Upper Saddle River, NJ: Pearson.

Carr, E. G., Levin, L., McConnachie, G., Carlson, J. I., Kemp, D. C., & Smith, C. E. (1994). *Communication-based interventions for problem behavior: A user's guide for producing positive change.* Baltimore: Brooks.

Carter, B. D., & von Weiss, R. T. (2005). Inpatient pediatric consultation-liaison: Applied child health psychology. In R. G. Steele & M. C. Roberts (Eds.), *Handbook of mental health services for children, adolescents, and families* (pp. 63–83). New York: Kluwer Academic/Plenum.

Chamberlain, P. (2003). *Treating chronic juvenile offenders: Advances made through the Oregon multidimensional treatment foster care model.* Washington, DC: American Psychological Association.

Chambless, D. L. (1996). In defense of dissertation of empirically supported psychological interventions. *Clinical Psychology: Science and Practice, 3,* 270–235.

Chambless, D. L., Baker, M. J., Baucom, D. H., Beutler, L., Calhoun, K. S., Crits-Christoph, P., et al. (1998). Update on empirically validated therapies, II. *Clinical Psychologist, 51,* 3–16.

Chambless, D. L., & Hollon, S. D. (1998). Defining empirically supported therapies. *Journal of Consulting and Clinical Psychology, 66,* 7–18.

Chambless, D. L., & Ollendick, T. H. (2001). Empirically supported psychological interventions: Controversies and evidence. *Annual Review of Psychology, 52,* 685–716.

Chang, E. C., D'Zurilla, T. J., & Sanna, L. J. (Eds.). (2004). *Social problem solving: Theory, research, and training.* Washington, DC: American Psychological Association.

Chemtob, C. M., Nakashima, J. P., & Hamada, R. S. (2002). Psychosocial intervention for postdisaster trauma symptoms in elementary school children: A controlled community field study. *Archives of Pediatrics and Adolescent Medicine, 156,* 211–216.

Chorpita, B. F., & Nakamura, B. J. (2004). Four considerations for dissemination of intervention innovations. *Clinical Psychology: Science and Practice, 11,* 364–367.

Chorpita, B. F., & Southam-Gerow, M. A. (2006). Fears and anxieties. In E. J. Mash & R. A. Barkley (Eds.), *Treatment of childhood disorders* (3rd ed., pp. 271–335). New York: Guilford.

Christophersen, E. R. (1994). *Pediatric compliance: A guide for the primary care physician.* New York: Plenum Medical.

Chu, B. C. (2008). Empirically supported training approaches: The who, what, and how of disseminating psychological interventions. *Clinical Psychology: Source and Practice, 15,* 308–312.

Chu, B. C., Choudhury, M. S., Shortt, A. L., Pincus, D. B., Creed, T. A., & Kendall, P. C. (2004). Alliance, technology, and outcome in the treatment of anxious youth. *Cognitive and Behavioral Practice, 11,* 44–55.

Cicchetti, D., & Cohen, D. (1995). Perspectives on developmental psychopathology. In D. Cicchetti & D. Cohen (Eds.), *Developmental psychopathology: Vol. 1. Theory and methods* (pp. 3–30). New York: Wiley.

Coatsworth, J. D., Santisteban, D. A., McBridge, C. K., & Szapocznik, J. (2001). Brief strategic family therapy versus community control: Engagement, retention, and an exploration of the moderating role of adolescent symptom severity. *Family Process, 40,* 313–332.

Cohen, L. L., MacLaren, J. E., & Lim, C. S. (2008). Pain and pain management. In R. G. Steele, T. D. Elkin, & M. C. Roberts (Eds.), *Handbook of evidence-based therapies for children and adolescents* (pp. 283–295). New York: Springer.

Commission for the Recognition of Specialties and Proficiencies in Professional Psychology (CRSPPP). (2010a). The historical roots of CRSPPP and its mission to recognize specialties and proficiencies in professional psychology. Retrieved from http://www.apa.org/ed/graduate/specialize/history.aspx

Commission for the Recognition of Specialties and Proficiencies in Professional Psychology (CRSPPP). (2010b). Public description of clinical child psychology. Retrieved from www.apa.org/ed/graduate/specialize/child-clinical.aspx

Commission for the Recognition of Specialties and Proficiencies in Professional Psychology (CRSPPP). (2010c). Public description of clinical health psychology. Retrieved from www.apa.org/ed/graduate/specialize/health.aspx

Commission for the Recognition of Specialties and Proficiencies in Professional Psychology (CRSPPP). (2010d). Public description of clinical psychology. Retrieved from www.apa.org/ed/graduate/specialize/clinical.aspx

Commission for the Recognition of Specialties and Proficiencies in Professional Psychology (CRSPPP). (2010e). Public description of school psychology. Retrieved from www.apa.org/ed/graduate/specialize/school.aspx

Connell, A. M., & Goodman, S. H. (2002). The association between psychopathology in fathers versus mothers and children's internalizing and externalizing behavior problems: A meta-analysis. *Psychological Bulletin, 128,* 746–773.

Conners, C. K. (1990). *Manual for Conners' Rating Scales.* North Tonawanda, NY: Multi Health Systems.

Costa, M. L., Van Rensburg, L., & Rushton, N. (2007). Does teaching style matter? A randomized trial of group discussion versus lectures in orthopaedic undergraduate teaching. *Medical Education, 41,* 214–217.

Council of National Psychological Associations for the Advancement of Ethnic Minority Interests (CNPAAEMI). (2009). *Psychology education and training from culture-specific and multiracial perspectives: Critical issues and recommendations.* Washington, DC: American Psychological Association.

Council of Specialties in Professional Psychology. (2005). Clinical child psychology formal specialty definition. Retrieved from http://cospp.org/specialties/clinical-child-psychology

Council of Specialties in Professional Psychology. (2010). CoS definition of a specialty in professional psychology. Retrieved from http://www.cospp.org

Crick, N. R., & Dodge, K. A. (1994). A review and reformulation of social information-processing mechanisms in children's social adjustment. *Psychological Bulletin, 115,* 74–101.

Crocker, J., & Major, B. (1989). Social stigma and self-esteem: The self-protective properties of stigma. *Psychological Review, 96,* 608–630.

Crouter, A. C. (2006). Mothers and fathers at work: Implications for families and children. In A. Clarke-Stewart & J. Dunn (Eds.), *Families count: Effects on child and adolescent development* (pp. 135–154). New York: Cambridge University Press.

Cunningham, C. (1995). Collaborative psychological practice in pediatric gastroenterology: Clinical issues and professional opportunities. In D. Drotar, *Consulting with pediatricians: Psychological perspectives* (pp. 173–184). New York: Plenum.

Daleiden, E. L., & Vasey, M. W. (1997). An information-processing perspective on childhood anxiety. *Clinical Psychology Review, 4*, 407–429.

D'Augelli, A. R. (1973). Group composition using interpersonal skills: An analogue study on the effects of members' interpersonal skills on peer ratings and group cohesiveness. *Journal of Counseling Psychology, 20*, 531–534.

Davies, D. (2001). *Child development: A practitioner's guide* (3rd ed.). New York: Guilford Press.

Davis, A. M. M., & Vuong, N. (2005). Mental health services for children with chronic illness. In R. G. Steele & M. C. Roberts (Eds.), *Handbook of mental health services for children, adolescents, and families* (pp. 259–275). New York: Kluwer Academic/Plenum.

Daviss, W. B., Coon, H., Whitehead, P., Ryan, K., Burkley, M., & McMahon, W. (1995). Predicting diabetic control from competence, adherence, adjustment, and psychopathology. *Journal of the American Academy of Child and Adolescent Psychiatry, 34*, 1629–1636.

DeAngelis, T. (2010). Closing the gap between practice and research. *Monitor on Psychology, 41*, 42–45.

Department of Health and Human Services. (2005). *Transforming mental health care in America: Federal action agenda: First steps* (DHHS Pub. No. SMA-05-4060). Rockville, MD: Substance Abuse and Mental Health Services Administration.

DeRoma, V. (2006). Family therapy. In A. J. Finch, W. M. Nelson, & K. Hart (Eds.), *Conduct disorders: A practitioner's guide to comparative treatments.* New York: Springer.

Dodge, K. A. (1993). Social cognitive mechanisms in the development of conduct disorder and depression. *Annual Review of Psychology, 44*, 558–584.

Dodge, K. A., & Pettit, G. S. (2003). A biopsychosocial model of development of chronic conduct problems in adolescence. *Developmental Psychology, 39*(2), 349–371.

Dodge, K. A., Pettit, G. S., & Bates, J. E. (1994). Effects of physical maltreatment on the development of peer relations. *Development and Psychopathology, 6*, 43–55.

Dollard, J., & Miller, N. (1950). *Personality and psychotherapy*. New York: McGraw-Hill.

Dougherty, A. M. (2009). *Psychological consultation and collaboration in school and community settings* (5th ed.). Belmont, CA: Brooks/Cole.

Dozier, M., Lindheim, O., & Ackerman, J. P. (2005). Attachment and biobehavioral catch-up: An intervention targeting empirically identified needs of foster children. In L. J. Berlin, Y. Ziv, L. M. Amaya-Jackson, & M. T. Greenberg (Eds.), *Enhancing early attachment: Theory, research, intervention and policy* (pp. 178–194). New York: Guilford.

Drotar, D. (1978). Training psychologists to consult with pediatricians: Problems and prospects. *Journal of Clinical Child Psychology, 7*, 57–61.

Drotar, D. (1995). *Consulting with pediatricians: Psychological perspectives.* New York: Plenum.

Drotar, D. (2008). Ethical issues in treatment and intervention research with children and adolescents with behavioral and mental disorders. *Ethics and Behavior, 18* (2 & 3), 119–126.

Drotar, D., Palermo, T., & Barry, C. (2004). Collaboration with schools: Models and methods in pediatric psychology and pediatrics. In R. T. Brown (Ed.), *Handbook of pediatric psychology in school settings* (pp. 21–36). Mahwah, NJ: Erlbaum.

Dumas J. E., & Nilsen, W. J. (2003). *Abnormal child and adolescent psychology.* Boston: Allyn & Bacon.

Dunn, J. (2007). Siblings and socialization. In J. E. Grusec & P. D. Hastings (Eds.), *Handbook of socialization.* New York: Guilford.

DuPaul, G. J., Power, T. J., & Shapiro, E. S. (2009). Schools and integration/reintegration into schools. In M. C. Roberts & R. G. Steele (Eds.), *Handbook of pediatric psychology* (4th ed., pp. 689–702). New York: Guilford.

Durand, V. M. (1987). In response: "Look homeward angel": A call to return to our (functional) roots. *The Behavior Analyst, 10,* 299–302.

D'Zurilla, T. J., & Goldfried, M. R. (1971). Problem solving and behavior modification. *Journal of Abnormal Psychology, 78,* 107–126.

D'Zurilla, T. J., & Nezu, A. M. (1982). Social problem solving in adults. In P. Kendall (Ed.), *Advances in cognitive-behavioral research and therapy* (Vol. 1, pp. 285–315). New York: Academic Press.

D'Zurilla, T. J., & Nezu, A. M. (1999). *Problem-solving therapy: A social competence approach to clinical intervention* (2nd ed.). New York: Springer.

D'Zurilla, T. J., & Nezu, A. M. (2001). Problem-solving therapies. In K. S. Dobson (Ed.), *Handbook of cognitive-behavioral therapies* (2nd ed., pp. 211–245). New York: Guilford.

D'Zurilla, T. J., & Nezu, A. M. (2007). *Problem-solving therapy: A positive approach to clinical intervention.* New York: Springer.

Edgar, K. A., & Skinner, T. C. (2003). Illness representations and coping as predictors of emotional well-being in adolescence with type-1 diabetes. *Journal of Pediatric Psychology, 28,* 485–493.

Eells, T. D. (1997). Psychotherapy case formulation: History and current status. In T. Eells (Ed.), *Handbook of psychotherapy case formulation* (pp. 1–25). New York: Guildford Press.

Eells, T. D., Kendjelic, E. M., & Lucas, C. P. (1998). What's in a case formulation? Development and use of a content coding manual. *Journal of Psychotherapy Practice, 7, 144–153.*

Eisler, I., Dare, C., Hodes, M., Russell, G. F. M., Dodge, E., & Le Grange, D. (2000). Family therapy for adolescent anorexia nervosa: The results of a controlled comparison of two family interventions. *Journal of Child Psychology and Psychiatry, 41,* 727–736.

Eisler, I., & Lask, J. (2008). Family interviewing and family therapy. In M. Rutter, D. Bishop, D. Pine, S. Scott, J. Stevenson, E. Taylor, et al. (Eds.), *Rutter's child and adolescent psychiatry* (5th ed., pp. 1062–1078). London: Blackwell.

Eisler, I., Simic, M., Russell, G. F. M., & Dare, C. (2007). A randomized controlled treatment trial of two forms of family therapy in adolescent anorexia nervosa: A five-year follow-up. *Journal of Child Psychology and Psychiatry, 48,* 552–560.

Ellis, M. V., & Ladany, N. (1997). Inferences concerning supervisees and clients in clinical supervision: An integrative review. In C. E. Watkins, Jr. (Ed.), *Handbook of psychotherapy supervision* (pp. 447–507). New York: Wiley.

Embry, D. D. (2002). The Good Behavior Game: A best practice candidate as a universal behavioral vaccine. *Clinical Child & Family Psychology Review, 5,* 273–297.

Epstein, N. B., Schlesinger, S. E., & Dryden, W. (Eds.). (1988). Concepts and methods of cognitive-behavioral family treatment. In N. Epstein, S. E. Schlesinger, & W. Dryden (Eds.), *Cognitive-behavioral therapy with families.* New York: Brunner/Mazel.

Epstein, R. M., & Hundert, E. M. (2002). Defining and assessing professional competence. *Journal of the American Medical Association, 287,* 226–235.

Erchul, W. P., & Martens, B. K. (2002). *School consultation: Conceptual and empirical bases of practice* (2nd ed.). New York: Kluwer Academic/Plenum.

Erchul, W. P., & Martens, B. K. (2010). *School consultation: Conceptual and empirical bases of practice* (3rd ed.). New York: Springer.

Erdley, C. A., Nangle, D. W., Burns, A. M., Holleb, L. J., & Kaye, A. J. (2010). Assessing children and adolescents. In D. W. Nangle, D. J. Hansen, C. A. Erdley, & P. J. Norton (Eds.). *Practitioner's guide to empirically based measures of social skills* (pp. 69–85). New York: Springer.

Ethical principles of psychologists and code of conduct with the 2010 amendments. Retrieved from http://www.apa.org/news/press/releases/2010/02/ethics-code.aspx

Evans, I. M., & Meyer, L. H. (1985). *An educative approach to behavior problems: A practical decision model for interventions with severely handicapped learners*. Baltimore: Brookes.

Eyberg, S. M., Nelson, M. M., & Boggs, S. R. (2008). Evidence-based psychosocial treatments for children and adolescents with disruptive behavior. *Journal of Clinical Child and Adolescent Psychology, 37,* 215–237.

Eysenck, H. J. (Eds.). (1960). *Behaviour therapy and neurosis*. London: Pergamon.

Fabiano, G. A., Pelham, W. E., Manos, M. J., Gnagy, E. M., Chronis, A. M., Onyango, A. N., et al. (2004). An evaluation of three time-out procedures for children with attention deficit/hyperactivity disorder. *Behavior Therapy, 35,* 449–469.

Falender, C. A., Erickson Cornish, J. A., Goodyear, R., Hatcher, R., Kaslow, N.J., Leventhal, G., et al. (2004). Defining competencies in psychology supervision: A consensus statement. *Journal of Clinical Psychology, 60,* 771–785.

Falender, C. A., & Shafranske, E. P. (2004). *Clinical supervision: A competency-based approach*. Washington, DC: American Psychological Association.

Falender, C. A., & Shafranske, E. P. (2007). Competence in competency-based supervision practice: Construct and application. *Professional Psychology: Research and Practice, 38,* 232–240.

Farmer, E. M. Z., Compton, S. N., Burns, B., & Robertson, E. (2002). Review of evidence base for treatment of childhood psychopathology: Externalizing disorders. *Journal of Consulting and Clinical Psychology, 70,* 1267–1302.

Fein, L. G. (1974). *The changing school scene: Challenge to psychology*. New York: Wiley.

Fernandez-Ballesteros, R., De Bruyn, E. E. J., Godoy, A., Hornke, L. F., Ter Laak, J., Vizcarro, C., et al. (2001). Guidelines for the Assessment Process (GAP): A proposal for discussion. *European Journal of Psychological Assessment, 17*(3), 187–200.

Finch, A. J., Jr. (2009). Professional development and lifelong learning. In C. M. Nezu, A. J. Finch, Jr., & N. P. Simon (Eds.), *Becoming board certified by the American Board of Professional Psychology*. New York: Oxford.

Finch, A. J., Jr. & Politano, P. M. (1994). Projective techniques. In T. H. Ollendick, N. J. King, & W. Yule (Eds.), *International handbook of phobic and anxiety disorders in children and adolescents*. New York: Plenum.

Finch, A. J. Jr., & Robbins, R. L. (1985). Internship training in clinical child psychology. *Proceedings of the National Conference on Training of Clinical Child Psychologist*. Section on Clinical Child Psychology, Division of Clinical Psychology, American Psychological Association.

Fincham, F. D. (1998). Child development and marital relations. *Child Development, 69,* 543–574.

Finn, S. E. (2007). *In our clients' shoes: Theory and techniques of therapeutic assessment.* Mahwah, NJ: Erlbaum.

Flanagan, R., & Miller, J. A. (2010). *Specialty competencies in school psychology.* New York: Oxford University Press.

Flannery-Schroeder, E., & Kendall, P. C. (2000). Group and individual cognitive-behavioral treatments for youth with anxiety disorders: A randomized clinical trial. *Cognitive Therapy and Research, 24,* 251–278.

Frick, P. J. (2006). Developmental pathways to conduct disorder. *Child and Adolescent Psychiatric Clinics of North America, 15*(2), 311–331.

Friman, P. C. (2008). Evidence-based therapies for enuresis and encopresis. In R. G. Steele, T. D. Elkin, & M. C. Roberts (Eds.), *Handbook of evidence-based therapies for children and adolescents* (pp. 311–334). New York: Springer.

Frisby, C. L. (2009). Cultural competence in school psychology: Established or elusive construct? In T. B. Gutkin & C. R. Reynolds (Eds.), *The handbook of school psychology* (4th ed, pp. 855–885). Hoboken, NJ: Wiley.

Fuligni, A. J., Witkow, M., & Garcia, C. (2005). Ethnic identity and the academic adjustment of adolescents from Mexican, Chinese, and European backgrounds. *Developmental Psychology, 41,* 799–811.

Gallessich, J. (1985). Toward a meta-theory of consultation. *The Counseling Psychologist, 13,* 336–354.

Giancola, P. R., Zeichner, A., Yarnell, J. E., & Dickson, K. E. (1996). Relation between executive functioning and adverse consequences of alcohol use in social drinkers. *Alcoholism, Clinical, and Experimental Research, 20*(6), 1094–1098.

Gil, K., Carson, J. W., Porter, L. S., Ready, J., Valrie, C., Redding-Lallinger, R., et al. (2003). Daily stress and mood and their association with pain, health-care use and school activity in adolescents with sickle cell disease. *Journal of Pediatric Psychology, 28,* 363–373.

Gil, K. M., Wilson, J., Edens, J., Workman, E., Ready, J., & Sedway, J. (1997). Cognitive coping skills training in children with sickle-cell disease pain. *International Journal of Behavioral Medicine, 4,* 364–377.

Gladstone, T. R. G., & Kaslow, N. J. (1995). Depression and attributions in children and adolescents: A meta-analytic review. *Journal of Abnormal Child Psychology, 23,* 597–606.

Glazener, C. M. A., Evans, J. H. C., & Peto, R. E. (2005). Alarm interventions for nocturnal enuresis in children. *Cochrane Database of Systematic Reviews,* CD02911, 1.

Goodheart, C. D., Kazdin, A. E., & Sternberg, R. J. (2006). *Evidence-based psychotherapy: Where practice and research meet.* Washington, DC: American Psychological Association.

Goodyear, R. K., & Bernard, J. M. (1998). Clinical supervision: Lessons from the literature. *Counselor Education and Supervision, 38,* 6–22.

Graham, P. (2005). Jack Tizard lecture: Cognitive behavior therapies for children: Passing fashion or here to stay? *Child and Adolescent Mental Health, 10,* 57–62.

Graue, M. E., & Walsh, D. J. (1998). *Studying children in context: Theories, methods, and ethics.* Beverly Hills, CA: Sage.

Graves, D. A., & Graves, S. B. (2008). Multicultural issues in the lives of developing children in the 21st century. In J. K. Asamen, M. L. Ellis, & G. L. Berry (Eds.), *Child development, multiculturalism, and media* (pp. 83–99). Los Angeles, CA: Sage.

Gray, L. A., Ladany, N., Walker, J. A., & Ancis, J. R. (2001). Psychotherapy trainees' experience of counterproductive events in supervision. *Journal of Counseling Psychology, 48,* 371–383.

Green, B. A., & Dohrn, B. (1996). Children and the ethical practice of law. *Fordham Law Review, 64,* 1281.

Green, J. (2006). Annotation: The therapeutic alliance—a significant but neglected variable in child mental health treatment studies. *Journal of Child Psychology and Psychiatry, 47,* 425–435.

Greenberg, M. T., & Kusché, C. A. (2006). Building social and emotional competence: The PATHS curriculum. In S. R. Jimerson & M. Furlong (Eds.), *Handbook of school violence and school safety: From research to practice* (pp. 395–412). Mahwah, NJ: Erlbaum.

Gresham, F. M., & Lochman, J. E. (2008). Methodological issues in research using cognitive-behavioral interventions. In M. J. Mayer, R. Van Acker, J. E. Lochman, & F. M. Gresham (Eds.), *Cognitive behavioral interventions for emotional and behavioral disorders: School-based practice* (pp. 58–81). New York: Guilford.

Grey, M., Boland, E. A., Davidson, M., Li, J., & Tamborlane, W. V. (2000). Coping skills training for youth with diabetes mellitus has long-lasting effects on metabolic control and quality of life. *Journal of Pediatrics, 137,* 107–113.

Groark, C. J., & McCall, R. B. (2008). Community-based intervention and services. In M. Rutter, D. Bishop, D. Pine, S. Scott, J. Stevenson, E. Taylor, et al. (Eds.), *Rutter's child and adolescent psychiatry* (5th ed., pp. 971–988). London: Blackwell.

Groth-Marnat, G. (2003). *Handbook of psychological assessment* (4th ed.). Hoboken, NJ: Wiley.

Guest, P. D., & Beutler, L. E. (1988). Impact of psychotherapy supervision on therapist orientation and attitudes. *Journal of Consulting and Clinical Psychology, 56,* 653–658.

Hadjistavropoulos, T., & Koocher, G.P. (2009). Ethics in assessment, treatment, and research. In D. C. S. Richard & S. K. Huprich (Eds.), *Clinical psychology: Assessment, treatment and research* (pp. 31–50). San Diego: Elsevier.

Hamlett, K. W., & Stabler, B. (1995). The developmental progress of pediatric psychology consultation. In M. C. Roberts (Ed.), *Handbook of pediatric psychology* (2nd ed., pp. 39–54). New York: Guilford.

Hammond, W. R., & Yung, B. R. (1991). Preventing violence in at-risk African-American youth. *Journal of Health Care for the Poor and Underserved, 2,* 359–373.

Hanson, J. M., & Sinclair, K. E. (2008). Social constructivist teaching methods in Australian universities—reported uptake and perceived learning effects: A survey of teachers. *Higher Education Research and Development, 27,* 169–186.

Hart, B., & Risley, T. R. (1995). *Meaningful differences in everyday experiences of young Americans.* Baltimore: Paul H. Brookes.

Hart, D., Burock, D., London, B., & Atkins, R. (2003). Prosocial development, antisocial development, and moral development. In A. M. Slater & G. Bremner (Eds.). *An introduction to developmental psychology* (pp. 646–718). Malden, MA: Blackwell.

Hawkins, R. P. (1986). Selection of target behaviors. In R. O. Nelson & S. C. Hayes (Eds.), *Conceptual foundations of behavioral assessment* (pp. 329–385). New York: Guildford.

Hayes, S. C., Luoma, J. B., Bond, F.W., Masuda, A., & Lilllis, J. (2006). Acceptance and commitment therapy: Model, processes and outcomes. *Behaviour Research and Therapy, 44,* 1–25.

Haynes, S. N. (1998). The changing nature of behavioral assessment. In A. S. Bellack & M. Hersen (Eds.), *Behavioral assessment: A practical handbook* (4th ed., pp. 1–21). Boston: Allyn & Bacon.

Haynes, S. N., & O'Brien, W. (2000). *Principles and practice of behavioral assessment.* New York: Plenum.

Henderson, C. E., Cawyer, C. S., & Watkins, C. E., Jr. (1999). A comparison of student and supervisor perceptions of effective practicum experiences. *The Clinical Supervisor, 18,* 47–74.

Henggeler, S. W. (1999). Multisystemic therapy: An overview of clinical procedures, outcomes and policy implications. *Child Psychology and Psychiatry Review, 4,* 2–10.

Hergenhahn, B. R. (2009). *An introduction to the history of psychology.* Belmont, CA: Wadsworth.

Hersen, M. (2006). *Clinician's handbook of child behavioral assessment.* San Diego: Elsevier Academic Press.

Hersen, M., & Bellack, A. S. (1976). *Behavioral assessment: A practical handbook.* New York: Pergamon Press.

Hetherington, E. M. (2006). The influence of conflict, martial problem solving, and patterning on children's adjustment in nondivorced, divorced, and remarried families. In A. Clarke-Steward & J. Dunn (Eds.), *Families count.* New York: Oxford University Press.

Hocking, M. C., & Lochman, J. E. (2005). Applying the transactional stress and coping model to sickle cell disorder and insulin-dependent diabetes mellitus: Identifying psychosocial variables related to adjustment and intervention. *Clinical Child and Family Psychology Review, 8,* 221–246.

Hogg, M. (2003). Social identity. In M. R. Leary & J. P. Tangney (Eds.), *Handbook of self and identity* (pp. 462–479). New York: Guilford.

Holloway, E. L. (1995). *Clinical supervision: A systems approach.* Thousand Oaks, CA: Sage.

Holmes, K. J., & Lochman, J. E. (2009). Ethnic identity in African American and European American preadolescents: Relation to self-worth, social goals, and aggression. *Journal of Early Adolescence, 29,* 476–496.

Houts, A. C. (2003). Behavioral treatments for enuresis. In A. Kazddin & J. Weisz (Eds.), *Evidence-based psychotherapies for children and adolescents* (pp. 389–406). New York: Guilford.

Hudley, C., & Graham, S. (1993). An attributional intervention to reduce peer-directed aggression among African-American boys. *Child Development, 64,* 124–138.

Hunsley, J., & Bailey, J. M. (1999). The clinical utility of the Rorschach: Unfulfilled promises and an uncertain future. *Psychological Assessment, 11,* 266–277.

Hunsley, J., & Mash, E. J. (2008). *A guide to assessments that work.* New York: Oxford University Press.

Hunsley, J. & Mash, E. J. (2010). Role of assessment in evidence-based practice. In M. M. Antony & D. H. Barlow (Eds.), *Handbook of assessment and treatment planning for psychological disorders* (2nd ed., pp. 3–22). New York: Guilford Press.

Hupp, S. D. A., Jewell, J., Reitman, D., & LeBlanc, M. (2010). Competencies in clinical child psychology. In J. C. Thomson & M. Hersen (Eds.), *Handbook of clinical psychology competencies* (pp. 43–72). New York: Springer.

Hurtig, A. L., Koepke, D., & Park, K. B. (1989). Relation between severity of chronic illness and adjustment in children and adolescents with sickle cell disease. *Journal of Pediatric Psychology, 14,* 117–132.

Hurtig, A. L., & White, L. S. (1986). Psychosocial adjustment in children and adolescents with sickle cell disease. *Journal of Pediatric Psychology, 11,* 411–427.

Ialongo, N. S., Werthamer, L., Kellam, S. G., Brown, C. H., Wang, S., & Lin, Y. (1999). Proximal impact of two first-grade preventive interventions on the early risk behaviors for later substance abuse, depression, and antisocial behavior. *American Journal of Community Psychology, 27,* 599–641.

Institute of Medicine. (1994). *Reducing risks for mental disorders: Frontiers for preventive intervention research.* Washington, DC: National Academy Press.

Iwata, B. A., Dorsey, M. F., Slifer, K. J., Bauman, K. E., & Richman, G. S. (1982). Toward a functional analysis of self-injury. *Analysis and Intervention in Developmental Disabilities, 2,* 3–20.

Jackson, Y., Alberts, F. L., & Roberts, M. C. (2010). Clinical child psychology: A practice specialty serving children, adolescents, and their families. *Professional Psychology: Research and Practice, 41,* 75–81.

Jacob, S., & Hartshorne, T. S. (2003). *Ethics and law for school psychologists* (5th ed.). Hoboken, NJ: Wiley.

Jahoda, M. (1958). *Current concepts of positive mental health.* New York: Basic Books.

Johnson, C., & Murray, C. (2003). Incremental validity in the psychological assessment of children and adolescents. *Psychological Assessment, 15,* 496–507.

Johnson, J. H. (2003). Training issues. In T. Ollendick & C. Schroeder (Eds.), *Encyclopedia of clinical child and pediatric psychology* (pp. 674–676). New York: Kluwer Academic/Plenum.

Johnson, J. H., Janicke, D. M., & Reader, S. K. (2008). Professional roles. In M. Hersen & A. M. Gross (Eds.), *Handbook of clinical psychology, Vol. 2: Children and adolescents* (pp. 138–170). Hoboken, NJ: Wiley.

Jones, M. C. (1924). A laboratory study of fear: The case of Peter. *Pedagogical Seminary, 31,* 308–315.

Jones, R. T., Kephart, C., Langley, A. K., Parker, M. N., Shenoy, U., & Weeks, C. (2001). Cultural and ethnic diversity issues in clinical child psychology. In C. E. Walker & M. C. Roberts (Eds.), *Handbook of clinical child psychology* (3rd ed., pp. 955–973). New York: Wiley.

Kabot, S., Masi, W., & Segal, M. (2003). Advances in the diagnosis and treatment of autism spectrum disorders. *Professional Psychology: Research and Practice, 34,* 26–33.

Kamphaus, R. W., & Frick, P. J. (1996). *Clinical assessment of child and adolescent personality and behavior.* Boston: Allyn & Bacon.

Kane, P., & Garber, J. (2004). The relations among depression in fathers, children's psychopathology, and father-child conflict: A meta-analysis. *Clinical Psychology Review, 24,* 339–360.

Kanner, L. (1943). Autism disturbances of affective contact. *Nervous Child, 2,* 217–250.

Kaslow, N. J., Celano, M. P., & Stanton, M. (2009). Training in family psychology: A competencies-based approach. In J. H. Bray & M. Stanton (Eds.), *The Wiley-Blackwell handbook of family psychology* (pp. 112–128). Malden, MA: Wiley-Blackwell.

Kaslow, N. J., Rubin, N. J., Leigh, I. W., Portnoy, S., Lichtenberg, I., Smith, I. L., et al. (2006). *American Psychological Association Task Force on the Assessment of Competency in Professional Psychology.* Washington, DC: American Psychological Association.

Kaufman, R. A. (1971). A possible integrative model for the systematic and measurable improvement of education. *American Psychologist, 26,* 250–256.

Kazak, A. E. (2006). Pediatric Psychosocial Preventative Health Model (PPHM): Research, practice and collaboration in pediatric family systems medicine. *Families, Systems, & Health, 24*, 381–395.

Kazak, A. E., Hoagwood, K., Weisz, J. R., Hood, K., Kratochwill, T. R., Vargas, L. A., et al. (2010). A meta-systems approach to evidence-based practice for children and adolescents. *American Psychologist, 65*, 85–97.

Kazdin, A. E. (2001). Progression of therapy research and clinical application of treatment require better understanding of the change process. *Clinical Psychology: Science and Practice, 8*(2), 143–151.

Kazdin, A. (2008). Evidence-based treatment and practice: New opportunities to bridge clinical research and practice, enhance the knowledge base, and improve patient care. *American Psychologist, 63*, 146–159.

Kazdin, A. E., & Benjet, C. (2003). Spanking children: Evidence and issues. *Current Directions in Psychological Science, 12*, 99–103.

Kazdin, A. E., Siegel, T. C., & Bass, D. (1990). Drawing on clinical practice to inform research on child and adolescent psychotherapy: Survey of practitioners. *Professional Psychology: Research and Practice, 21*, 189–198.

Kazdin, A. E., & Weisz, J. R. (1998). Identifying and developing empirically supported child and adolescent treatments. *Journal of Consulting and Clinical Psychology, 66*, 19–36.

Kazdin, A. E., & Weisz, J. R. (2003). *Evidence-based psychotherapies for children and adolescents*. New York: Guilford.

Kazdin, A. E., & Whitley, M. K. (2006). Pretreatment social relations, therapeutic alliance, and improvements in parenting practices in parent management training. *Journal of Consulting and Clinical Psychology, 74*, 346–355.

Kazdin, A. E., Whitley, M., & Marciano, P. L. (2006). Child-therapist and parent-therapist alliance and therapeutic change in the treatment of children referred for oppositional, aggressive, and antisocial behavior. *Journal of Child Psychology and Psychiatry, 47*, 436–445.

Kearney, C., & Silverman, W. (1993). Measuring the function of school refusal behavior: The Social Assessment Scale. *Journal of Clinical Child Psychology, 22*, 85–96.

Kearney, C. A., & Albano, A. M. (2000). *Target manual for when children refuse school: A cognitive behavioral approach*. New York: Oxford University Press.

Kees, M. R., & Bonner, B. L. (2005). Child abuse prevention and intervention services. In R. G. Steele & M. C. Roberts (Eds.), *Handbook of mental health services for children, adolescents, and families* (pp. 151–166). New York: Kluwer Academic/Plenum.

Keith-Spiegel, P. C., & Koocher, G. P. (1985). *Ethics and in psychology: Professional standards and cases*. New York: Random House.

Kendall, P. C. (1994). Treating anxiety disorders in children: Results of a randomized clinical trial. *Journal of Consulting and Clinical Psychology, 62*, 100–110.

Kendall, P. C., Flannery-Schroeder, E., Panichelli-Mindel, S., Southam-Gerow, M., Henin, A., & Warman, M. (1997). Therapy for youths with anxiety disorders: A second randomized clinical trial. *Journal of Consulting and Clinical Psychology, 65*, 366–380.

Kendall, P. C., & Hedtke, K. A. (1992). *The coping cat workbook* (2nd ed.). Ardmore, PA: Workbook.

Kendall, P. C., & Southam-Gerow, M. (1996). Long-term follow-up of treatment for anxiety disordered youth. *Journal of Consulting and Clinical Psychology, 65*, 883–888.

Kendall, P. C., & Suveg, C. (2008). Treatment outcome studies with children: Principles for proper practice. *Ethics & Behavior, 18*, 215–233.

Kendell, R., & Jablensky, A. (2003). Distinguishing between the validity and utility of psychiatric diagnoses. *American Journal of Psychiatry, 160*, 4–12.

Kennedy, W. A. (1965). School phobia: Rapid treatment of fifty cases. *Journal of Abnormal Psychology, 70*, 285–289.

King, A. (1992). Facilitating elaborative learning through guided student-generated questioning. *Educational Psychologist, 27*, 111–126.

Kirschman, K. J. B., Mayes, S., & Perciful, M. S. (2009). Prevention of unintentional injury in children and adolescents. In M. C. Roberts & R. G. Steele (Eds.), *Handbook of pediatric psychology* (4th ed., pp. 586–602). New York: Guilford Press.

Kleinsorge, C. A., Roberts, M. C., Roy, K. M., & Rapoff, M. A. (2010). The program evaluation of services in a primary care clinic: Attaining a medical home. *Clinical Pediatrics, 49*, 548–559.

Koocher, G. P. (Ed.). (1976). *Children's rights and the mental health professions.* New York: Wiley.

Koocher, G. P., & Keith-Spiegel, P. C. (1990). *Children, ethics, and the law*. Lincoln: University of Nebraska Press.

Kovacs, M. (1999). *The Children's Depression Inventory (CDI).* New York: Multi-Health Systems.

Kramer, L. (2006, July 10). Commentary in "How your siblings make you who you are" by J. Kluger. *Time*, pp. 46–51.

Kusche, C., & Greenberg, M. (1994). *The PATHS curriculum: Promoting Alternative Thinking Strategies*. Seattle, WA: Developmental Research and Programs.

Kuyken, W., Padesky, C. A., & Dudley, R. (2009). *Collaborative case conceptualization: Working effectively with clients in cognitive-behavioral therapy*. New York: Guilford.

Labay, L. E., & Walco, G. A. (2004). Brief report: Empathy and psychological adjustment in siblings of children with cancer. *Journal of Pediatric Psychology, 29*, 309–314.

Ladany, N., & Lehrman-Waterman, D. (1999). The content and frequency of supervisor self-disclosures and their relationship to supervisor style and the supervisory working alliance. *Counselor Education and Supervision, 38*, 143–160.

Ladany, N., & Walker, J. A. (2003). Supervisor self-disclosure: Balancing the uncontrollable narcissist with the indomitable altruist. *JCLP/In Session, 59*, 611–621.

La Greca, A. M., & Hughes, J. N. (1999). United we stand, divided we fall: The education and training needs of clinical child psychologists. *Journal of Clinical Child Psychology, 28*(4), 435–447.

La Greca, A. M., & Stone, W. L. (1993). Social Anxiety Scale for Children Revised: Factor structure and concurrent validity. *Journal of Clinical Child and Adolescent Psychology, 22*(1), 17–27.

Lahey, B. B., Applegate, B., Waldman, I. D., Loft, J. D., Hankin, B. L., & Rick, J. (2004). The structure of child and adolescent psychopathology: Generating new hypotheses. *Journal of Abnormal Psychology, 113*, 358–385.

Landolf, B. M. (2005). Outpatient-private practice model. In R. G. Steele & M. C. Roberts (Eds.), *Handbook of mental health services for children, adolescents, and families* (pp. 117–131). New York: Springer.

Last, C. G., & Perrin, S. (1993). Anxiety disorders in African-American and white children. *Journal of Abnormal Child Psychology, 21*, 153–164.

Lazarus, A. A., Davison, G. C., & Polefka, D. A. (1965). Classical and operant factors in the treatment of a school phobia. *Journal of Abnormal Psychology, 70*(3), 225–229.

Leigh, I. W., Smith, I. L., Bebeau, M. J., Lichtenberg, J. W., Nelson, P. D., Portnoy, S., et al. (2007). Competency assessment models. *Professional Psychology: Research and Practice, 38*, 463–473.

Lescano, C., Plante, W., & Spirito, A. (2004). Training in the delivery of pediatric psychology services in school systems. In R. T. Brown (Ed.), *Handbook of pediatric psychology in school settings* (pp. 701–712). Mahwah, NJ: Erlbaum.

Liaupsin, C. J., Jolivette, K., & Scott, T. M. (2004). Schoolwide systems of behavior support: Maximizing student success in schools. In R. B. Rutherford, M. M. Quinn, & S. R. Mathur (Eds.), *Handbook of Research in Emotional and Behavioral Disorders* (pp. 487–501). New York: Guilford Press.

Liddle, H. A., & Hogue, A. (2001). Multidimensional family therapy: Pursuing empirical support through planful treatment development. In E. Wagner & H. Waldron (Eds.), *Adolescent substance use.* Needham Heights, MA: Allyn & Bacon.

Lieberman, D. A. (2000). *Learning behavior and cognition* (3rd ed.). Belmont, CA: Wadsworth/Thomson Learning.

Liese, B. S., & Beck, J. S. (1997). Cognitive therapy supervision. In C. E. Watkins, Jr. (Ed.), *Handbook of psychotherapy supervision* (pp. 114–133). New York: Wiley.

Linehan, M. M. (1993). *Cognitive-behavioral treatment of borderline personality disorder.* New York: Guilford.

Lochman, J. E. (1983). Factors related to patients' satisfaction with their medical care. *Journal of Community Health, 9*, 91–109.

Lochman, J. E. (1992). Cognitive-behavioral intervention with aggressive boys: Three-year follow-up and preventive effects. *Journal of Consulting and Clinical Psychology, 60*, 426–432.

Lochman, J. E., Barth, J. M., & Mager, W. (2005, June). Effects of therapeutic alliance in preventive intervention with aggressive children. Paper presented at the Twelfth Scientific Meeting of the International Society for Research in Child and Adolescent Psychopathology, New York, NY.

Lochman, J. E., Boxmeyer, C., Powell, N., Qu, L., Wells, K., & Windle, M. (2009). Dissemination of the Coping Power Program: Importance of intensity of counselor training. *Journal of Consulting and Clinical Psychology, 77*, 397–409.

Lochman, J. E., Burch, P. P., Curry, J. F., & Lampron, L. B. (1984). Treatment and generalization effects of cognitive-behavioral and goal setting interventions with aggressive boys. *Journal of Consulting and Clinical Psychology, 52*, 915–916.

Lochman, J. E., & Dain, R. N. (1982). Behavioral context of perceived physician empathy. *Family Practice Research Journal, 2*, 28–36.

Lochman, J. E., Dain, R. N., & Babick, K. (1984). Interactive effects of cognitive sets, physician interviewing styles and subject expectancies upon perceived satisfaction. *Family Practice Research Journal, 4*, 110–121.

Lochman, J. E., Holmes, K., & Wojnaroski, M. (2008). Children and cognition: Development of social schema. In J. K. Asamen, M. L. Ellis, & G. L. Berry (Eds.), *Handbook of child development, multiculturalism, and media* (pp. 33–46). Thousand Oaks, CA: Sage.

Lochman, J. E., & Pardini, D. A. (2008). Cognitive-behavioral therapies. In M. Rutter, D. Bishop, D. Pine, S. Scott, J. Stevenson, E. Taylor, et al. (Eds.), *Rutter's child and adolescent psychiatry,* (5th ed., pp. 1026–1045). London: Blackwell.

Lochman, J. E., & Wells, K. C. (2002a). The Coping Power Program at the middle school transition: Universal and indicated prevention effects. *Psychology of Addictive Behaviors, 16,* S40–S54.

Lochman, J. E., & Wells, K. C. (2002b). Contextual social-cognitive mediators and child outcome: A test of the theoretical model in the Coping Power program. *Development and Psychopathology, 14,* 945–967.

Lochman, J. E., & Wells, K. C. (2003). Effectiveness study of Coping Power and classroom intention with aggressive children: Outcomes at a one-year follow-up. *Behavior Therapy, 34,* 493–515.

Lochman, J. E., & Wells, K. C. (2004). The Coping Power Program for preadolescent aggressive boys and their parents: Outcome effects at the 1-year follow-up. *Journal of Consulting and Clinical Psychology, 72,* 571–578.

Lochman, J. E., Wells, K. C., & Lenhart, L. A. (2008). *Coping power child group program.* New York: Oxford University Press.

Lochner, B. T., & Melchert, T. P. (1997). Relationship of cognitive style and theoretical orientation to psychology interns' preferences for supervision. *Journal of Counseling Psychology, 44,* 256–260.

Lonigan, C. J., Elbert J. C., & Johnson, S. B. (1998). Empirically supported psychosocial interventions for children: An overview. *Journal of Clinical Child Psychology, 27,* 138–145.

Loo, C. (1979). Measures for predicting therapeutic skill and the effects of training. *Psychotherapy: Theory, Research and Practice, 16,* 460–466.

Louttit, C. M. (1936). *Clinical psychology: A handbook of children's behavior problems.* New York: Harper & Brothers.

Lovaas, O. I., & Smith, T. (2003). Early and intensive behavioral intervention in autism. In A. Kazddin & J. Weisz (Eds.), *Evidence-based psychotherapies for children and adolescents* (pp. 325–400). New York: Guilford.

Magnuson, S., Wilcoxon, S.A., & Norem, K. (2000). A profile of lousy supervision: Experienced counselors' perspectives. *Counselor Education and Supervision, 39,* 189–202.

Malgady, R. G., & Costantino, G. (2003). Narrative therapy for Hispanic children and adolescents. In A. E. Kazdin & J. R. Weisz (Eds.), *Evidence-based psychotherapies for children and adolescents* (pp. 425–435). New York: Guilford.

March, J. S., Silva, S., Petrycki, S., Curry, J., Wells, K., Fairbank, J., et al. (2004). The Treatment for Adolescents with Depression Study (TADS): Short-term effectiveness and safety outcomes. *Journal of the American Medical Association, 292,* 807–820.

Markie-Dadds, C., & Sanders, M. R. (2006). Self-directed Triple P (Positive Parenting Program) for mothers with children at-risk of developing conduct problems. *Behavioural and Cognitive Psychotherapy, 34,* 259–275.

Marks, E. S. (1995). *Entry strategies for school consultation.* New York: Guilford.

Marmorstein, N. R., & Iacono, W. G. (2004). Major depression and conduct disorder in youth: Associations with parental psychopathology and parent-child conflict. *Journal of Child Psychology and Psychiatry, 45,* 377–386.

Martin, G., & Pear, J. (2003). *Behavior modification: What it is and how to do it.* Upper Saddle River, NJ: Prentice Hall.

Mash, E. J., & Barkley, R. (2006). *Treatment of childhood disorders.* New York: Guilford.

Mash, E. J., & Hunsley, J. (2005a). Evidence-based assessment of child and adolescent disorders: Issues and challenges. *Journal of Clinical Child and Adolescent Psychology, 34,* 362–379.

Mash, E. J., & Hunsley, J. (Eds.). (2005b, September). Special section: Developing guidelines for evidence-based assessment of child and adolescent disorders. *Journal of Adolescent and Child Psychology, 34*(3), 362–379.

Mash, E. J., & Terdal, L. G. (1997). *Assessment of childhood disorders* (3rd ed.) New York: Guilford.

Mash E. J., & Wolfe, D. A. (2010). *Abnormal child psychology.* Belmont, CA: Wadsworth.

Masten, A. S. (2007). Resilience in developing systems: Progress and promise as the fourth wave rises. *Development and Psychopathology, 19*(3), 921–930.

Masten, A. S., & Braswell, L. (1991). Developmental psychopathology: An integrative framework. In P. R. Martin (Ed.), *Handbook of behavior therapy and psychological science: An integrative approach.* New York: Pergamon.

Masten, A. S., & Coatsworth, J. D. (1988). The development of competence in favorable and unfavorable environments: Lessons from research on successful children. *American Psychologist, 53,* 205–220.

Masters, J., Burish, T., Hollon, S., & Rimm, D. (1987). *Behavior therapy: Technique and empirical findings* (3rd ed.) San Diego: Harcourt.

Mayer, M. J., Van Acker, R., Lochman, J. E., & Gresham, F. M. (Eds.). (2008). *Cognitive behavioral interventions for emotional and behavioral disorders: School-based practice.* New York: Guilford.

McCart, M. R., Priester, P. E., Davies, W. H., & Azen, R. (2006). Differential effectiveness of behavioral parent-training and cognitive-behavioral therapy for antisocial youth: A meta-analysis. *Journal of Abnormal Child Psychology, 34,* 527–543.

McEachin, J. J., Smith, T., & Lovaas, O. I. (1993). Long-term outcome for children with autism who received early intensive behavioral treatment. *American Journal of Mental Retardation, 97,* 359–372.

McElroy, H. K., & Prentice-Dunn, S. (2005). Graduate students' perceptions of a teaching of psychology course. *Teaching of Psychology, 32,* 122–124.

McGrath, R. E. (2001). Toward more clinically relevant assessment research. *Journal of Personality Assessment, 77,* 307–332.

McHugh, R. K., & Barlow, D. H. (2010). The dissemination and implementation of evidence-based psychological treatments: A review of current efforts. *American Psychologist, 65,* 73–84.

McMahon, R. J., & Forehand, R. L. (2003). *Helping the noncompliant child: Family-based treatment for oppositional behavior* (2nd ed.). New York: Guilford.

McMahon, S. D., Grant, K. E., Compas, B. E., Thurm, A. E., & Ey, S. (2003). Stress and psychopathology in children and adolescents: Is there evidence of specificity? *Journal of Child Psychology and Psychiatry, 44,* 107–133.

McMahon, S. D., & Watts, R. J. (2002). Ethnic identity in urban African American youth: Exploring links with self-worth, aggression, and other psychosocial variables. *Journal of Community Psychology, 30,* 411–431.

McReynolds, P. (1987a). Lightner Witmer: Father of clinical psychology. In G. A. Kimble, C. A. Boneau, & M. Wertheimer (Eds.), *Portraits of pioneers in psychology* (Vol. 2). Washington, DC: American Psychological Association.

McReynolds, P. (1987b). Lightner Witmer: Little-known founder of clinical psychology. *American Psychologist, 42*, 849–858.

Meichenbaum, D. H., & Goodman, J. (1969). The developmental control of operant motor responding by verbal operants. *Journal of Experimental Child Psychology, 7*, 553–565.

Meichenbaum, D. H., & Goodman, J. (1971). Training impulsive children to talk to themselves: A means of developing self-control. *Journal of Abnormal Psychology, 77*, 115–126.

Melton, G. B., Koocher, G. P., & Saks, M. (Eds.). (1983). *Children's competence to consent.* New York: Plenum.

Melvin, G. A., Tonge, B. J., King, N. J., Heyne, D., Gordon, M. S., & Klimkeit, E. (2006). A comparison of cognitive-behavioral therapy, sertraline, and their combination for adolescent depression. *Journal of the American Academy of Child and Adolescent Psychiatry, 45*, 1151–1161.

Merrell, K. W. (2003). *Behavioral, Social, and emotional assessment of children and adolescents* (2nd ed.). Mahwah, NJ: Erlbaum.

Milne, D. (2007). An empirical definition of clinical supervision. *British Journal of Clinical Psychology, 46*, 437–447.

Milne, D. L., & James, I. A. (2002). The observed impact of training on competence in clinical supervision. *British Journal of Clinical Psychology, 41*, 55–72.

Minuchin, S., Montalvo, B., Guerney, B., Rosman, B., & Schumer, F. (1967). *Families of the slums.* New York: Basic Books.

Minuchin, S., Rosman, B. L., & Baker, L. (1978). *Psychosomatic families: Anorexia nervosa in context.* Cambridge, MA: Harvard University Press.

Mischel, W. (1973). Toward a cognitive social learning conceptualization of personality. *Psychological Review, 80*, 252–283.

Moskowitz, S. A., & Rupert, P. A. (1983). Conflict resolution within the supervisory relationship. *Professional Psychology: Research and Practice, 14*, 632–641.

Mowrer, O. H. (1980). Enuresis: The beginning work: What really happened. *Journal of the History of the Behavioral Sciences, 16*, 25–30.

MTA Cooperative Group. (1999). A 14-month randomized clinical trial of treatment strategies for attention-deficit/hyperactivity disorder. *Archives of General Psychiatry, 56*, 1073–1086.

Mullins, L. L., Gillman, J., & Harbeck, C. (1992). Multiple-level interventions in pediatric psychology settings: A behavioral systems perspective. In A. M. La Greca, L. J. Siegel, J. L. Wallander, & C. E. Walker (Eds.), *Stress and coping in child health* (pp. 377–399). New York: Guilford.

Murphy, W. D., Page, J., & Ettelson, R. (2005). Adolescent sex offender programs. In R. G. Steele & M. C. Roberts (Eds.), *Handbook of mental health services for children, adolescents, and families* (pp. 167–179). New York: Kluwer Academic/Plenum.

Nagy, Thomas F. (2005). *Ethics in plain English: An illustrative casebook for psychologists* (2nd ed.). Washington, DC: American Psychological Association Press.

Neddleman, L. D. (1999).*Cognitive case conceptualization: A guidebook for practitioners.* Mahwah, NJ: Erlbaum.

Neisser, U. (1967). *Cognitive psychology.* New York: Wiley Press.

Nelson, C. A. (2003). Neural development and lifelong plasticity. In R. M. Lerner, F. Jacobs, & D. Wertlieb (Eds.), *Handbook of applied developmental science* (Vol. 1). Thousand Oaks, CA: Sage.

Nelson, R. O. (1983). Behavioral assessment: Past, present, and future. *Behavioral Assessment, 5,* 195–206.

Nelson, W. M., III. (1982). Behavior treatment of childhood trichotillomania: A case study. *Clinical Child Psychology, 11,* 227–230.

Nelson, W. M., III, & Finch, A. J., Jr. (2000). *The Children's Inventory of Anger (ChIA).* Los Angeles: Western Behavioral Sciences.

Nelson, W. M., III, & Finch, A. J., Jr. (2008a). *Cognitive-behavioral therapy for aggressive children: Therapist manual.* Ardmore, PA: Workbook.

Nelson, W. M., III, & Finch, A. J., Jr. (2008b). *"Keeping your cool": The anger management workbook* (Parts 1 and 2, 2nd ed.). Ardmore, PA: Workbook.

Nelson, W. M., III, & Finch, A. J., Jr. (2008c). *Therapist manual for "Keeping Your Cool: The Anger Management Workbook"* (2nd ed.). Ardmore, PA: Workbook.

Nelson, W. M., & Politano, P. M. (1993). The goal is to say "good-bye" and have the treatment effects generalize and maintain: A cognitive-behavioral view of termination. *Journal of Cognitive Psychology, 7,* 249–261.

Nerdrum, P., & Ronnestad, M. H. (2002). The trainees' perspective: A qualitative study of learning empathic communication in Norway. *The Counseling Psychologist, 30,* 609–629.

Nezu, A. M. (1993). Identifying and selecting target problems for clinical interventions: A problem-solving model. *Psychological Assessment, 5,* 254–263.

Nezu, A. M., Nezu, C. M., & Cos, T. A. (2007). Case formulation for the behavioral and cognitive therapies: A problem-solving perspective. In T. D. Ells (Ed.), *Handbook of psychotherapy case formulation.* New York: Guilford Press.

Nichols, M. P. (2010). *Family therapy and methods.* New York: Allyn & Bacon.

Nock, M. K. (2003). Progress review of the psychosocial treatment of child conduct problems. *Clinical Psychology: Science and Practice, 10,* 1–28.

Norcross, J. C. (Ed.) (2002). *Psychotherapy relationships that work: Therapist contributions and responsiveness to patients.* New York: Oxford University Press.

O'Donohue, W., & Ferguson, K. (Eds.). (2003). *Handbook of professional ethics for psychologists: Issues, questions, and controversies.* Thousand Oaks, CA: Sage.

Olds, D. L., Henderson, C. R., Jr., Kitzman, H. J., Eckenrode, J. J., Cote, R. E., & Tatelbaum, R. C. (1999). In R. E. Behrman (Ed.), *Home visiting: Recent program evaluations. The Future of Children* (Vol. 9, pp. 44–65). Los Angeles: David and Lucile Packard Foundation.

Ollendick, T. H. (1983). Reliability and validity of the Revised Fear Survey Schedule for Children (FSSC-R). *Behaviour Research and Therapy, 21,* 685–692.

Ollendick, T. H. (1984). Training in clinical child psychology: A proposal for the role of continuing education. In J. M. Tuma (Ed.), *Proceedings: Conference on training clinical child psychologists* (pp. 90–91). Baton Rouge, LA: Section on Child Psychology, American Psychological Association.

Ollendick, T. H., & Hersen, M. (1984). *Child behavioral assessment: Principles and procedures.* New York: Pergamon Press.

Ollendick, T. H., & King, N. J. (2000). Empirically supported treatments for children with phobic and anxiety disorders: Current status. *Journal of Clinical Child Psychology, 27,* 156–167.

Ollendick, T. H., & Schroeder, C. S. (Eds.). (2003). *Encyclopedia of clinical child and pediatric psychology*. New York: Kluwer/Plenum.

Ortiz, S. O., & Dynda, A.M. (2003). Use of intelligence tests with culturally and linguistically diverse populations. In D. P. Flanagan & P. L. Harrison (Eds.), *Contemporary intellectual assessment: Theories, tests, and issues* (2nd ed., pp. 545–556). New York: Guilford.

Orvaschel, H., Faust, J., & Hersen, M. (2001a). General issues in conceptualization and treatment. In H. Orvaschel, J. Faust, & M. Hersen (Eds.), *Handbook of conceptualization and treatment of child psychopathology* (pp. 3–7). Oxford: Elsevier.

Orvaschel, H., Faust, J., & Hersen, M. (2001b). *Handbook of conceptualization and treatment of child psychopathology*. Oxford, UK: Elsevier Science.

Oster, G. D., Caro, J. E., Eagen, D. R., & Lillo, M. A. (1988). *Assessing adolescents*. Elmsford, NY: Pergamon Press.

O'Sullivan, P., Chao, S., Russell, M., Levine, S., & Fabiny, A. (2008). Development and implementation of an objective structured clinical examination to provide formative feedback on communication and interpersonal skills in geriatric training. *Journal of the American Geriatric Society, 56,* 1730–1735.

Oyserman, D., Harrison, K., & Bybee, D. (2001). Can racial identity be promotive of academic efficacy? *International Journal of Behavioral Development, 25,* 379–385.

Pagliocca, P. M., Melton, G. G., Weisz, V., & Lyons, P. M., Jr. (1995). Parenting and the law. In M. H. Bornstein (Ed.), *Handbook of parenting*. Hillsdale, NJ: Lawrence Erlbaum.

Palazzoli, M. S., Boscolo, L., Cecchin, G., & Prata, G. (1980). Hypothesizing-circularity-neutrality: Three guidelines for the conductor of the session. *Family Process, 19,* 3–12.

Panerai, S., Ferrante, L., & Zingale, M. (2002). Benefits of the Treatment and Education of Autistic and Communication Handicapped Children (TEACCH) program as compared worth a non-specific approach. *Journal of Intellectual Disability Research, 46,* 318–327.

Parron, D. L. (1994). DSM-IV: Making it culturally relevant. In S. Friedman (Ed.), *Anxiety disorders in African Americans* (pp. 149–165). New York: Springer.

Parry, A., & Doane, R. (1994). *Story re-visions: Narrative therapy in the postmodern world*. New York: Guilford.

Paschall, M. J., & Flewlling, R. L. (1997). Measuring intermediate outcomes of violence prevention program targeting African-American male youth: An exploratory assessment of the psychometric properties of six psychological measures. *Health Education Research: Theory and Practice, 12,* 117–128.

Paulhus, D. L. (2008). Birth order. In M. M. Haith & J. B. Benson (Eds.). *Encyclopedia of infant and early childhood development*. Oxford, UK: Elsevier.

Pernell-Arnold, A., & Finley, L. (1999). Integrating multicultural competence into psychosocial rehabilitation. In R. Hughes & D. Weinstein (Eds.), *Best practices in psychosocial rehabilitation* (pp. 213–244). Columbia, MD: International Association of Psychosocial Rehabilitation Services.

Persons, J. B. (2008). *The case-formulation approach to cognitive-behavior therapy*. New York: Guilford.

Phinney, J. (1990). Ethnic identity in adolescents and adults: A review of research. *Psychological Bulletin, 108,* 499–514.

Potash J. B., Toolan J., Steele, J., Miller, E. B., Pearl, J., Zandi, P. P., et al. (2007). The bipolar disorder phenome database: A resource for genetic studies. *American Journal of Psychiatry, 164,* 1229–1237.

Practice Directorate, American Psychological Association. (1994). Guidelines for child custody evaluations in divorce proceedings. *American Psychologist, 49,* 677–680.

Premack, D. (1965). Reinforcement theory. In D. Levine. (Ed.), *Nebraska symposium on motivation* (pp. 123–180). Lincoln: University of Nebraska Press.

Pressley, M., McDaniel, M. A., Turnure, J. E., Wood, E., & Ahmad, M. (1987). Generation and practice of elaboration: Effects on intentional and incidental learning. *Journal of Experimental Psychology: Learning, Memory, and Cognition, 13,* 291–300.

Pressley, M., Wood, E., Woloshyn, V. E., Martin, V., King, A., & Menke, D. (1992). Encouraging mindful use of prior knowledge: Attempting to construct explanatory answers facilitates learning. *Educational Psychologist, 27,* 91–109.

Pringle, B., & Flanzer, J. (2005). Treatment services for adolescent substance abuse. In R. G. Steele & M. C. Roberts (Eds.), *Handbook of mental health services for children, adolescents, and families* (pp. 231–243). New York: Kluwer Academic/Plenum.

Prinstein, M. J., & Roberts, M. C. (2006). The professional adolescence of clinical child and adolescent psychology and pediatric psychology: Grown up and striving for autonomy. *Clinical Psychology: Science and Practice, 13,* 263–268.

Prochaska, J. O., & Diclemente, C. C. (2005). The transtheoretical approach. In J. C. Norcross & M. R. Goldfried (Eds.), *Handbook of psychotherapy integration* (pp. 300–334). New York: Oxford.

Pumariega, A. J. (2001). Cultural competence in treatment interventions. In H. B. Vance & A. J. Pumariega (Eds.), *Clinical assessment of child and adolescent behavior* (pp. 494–512). New York: Wiley.

Rae, W. A. (2003). Licensure. In T. H. Ollendick & C. S. Schroeder (Eds.), *Encyclopedia of clinical child and pediatric psychology* (pp. 343–344). New York: Kluwer/Plenum.

Ramos-Sanchez, L., Esnil, E., Goodwin, A., Riggs, S., Touster, L. O., Wright, L. K., et al. (2002). Negative supervisory events: Effects on supervision satisfaction and supervisory alliance. *Professional Psychology: Research and Practice, 33,* 197–202.

Rappaport, J., Chinsky, J., & Cowen, E. (1971). *Innovations in helping chronic patients: College students in a mental institution.* New York: Academic Press.

Reilly, D. H. (1973). School psychology: A view from the second generation. *Psychology in the Schools, 11,* 165–170.

Reilly, D. H. (1974). A conceptual model for school psychology. *Psychology in the Schools, 11,* 151–155.

Reinecke, M. A., Ryan, N. E., & DuBois, D. L. (1998). Cognitive-behavioral therapy of depression and depressive symptoms during adolescence: A review and meta-analysis. *Journal of the American Academy of Child and Adolescent Psychiatry, 37,* 26–34.

Reitman, D. (2006). Overview of behavioral assessment with children. In M. Hersen (Ed.), *Clinician's handbook of behavioral assessment, Vol. 2: Child assessment.* New York: Elsevier.

Reynolds C. R., & Gutkin, T. B. (1999). *The handbook of school psychology* (3rd ed.). New York: Wiley.

Reynolds, C. R., & Kaiser, S. M. (2003). Bias in the assessment of aptitude. In C. R. Reynolds & R. W. Kamphaus (Eds.), *Handbook of psychological and educational assessment of children: Intelligence, aptitude, and achievement* (pp. 519–562). New York: Guilford.

Rhodes, P., Gosbee, M., Madden, S., & Brown, J. (2005). "Communities of concern" in the family based treatment of anorexia nervosa: Toward a consensus in the Maudsley model. *European Eating Disorders Review, 13,* 392–398.

Robbins, M. S., Szapocznik, J., Santisteban, D. A., Hervis, O. E., Mitrani, V. B., & Schwartz, S. J. (2003). Brief strategic family therapy for Hispanic youth. In A. E. Kazdin & J. R. Weisz (Eds.), *Evidence-based psychotherapies for children and adolescents* (pp. 407–424). New York: Guilford.

Roberts, M. C. (1986). *Pediatric psychology: Psychological interventions and strategies for pediatric problems.* New York: Pergamon Press.

Roberts, M. C. (2006). Essential tension: Specialization with broad and general training in psychology. *American Psychologist, 61*(8), 862–862.

Roberts, M. C., Biggs, B. K., Jackson, Y., & Steele, R. G. (2011). Clinical child psychology: Research and practice applications. In P. Martin, F. Cheung, M. Kyrios, L. Littlefield, M. Knowles, B. Overmeier et al. (Eds.), *The IAAP handbook of applied psychology.* Hoboken, NJ: Wiley-Blackwell.

Roberts, M. C., Carlson, C. I., Erickson, M. T., Friedman, R. M., La Greca, A. M., Lemanek, K. L., et al. (1998). A model for training psychologists to provide services for children and adolescents. *Professional Psychology: Research and Practice, 29*(3), 293–293.

Roberts, M. C., Erickson, M. T., & Tuma, J. M. (1985). Addressing the needs: Guidelines for training psychologists to work with children, youth, and families. *Journal of Clinical Child Psychology, 14,* 70–79.

Roberts, M. C., Jacobs, A. K., Puddy, R. W., Nyre, J. E., & Vernberg, E. M. (2003). Treating children with serious emotional disturbances in schools and community: The Intensive Mental Health Program. *Professional Psychology: Research and Practice, 34,* 519–526.

Roberts, M. C., & James, R. L. (2008). Empirically supported treatments and evidence-based practice for children and adolescents. In R. G. Steele, T. D. Elkin, & M. C. Roberts (Eds.), *Handbook of evidence-based therapists for children and adolescents: Bridging science and practice* (pp. 9–24). New York: Springer.

Roberts, M. C., & Steele, R. G. (Eds.). (2010). *Handbook of pediatric psychology* (4th ed.). New York: Guilford.

Roberts, M. C., & Wright, L. (1982). The role of the pediatric psychologist as consultant to pediatricians. In J. M. Tuma (Ed.), *Handbook for the practice of pediatric psychology* (pp. 251–289). New York: Wiley.

Robiner, W. N. (2008). Addressing professional competence problems in trainees: Managing hot potatoes with heightened ethical awareness. *Professional Psychology: Research and Practice, 39,* 594–597.

Rogers, C. R. (1942). *Counseling and psychotherapy: Newer concepts in practice.* Boston: Houghton Mifflin.

Rogers, M. R., & Lopez, E. C. (2002). Identifying cross-cultural school psychology competencies. *Journal of School Psychology, 40,* 115–141.

Ronan, K. R., Kendall, P. C., & Rowe, M. (1994). Negative affectivity in children: Development and validation of a self-statement questionnaire. *Cognitive Therapy and Research, 18,* 509–528.

Rosenthal, S. L. (1995). Consultation in an adolescent medicine clinic. In D. Drotar, *Consulting with pediatricians: Psychological perspectives* (pp. 185–194). New York: Plenum.

Ross, A. O. (1959). *The practice of clinical child psychology.* New York: Grune & Stratton.

Rotter, J. B. (1954). *Social learning and clinical psychology,* Englewood Cliffs, NJ: Prentice Hall.

Rotter, J. B., Chance, J. E., & Pharres, E. J. (1972). *Applications of a social learning theory of personality*. New York: Holt, Rinehart, & Winston.

Routh, D. K. (1994). *Clinical psychology since 1917*. New York: Plenum.

Rubin, N. J., Bebeau, M., Leigh, I. W., Lichtenberg, J. W., Nelson, P. D., Portnoy, S., et al. (2007). The competency movement within psychology: An historical perspective. *Professional Psychology: Research and Practice, 38*, 452–462.

Russell, G. F. M., Szmukler, G. I., Dare, C., & Eisler, I. (1987). An evaluation of family therapy in anorexia nervosa and bulimia nervosa. *Archives of General Psychiatry, 44*, 1047–1056.

Rutter, M. (1999). Resilience concepts and findings: Implications for family therapy. *Journal of Family Therapy, 21*, 119–144.

Rutter, M., Silberg, J., O'Connor, T., & Simonoff, E. (1999). Genetics and child psychiatry. I. Advances in quantitative and molecular genetics. *Journal of Child Psychiatry and Psychiatry, 40*, 3–18.

Sacco, W. P., & Beck, A. T. (1995). Cognitive theory and therapy. In E. E. Beckham & W. R. Leber (Eds.), *Handbook of depression* (2nd ed., pp. 329–351). New York: Guilford.

Santrock, J. W. (2009). *Life-span development* (12th ed.). Boston: McGraw Hill.

Sarason, S. B. (1971). *The culture of the school and the problem of change*. Boston: Allyn & Bacon.

Scaramella, L. V., & Leve, L. D. (2004). Clarifying parent-child reciprocities during early childhood: The early childhood coercion model. *Clinical Child and Family Psychology Review, 7*, 89–107.

Schmuck, S., Martell, R., & Derr, C. (1972). *Handbook of organizational development in schools*. Palo Alto, CA: Mayfield.

Schroeder, C. S. (1996). Mental health services in pediatric primary care. In M. C. Roberts & Task Force on Model Programs in Service Delivery (Eds.), *Model programs in child and family mental health* (pp. 265–284). Mahwah, NJ: Erlbaum.

Schroeder, C. S. (2005). A collaborative practice in primary care: Lessons learned. In B. G. Wildman & T. Stancin (Eds.), *Treating children's psychosocial problems in primary care* (pp. 1–34). Greenwich, CT: Information Age.

Scott, S. (2008). Parenting programs. In M. Rutter, D. Bishop, D. Pine, S. Scott, J. Stevenson, E. Taylor, et al. (Eds.), *Rutter's child and adolescent psychiatry* (5th ed., pp. 1046–1061). London: Blackwell.

Scott, S., & Yule, W. (2008). Behavioral therapies. In M. Rutter, D. Bishop, D. Pine, S. Scott, J. Stevenson, E. Taylor, et al. (Eds.), *Rutter's child and adolescent psychiatry* (5th ed., pp. 1009–1025). London: Blackwell.

Segal, Z. V., Williams, J. M. G., & Teasdale, J. T. (2001). *Mindfulness cognitive therapy for depression: A new approach to preventing relapse*. New York: Guilford.

Sexton, T. L., & Coop Gordon, K. (2009). Science, practice, and evidence-based treatments in the clinical practice of family psychology. In J. H. Bray & M. Stanton (Eds.), *The Wiley-Blackwell handbook of family psychology* (pp. 314–326). Malden, MA: Wiley-Blackwell.

Seymour, F. W., & Epston, D. (1989). An approach to childhood stealing with evaluation of 45 cases. *Australian and New Zealand Journal of Family Therapy, 10*, 137–143.

Sheridan, S. M., & Kratochwill, T. R. (2008). *Conjoint behavioral consultation: Promoting family-school connections and interventions* (2nd ed.). New York: Springer.

Shirk, S. R., & Karver, M. (2003). Prediction of treatment outcome from relationship variables in child and adolescent therapy: A meta-analytic review. *Journal of Consulting and Clinical Psychology, 71*, 452–464.

Shirk, S. R., & Russell, R. I. (1996). *Change processes in child psychotherapy: Revitalizing treatment and research*. New York: Guilford Press.

Shirk, S., & Saiz, C. (1992). Clinical, empirical, and developmental perspectives on the relationship in child psychotherapy. *Development and Psychopathology, 4*, 713–728.

Shriver, M. D., & Allen, K. D. (2008). *Working with parents of noncompliant children: A guide to evidence-based parent training for practitioners and students*. Washington, DC: American Psychological Association.

Shure, M. B. (1992). *I can problem solve (ICPS): An interpersonal problem-solving program. Kindergarten and primary grades*. Champaign, IL: Research Press.

Shure, M. B., & Spivack, G. (1980). Interpersonal problem solving as a mediator of behavioral adjustment in preschool and kindergarten children. *Journal of Applied Developmental Psychology, 1*, 29–44.

Silverman, A. H., Hains, A. H., Davies, W. H., & Parton, E. (2003). A cognitive behavioral adherence intervention for adolescents with type 1 diabetes. *Journal of Clinical Child Psychology in Medical Settings, 10*, 119–127.

Silverman, W. K., & Hinshaw, S. P. (2008). The second special issue on evidence-based psychosocial treatments for children and adolescents: A ten year update. *Journal of Clinical Child and Adolescent Psychology, 37*(whole issue 1).

Silverman, W. K., Kurtines, W. M., Ginsburg, G. S., Weems, C. F., Rabian, B., & Serafini, L. T. (1999). Contingency management, self control, and education support in the treatment of childhood phobic disorders: A randomized clinical trial. *Journal of Consulting and Clinical Psychology, 67*, 675–687.

Silverman, W. K., & Saavedra, L. M. (2004). Assessment and diagnosis in evidence-based practice. In P. M. Barrett & T. H. Ollendick (Eds.), *Handbook of interventions that work with children and adolescents: Prevention and treatment*. West Sussex, UK: Wiley.

Skinner, T. C., & Hampson, S. E. (2001). Personal models of diabetes in relation to self-care, well-being, and glycemic control. *Diabetes Care, 24*, 828–833.

Sloves, R. E., Docherty, E. M., & Schneider, K. C. (1979). A scientific problem-solving model of psychological assessment. *Professional Psychology, 10*, 28–35.

Smith, T., Groen, A., & Wynn, J. W. (2000). Randomized trial of intensive early intervention for children with pervasive developmental disorder. *American Journal of Mental Retardation, 105*, 269–285.

Smith-Boydston, J. M. (2005). Providing a range of services to fit the needs of youth in community mental health centers. In R. G. Steele & M. C. Roberts (Eds.), *Handbook of mental health services for children, adolescents, and families* (pp. 103–116). New York: Kluwer Academic/Plenum.

Smith-Boydston, J. M., & Nelson, T. D. (2008). Adoption of evidence-based treatments in community settings: Obstacles and opportunities. In R. G. Steele, T. D. Elkin, & M. C. Roberts (Eds.), *Handbook of evidence-based therapies for children and adolescents* (pp. 521–535). New York: Springer.

Sobel, A. B., Roberts, M. C., Rayfield, A., Barnard, M. U., & Rapoff, M. A. (2001). Evaluating outpatient pediatric psychology services in a primary care setting. *Journal of Pediatric Psychology, 26*, 395–405.

Society for Child and Family Policy and Practice (SCFPP). (2010). Division 37 of the American Psychological Association homepage. Retrieved from http://www.apa.org/divisions/div37/

Society for Child and Family Practice. (2010). Report of *Healthy Development: A Summit on Young Children's Mental Health*. Retrieved from http://www.apa.org/about/division/div37.aspx

Society of Behavioral Medicine (SBM). (2010) About SBM. Retrieved from http://www.sbm.org/about

Society of Clinical Psychology (SCP). (2010). About clinical psychology. Retrieved at http://www.div12.org/about-clinical-psychology

Society of Pediatric Psychology (SPP). (2010). Who we are. Retrieved from http://www.societyofpediatricpsychology.org/who/

Spiegler, M. D., & Guevremont, D. C. (2010). *Contemporary behavior therapy*. Belmont, CA: Wadsworth.

Spirito, A. (1999). Introduction to special series on empirically supported treatments in pediatric psychology. *Journal of Pediatric Psychology, 24*(2), 87–90.

Spirito, A. (2010a). Division 53 and the dissemination of evidence-based treatments. *InBalance, 25*(1), 1.

Spirito, A. (2010b). SCCAP and clinical treatment guidelines. *InBalance, 25*(2), 1.

Spirito, A., Brown, R. T., D'Angelo, E. J., Delamater, A. M., Rodrigue, J. R., & Siegel, L. J. (2003). Training pediatric psychologists for the 21st century. In M. C. Roberts (Ed.), *Handbook of pediatric psychology* (3rd ed., pp. 19–31). New York: Guilford Press.

Spivack, G., & Spotts, J. (1966). *Devereux child behavior rating scale*. Devon, PA: Devereux Foundation.

Spivack, G., Spotts, J., & Haimes, P. E. (1967). *Devereux adolescent behavior rating scale*. Devon, PA: Devereux Foundation.

Stabler, B. (1979). Emerging models of psychologist-pediatrician liaison. *Journal of Pediatric Psychology, 4*, 307–313.

Stahl, P. M. (1999). *Complex issues in child custody evaluations*. Thousand Oaks, CA: Sage.

Stancin, T. (2005). Mental health services for children in pediatric primary care settings. In R. G. Steele & M. C. Roberts (Eds.), *Handbook of mental health services for children, adolescents, and families* (pp. 85–101). New York: Kluwer Academic/Plenum.

Stancin, T., Perrin, E. C., & Ramirez, L. (2009). Pediatric psychology and primary care. In M. C. Roberts & R. G. Steele (Eds.), *Handbook of pediatric psychology* (4th ed., pp. 630–646). New York: Guilford.

Standards for Educational and Psychological Testing. (1999). Washington, DC: American Psychological Association.

Stanhope, V., Solomon, P., Finley, L., Pernell-Arnold, A., Bourjolly, J. N., & Sands, R. G. (2008). Evaluating the impact of cultural competency trainings from the perspective of people in recovery. *American Journal of Psychiatric Rehabilitation, 11*, 356–372.

Stark, K. D., Hargrave, J., Sander, J., Custer, G., Schoebelen, S., Simpson, J., et al. (2006). Treatment of childhood depression: The ACTION treatment program. In P. Kendall (Ed.), *Child and adolescent therapy: Cognitive-behavioral procedures* (3rd ed., pp. 169–216). New York: Guilford.

Stark, K. D., Sander, J., Hauser, M., Simpson, J., Schoebelen, S., Glenn, R., et al. (2006). Depressive disorders during adolescence. In E. J. Mash & R. A. Barkley (Eds.), *Treatment of childhood disorders* (3rd ed., pp. 336–407). New York: Guilford.

Stark, K. D., Simpson, J., Schnoebelen, S., Hargrave, J., & Molnar, J. (2007). *ACTION workbook: Cognitive-behavioral therapy for treating depressed girls.* Ardmore, PA: Workbook.

Steele, R. G., & Aylward, B. S. (2009). An overview of systems in pediatric psychology research and practice. In M. C. Roberts & R. G. Steele (Eds.), *Handbook of pediatric psychology* (4th ed., pp. 649–655). New York: Guilford.

Steele, R. G., Elkin, T. D., & Roberts, M. C. (Eds.). (2008). *Handbook of evidence-based therapies for children and adolescents: Bridging science and practice.* New York: Springer.

Steele, R. G., & Roberts, M. C. (Eds.). (2005). *Handbook of mental health services for children, adolescents, and families.* New York: Kluwer Academic/Plenum.

Steele, R. G., Roberts, M. C., & Elkin, T. D. (2008). Evidence-based therapies for children and adolescents: Problems and prospects. In R. G. Steele, T. D. Elkin, & M. C. Roberts (Eds.), *Handbook of evidence-based therapies for children and adolescents: Bridging science and practice* (pp. 3–8). New York: Springer.

Stein, B. D., Jaycox, L. H., Kataoka, S. H., Wong, M., Tu, W., Elliott, M. N., et al. (2003). A mental health intervention for schoolchildren exposed to violence: A randomized controlled trial. *Journal of the American Medical Association, 290,* 603–611.

Stines, L. R., & Feeny, N. C. (2008). Unique ethical concerns in clinical trials comparing psychosocial and psychopharmalogical interventions. *Ethics & Behavior, 18,* 234–246.

Stoiber, K., & Kratochwill, T. R. (2000). Empirically supported interventions and school psychology: Rationale and methodological issues—Part I. *School Psychology Quarterly, 15,* 75–105.

Stoltenberg, C. D. (2005). Enhancing professional competence through developmental approaches to supervision. *American Psychologist, 60,* 857–864.

Stoltenberg, C. D., McNeill, B. W., & Delworth, U. (1998). *IDM Supervision: An integrated developmental model for supervising counselors and therapists.* San Francisco, CA: Jossey-Bass.

Stuart, R. B. (1971). Behavioral contracting within the families of delinquents. *Journal of Behavior Therapy and Experimental Psychiatry, 2*(1), 1–11.

Sundin, E. C., Ogren, M. L., & Boethius, S. B. (2008). Supervisor trainees' and their supervisors' perceptions of attainment of knowledge and skills: An empirical evaluation of a psychotherapy supervisor training program. *British Journal of Clinical Psychology, 47,* 381–396.

Sweareer, S. M., Espelege, D. L., & Napolitano, S. A. (2009). *Bullying prevention and intervention.* New York: Guilford Press.

Szapocznik, J., & Kurtines, W. (1989). *Breakthroughs in family therapy with drug abusing and problem youth.* New York: Springer.

Szapocznik, J., & Williams, R. (2000). Brief strategic family therapy: Twenty-five years of interplay among theory, research and practice in adolescent behavior problems and drug abuse. *Clinical Child and Family Psychology Review, 3,* 117–134.

Tanaka-Matsumi, J., Seiden, D. Y., & Lam, K. N. (1996). The Culturally Informed Functional Assessment (CIFA) interview: A strategy for cross-cultural behavioral practice. *Cognitive and Behavioral Practice, 3,* 215–235.

Teutsch, C. (2003). Patient-doctor communication. *Medical Clinics of North America, 87,* 1115–1145.

Tharinger, D. J., Finn, S. E., Austin, C. A., Gentry, L. B., Bailey, K. E., Parton, V. T., et al. (2008). Family sessions as part of child psychological assessment: Goals, techniques, clinical utility, and therapeutic value. *Journal of Personality Assessment 90*(6), 547–558.

Tharinger, D. J., Finn, S. E., Gentry, L., Hamilton, A., Fowler, J., Matson, M., et al. (2009). Therapeutic assessment with children: A pilot study of treatment acceptability and outcome. *Journal of Personality Assessment, 91*(3), 238–244.

Tharinger, D. J., Finn, S. E., Hersh, B., Wilkinson, A., Christopher, G. B., & Tran, A. (2008). Assessment feedback with parents and preadolescent children: A collaborative approach. *Professional Psychology: Research and Practice, 39,* 600–609.

Thompson, R. J., Jr., & Gustafson, K. E. (1996). *Adaptation to chronic childhood illness.* Washington, DC: American Psychological Association.

Thompson, R. J., Jr., Gustafson, K. E., Gil, K. M., Godfrey, J., & Bennet Murphy, L. M. (1998). Illness specific patterns of psychological adjustment and cognitive adaptational processes in children with cystic fibrosis and sickle cell disease. *Journal of Clinical Psychology, 54,* 121–128.

Tipton, R. M. (1996). Education and training. In L. J. Bass, S. T. DeMers, J. R. P. Ogloff, C. Peterson, J. L. Pettifor, R. P. Reaves, et al. (Eds.), *Professional conduct and discipline in psychology* (pp. 17–37). Washington, DC: American Psychological Association.

Trowell, J., Joffe, I., Campbell, J., Clemente, C., Almqvist, F., Soininen, M., et al. (2007). Childhood depression: A place for psychotherapy. An outcome study comparing individual psychodynamic psychotherapy and family therapy. *European Child and Adolescent Psychiatry, 16,* 157–167.

Tuma, J. M. (Ed.). (1985). *Proceedings: Conference on training clinical child psychologists.* Baton Rouge, LA: Section on Clinical Child Psychology.

Ullmann, L. P., & Krasner, L. (1965). *Case studies in behavior modification.* New York: Holt, Rinehart & Winston.

Vargas, L. A., & Brambila, A. D. D. (2005). Inpatient treatment models. In R. G. Steele & M. C. Roberts (Eds.), *Handbook of mental health services for children, adolescents, and families* (pp. 133–149). New York: Kluwer Academic/Plenum.

Vargas, L. A., & de Dios Brambila, A. (2005). Inpatient treatment models. In R. G. Steele & M. C. Roberts (Eds.), *Handbook of mental health services for children, adolescents, and families* (pp. 133–149). New York: Springer.

Vega, W. (2005). Higher stakes ahead for cultural competence. *General Hospital Psychiatry, 27,* 446–450.

Velderman, M. K., Bakermans-Kranenburg, M. J., Juffer, F., van Ijzendoorn, M. H., Mangelsdorf, S. C., & Zevalkink, J. (2006). Preventing preschool externalizing behavior problems through video-feedback intervention in infancy. *Infant Mental Health Journal, 27,* 466–493.

Vermunt, J. D. (1998). The regulation of constructive learning processes. *British Journal of Educational Psychology, 68,* 149–171.

Vermunt, J. D., & Vermetten, Y. J. (2004). Patterns in student learning: Relationships between learning strategies, conceptions of learning, and learning orientations. *Educational Psychology Review, 16,* 359–384.

Vitaro, F., & Tremblay, R. E. (2008). Clarifying and maximizing the usefulness of targeted preventive interventions. In M. Rutter, D. Bishop, D. Pine, S. Scott, J. Stevenson, E. Taylor, et al. (Eds.), *Rutter's child and adolescent psychiatry* (5th ed., pp. 989–1008). London: Blackwell.

Vitello, B. (2008). Effectively obtaining informed consent for child and adolescent participation in mental health research. *Ethics & Behavior, 18,* 182–198.

Voorpostel, M., & Bleszner, R. (2008). Intergenerational solidarity and support between adult siblings. *Journal of Marriage and the Family, 70,* 157–167.

Wagner, B. M., & Reiss, D. (1995). Family systems and developmental psychopathology: Courtship, marriage, or divorce? In D. Cicchetti & D. J. Cohen (Eds.). *Developmental psychopathology: Vol. 1. Theory and methods.* New York: Wiley.

Walker, H. M., Ramsay, E., & Gresham, F. M. (2004). *Antisocial behavior at school: Evidence-based practices* (2nd ed.). Belmont, CA: Wadsworth/Thomson Learning.

Walker, C. E., & Roberts, M. C. (Eds.). (2001). *Handbook of clinical child psychology* (3rd ed.). New York: Wiley.

Walsh, M. E., & Jackson, J. H. (2005). Psychological services for children and families who are homeless. In R. G. Steele & M. C. Roberts (Eds.), *Handbook of mental health services for children, adolescents, and families* (pp. 277–292). New York: Kluwer Academic/Plenum.

Watkins, C. E., Jr. (1993). Development of the psychotherapy supervisor: Concepts, assumptions, and hypotheses of the supervisor complexity model. *American Journal of Psychotherapy, 49,* 568–581.

Watson, D. L., & Tharp, R. G. (2002). *Self-directed behavior: Self-modification for personal adjustment* (8th ed.). Pacific Grove, CA: Brooks/Cole.

Watson, J. B., & Rayner, R. (1920). Conditioned emotional reactions. *Journal of Experimental Psychology, 3,* 1–14.

Webster-Stratton, C., & Hammond, M. (1997). Treating children with early-onset conduct problems: A comparison of child and parent training interventions. *Journal of Consulting and Clinical Psychology, 65,* 93–109.

Webster-Stratton, C., & Reid, M. J. (2003). The Incredible Years Parent, Teacher, and Children Training Series. In A. E. Kazdin & J. R. Weisz (Eds.), *Evidence-based psychotherapies for children and adolescents* (pp. 224–240). New York: Guilford.

Webster-Stratton, C., Reid, M. J., & Hammond, M. (2004). Treating children with early-onset conduct problems: Intervention outcomes for parent, child and teacher training. *Journal of Clinical Child and Adolescent Psychology, 33,* 105–124.

Weersing, V. R., & Brent, D. A. (2003). Cognitive-behavioral therapy for adolescent depression. In A. E. Kazdin & J. R. Weisz (Eds.), *Evidence-based psychotherapies for children and adolescents* (pp. 135–147). New York: Guilford.

Weist, M. D., Evans, S. W., & Lever, N. A. (Eds.). (2003). *Handbook of school mental health: Advancing practice and research.* New York: Springer.

Weist, M. D., Finney, J. W., Barnard, M. U., Davis, C. D., & Ollendick, T. H. (1993). Empirical selection of psychosocial treatment targets for children and adolescents with diabetes. *Journal of Pediatric Psychology, 18,* 11–28.

Weisz, J. R., & Kazdin, A. E. (2010). *Evidence-based psychotherapies for children* (2nd ed.). New York: Guilford.

Weisz, J. R., Sandler, I. N., Durlak, J. A., & Anton, B. S. (2005). Promoting and protecting youth mental health through evidence-based prevention and treatment. *American Psychologist, 60,* 628–648.

Weithorne, L. A. & McCabe, M. A. (1987). Legal and ethical problems in pediatric psychology. In D. K. Routh (Ed.). *The handbook of pediatric psychology* (pp. 567–606). New York: Guilford.

Welch, T. D. (2003). *The therapeutic relationship: Listening and responding in a multicultural world.* Westport, CT: Praeger.

Werner, C. (1994). *Developmental psychopathology: From infancy through adolescence* (3rd ed.). New York: McGraw-Hill.

Werner, E. E. (2000). Protective factors and individual resilience. In J. P. Shonkoff & S. J. Meisels (Eds.), *Handbook of early childhood intervention* (2nd ed., pp. 115–132). Cambridge: Cambridge University Press.

Wilson, D. K., & Lawman, H. G. (2009). Health promotion in children and adolescents: An integration of the biopsychosocial model and ecological approaches to behavior change. In M. C. Roberts & R. G. Steele (Eds.), *Handbook of pediatric psychology* (4th ed., pp. 603–617). New York: Guilford.

Wittrock, M. (1990). Generative processes of comprehension. *Educational Psychologist, 24,* 345–376.

Wolfe, J. C., & Ollendick, T. H. (2006). The comorbidity of conduct problems and depression in childhood and adolescence. *Clinical Child and Family Psychology Review, 9,* 201–220.

Wolpe, J. (1958). *Psychotherapy by reciprocal inhibition.* Stanford, CA: Stanford University Press.

Wong, C. A., Eccles, J. S., & Sameroff, A. (2003). The influence of ethnic discrimination and ethnic identification on African American adolescents' school and socioemotional adjustment. *Journal of Personality, 71,* 1197–1232.

Woods, P. J., & Ellis, A. (1997). Supervision in rational emotive behavior therapy. In C. E. Watkins, Jr. (Ed.), *Handbook of psychotherapy supervision* (pp. 101–113). New York: Wiley.

Worthen, V. E., & McNeill, B. W. (1996). A phenomenological investigation of "good" supervision events. *Journal of Counseling Psychology, 43,* 25–34.

Wu, Y. P., Messner, B. M., & Roberts, M. C. (2010). Children's psychosocial problems presenting in a family medicine practice. *Journal of Clinical Psychology in Medical Settings, 17,* 203–210.

Wulf, J., & Nelson, M. L. (2000). Experienced psychologists' recollections of internship supervision and its contribution to their development. *The Clinical Supervisor, 19,* 123–145.

Wynne, L. C., McDaniel, S. H., & Weber, T. T. (Eds.). (1986). *Systems consultation: A new perspective for family therapy.* New York: Guilford.

Yates, B. T., & Taub, J. (2003). Assessing the costs, benefits, cost-effectiveness, and cost-benefit of psychological assessment: We should, we can, and here's how. *Psychological Assessment, 15,* 478–495.

Yourman, D. B., & Farber, B. A. (1996). Nondisclosure of distortion in psychotherapy supervision. *Psychotherapy: Theory, Research, Practice, Training, 33,* 567–575.

Zonnevylle-Bender, M. J. S., Matthys, W., van de Wiel, N. M. H., & Lochman, J. (2007). Preventive effects of treatment of DBD in middle childhood on substance use and delinquent behavior. *Journal of the American Academy of Child and Adolescent Psychiatry, 46,* 33–39.

KEY TERMS

Bioecological theory of human development—in this model of development, five environmental systems and the biological system interact to influence the development of the individual. The microsystem, the mesosystem, the exosystem, the chronosystem, and the macrosystem all have to be considered to understand the uniqueness of the individual child.

Biopsychosocial model—a widely used model of psychological problems that is designed to take into account the biological, psychological, and sociocultural influences associated with specific problems.

Chronosystem—this system consists of the events that happen in one's life and the changes that take place.

Classical conditioning—a basic form of learning, studied originally by Pavlov, involving the repeated association of a previously neutral stimuli with one that elicits a predictable response until the previously neutral stimuli comes to elicit a similar response.

Clinical child and adolescent psychology—a multisystems approach to assessing and treating children, adolescents, and their families.

Cognitive-behavioral therapy—treatment that integrates behavioral therapy approaches with the assumption that cognitions or thoughts can influence emotions and behaviors across a variety of situations.

Collaborative problem-solving model—a collaborative set of procedures designed to teach the client how to deal with stress and problems by engaging in various coping strategies including self-instruction, self-monitoring, cognitive rehearsal, distracting imagery, and so forth.

Developmental psychopathology—this approach views the development of psychological problems within the context of the developmental level of the child—psychological problems are disruption due to development encountering a problem and produced maladjustment.

Disease model—this model holds that psychological problems are diseases of the brain and nervous system that have distinct behavioral symptoms in the same way that physical diseases have biological symptoms.

Exosystem—this system involves the links between the various systems in which the child is involved and those systems that may influence his/her life but in which they are not directly involved.

Functional analysis—the systematic, empirical search for answers to relevant questions before implementing therapeutic interventions

Macrosystem—an individual's culture, which involves the beliefs and behaviors that are passed down through the generations.

Mesosystem—the interaction of the microsystems, such as the relationship between the parents and the school; the parents and the child's peers; the peers and the teachers; and the teachers and the neighborhood.

Microsystem—the system in which the child lives; it includes family, peers, school, and neighborhood.

Neurotransmitters—the messengers of the nervous system.

Operant conditioning—a form of learning that involves increasing or decreasing the probability of a given response being emitted by changing the consequence of the behavior. Most frequently associated with Skinner.

Principle of parsimony—in child/adolescent case formulation, attempting to identify the fewest number of causal mechanisms related to the problems that can comprehensively explain the child/adolescent's behavioral problems (Persons, 2008).

Psychological testing—basically, the measuring of psychology-related variables by means of devices, procedures, and/or tests designed to obtain relevant samples of behavior.

INDEX

ABOUT THE AUTHORS

Alfred J. Finch, Jr., PhD, ABPP, is a professor of psychology at The Citadel, where he was previously the head of the Department of Psychology and dean of the School of Humanities and Social Sciences. He was instrumental in the development of board certification in clinical child and adolescent psychology through the American Board of Professional Psychology (ABPP) and was the founding president of the clinical child and adolescent psychology board. Within ABPP he served also as president of the clinical board and as president of the board of trustees. In addition, he was previously the president of the Section on Clinical Child Psychology, which is now Division 53 of the American Psychological Association, and president of the Southeastern Psychological Association (SEPA); he is currently the administrative officer of SEPA.

John E. Lochman, PhD, ABPP, is a professor and Doddridge Saxon Chairholder in Clinical Psychology and directs the Center for Prevention of Youth Problem Behavior at the University of Alabama. In 2009, he received the International Collaborative Prevention Research Award from the Society for Prevention Research. Dr. Lochman has published over 300 items on risk factors and intervention research with aggressive children. Dr. Lochman is editor-in-chief of the *Journal of Abnormal Child Psychology* and is a fellow in the American Psychological Association, the American Psychological Society, and the Academy for Cognitive Therapy. He serves on a World Health Organization work group on the revision of the ICD classification system for mental and behavioral disorders for children and adolescents, and is past president of the American Board for Clinical Child and Adolescent Psychology. He will receive the 2011 Distinguished Career Award from the Clinical Child and Adolescent Psychology Division of the American Psychological Association.

W. Michael Nelson III, PhD, ABPP, is a professor and former chair of the Department of Psychology at Xavier University in Cincinnati, Ohio. He is board certified in both clinical psychology and in clinical child and adolescent psychology through the American Board of Professional Psychology, and he is a fellow in the American Psychological Association Divisions of Clinical Child Psychology and Clinical Psychology. After earning his degree in clinical psychology from the Virginia Commonwealth University, Dr. Nelson began his work with children and adolescents in low-income families at the University of Texas Health Science Center in Dallas. He also worked with inpatient children for 5 years at the Millcreek Psychiatric Center for Children, where he was also the director of psychology. He has always attempted to integrate research with practice, as evidenced in a book coauthored with Dr. Finch titled *Cognitive-Behavioral Procedures with Children and Adolescents: A Practical Guide* and in their psychoeducational workbook series *"Keeping Your Cool": The Anger Management Workbook*. His efforts to make empirically supported therapies more user-friendly are also reflected in the several videos he produced, including *"Keeping Your Cool": The Anger Management Video*, which serves as an accompaniment to the workbook. Dr. Nelson has taught for 33 years at Xavier University, including courses in the areas of childhood psychopathology, cognitive behavior therapy, and family therapy. Widely published, Dr. Nelson's research interests have primarily centered on assessment and cognitive-behavioral interventions with children and adolescents.

Michael C. Roberts, PhD, ABPP, is director of the Clinical Child Psychology Program at the University of Kansas. He graduated from Purdue University in clinical psychology with a specialization in clinical child psychology and interned at the University of Oklahoma Health Sciences Center. Dr. Roberts has published over 200 journal articles and book chapters on a variety of topics in clinical child and pediatric psychology. He is the current editor of *Professional Psychology: Research and Practice*; he previously served as editor for the *Journal of Pediatric Psychology*; *Children's Health Care*; and *Children's Services: Social Policy, Research, and Practice*. Roberts has authored and coedited 20 books, including *Handbook of Clinical Child Psychology*; *Handbook of Pediatric Psychology*; *Model Programs in Service Delivery in Child and Family Mental Health; Prevention of Problems in Childhood; Helping Children Cope with Disasters and Terrorism; Handbook of Research Methods in Clinical Psychology; Handbook of Mental Health Services for Children, Adolescents, and Families*; and *Handbook of Evidence-Based Therapies for Children and Adolescents: Bridging Science and Practice*.

ABOUT THE SERIES EDITORS

Arthur M. Nezu, PhD, ABPP, is a professor of psychology, medicine, and public health at Drexel University and Special Professor of Forensic Mental Health and Psychiatry at the University at Nottingham in the United Kingdom. He is a fellow of multiple professional associations including the American Psychological Association and board certified by the American Board of Professional Psychology in cognitive and behavioral Psychology, clinical psychology, and clinical health psychology. Dr. Nezu is widely published, is incoming editor of the *Journal of Consulting and Clinical Psychology*, and has maintained a practice for 3 decades.

Christine Maguth Nezu, PhD, ABPP, is a professor of psychology and medicine at Drexel University, and Special Professor of Forensic Mental Health and Psychiatry at the University at Nottingham in the United Kingdom. With over 25 years experience in clinical private practice, consultation/liaison, research, and teaching, Dr. Maguth Nezu is board certified by the American Board of Professional Psychology (ABPP) in cognitive and behavioral psychology and clinical psychology. She is also a past president of ABPP. Her research has been supported by federal, private, and state-funded agencies, and she has served as a grant reviewer for the National Institutes of Health.

www.ingramcontent.com/pod-product-compliance
Lightning Source LLC
LaVergne TN
LVHW022342051025
822766LV00028B/468